T0342069

Mastering
Strategic Risk

The Wiley Finance series contains books written specifically for finance and investment professionals as well as sophisticated individual investors and their financial advisers. Book topics range from portfolio management to e-commerce, risk management, financial engineering, valuation, and financial instrument analysis, as well as much more. For a list of available titles, visit our Web site at www.WileyFinance.com.

Founded in 1807, John Wiley & Sons is the oldest independent publishing company in the United States. With offices in North America, Europe, Australia and Asia, Wiley is globally committed to developing and marketing print and electronic products and services for our customers' professional and personal knowledge and understanding.

Mastering Strategic Risk

A Framework for Leading and Transforming Organizations

JOEL E. MCPHEE, JR.

WILEY

ISBN 9781118757291 (Hardcover)
ISBN 9781118772874 (ePDF)
ISBN 9781118772867 (ePub)

Printed in the United States of America
10 9 8 7 6 5 4 3 2 1

This book is dedicated to the Past and the Future:

*The Past, in memory of my maternal grandfather,
Arthur Leon Roach Sr., whose tremendous insight and
vision inspires me to this very day*

And

*The Future, in the form of my wonderful
daughters, Kimai and Kiori . . . It's a blessing and an honor
to be the father of two amazing human beings!*

Contents

Preface

If you've picked up this book, it's likely that you're someone who is a lot like the way I was: a senior executive at an organization charged with finding a way to help your group not merely survive but thrive in times of uncertainty. The challenge before us all is daunting. But the great news is that it can be done. And, in essence, nature has already shown us the way for it to happen.

For over 20 years I've been at the forefront of solving the critical challenges facing large, complex organizations. I've led organizations through troubled waters and changing market dynamics and I can help you lead yours through, too. Having held key executive assignments at industry leaders such as Wells Fargo Inc., and providing consulting services to top global brands, I possess an extensive background in understanding the keys to driving peak performance. Through these experiences I realize that more than ever before companies need new tools to manage the requirements and complexities of our new era. As we move steadily toward the future, I've also observed that, as individuals, we struggle to manage the intensity and pace of change we face.

But one of the most important things to realize is this: new challenges bring new opportunities, and markets yet to be culled and discovered. And the transformation of people, resources, and our world now lie within our reach in a way that we may have only dreamed about before.

Mastering Strategic Risk was written with these circumstances in mind. It provides a simple, yet effective solution to these formidable challenges. *Mastering Strategic Risk* offers a perspective that redesigns organizational systems to manage the risk and complexities of a radically different world. I believe CEOs, executives, leaders, managers, and employees of all types should read this book. So should any other professional or function tied to ensuring optimal corporate performance, including external auditors, consultants, board members, and suppliers of services to companies.

Mastering Strategic Risk is also a book for anyone who desires to understand how our world works and would like to explore new ways of thinking through the opportunities and common pitfalls we face today. My goal is to introduce a fresh perspective, one that provides readers with a new approach. More than just case studies, we will look at how successful companies have navigated challenges and take the wisdom they have learned from these experiences to help you apply it to the challenges you face day-in and day-out. You will be equipped with tangible tools that are relevant and can be applied for immediate results.

I hope you leverage the observations in the book and that these concepts will stimulate new thinking, that these new learnings will enable you to unleash the tremendous resources and promise that lie dormant in your organization. It is also my hope that this fresh new perspective will help you to see the world in a way you've never seen it before. That it will further your understanding of how truly integrated and connected as a world we are and why it is critical to manage holistically in these uncertain times.

I also aim to move beyond the typical methods to deliver a compelling new vision. It is a perspective that will enable you to harness our unique opportunity and time, realizing that we live in a truly special era in our modern world. I hope that, armed with this new information, leaders and managers, with a renewed intent, will move forward to consciously shape and mold their companies. We live in a world of amazing capabilities; let this new framework help you as you lead your organization in mastering the strategic risks of our new era.

Acknowledgments

In writing a book there are many people to thank, for you never complete an undertaking of this type without the support of some very special individuals. I would first like to thank my stellar literary agent, John Willig. Without his keen understanding of how to position this work, the publication of this book would not have been possible. A hearty thanks to the amazing team at Wiley. Thanks to Executive Editor Bill Falloon, Senior Editorial Assistant Lia Ottaviano, Editorial Program Coordinator Tiffany Charbonier, Senior Production Editor Stacey Fischkelta, and to Susan McDermott, and Jennifer Macdonald.

I would like to recognize the wonderful team of individuals who came together to assemble critical components of the book: Kristin Everidge of Everidge Designs, Tammy McGee Anderson, James Sokolowski, Mark Little, Stephen Sopher, and Karen Poimbeuf. A special thank you to Tony Elwood and Paul Barrett of Elwood Design. Without Tony's constant pushing and prodding, I'm not sure I would have written this book. I'd also like to thank Alison Woo for her knowledge and guidance along the way, and Randy Peyser, Kevin Killabrew, Roger Ryan, Brian McCullers and Dr. Ali Solomon. I'd like to thank my publicist Yolanda Harris, and Jonna Palmer and Tommy Pruitt of The Keynote Group.

Last and definitely not least, I'd like to thank my family, who have nurtured and supported me through the years. I would like to first thank my parents: my mother, Dr. Clara McPhee, for being my hero and for providing me with so many important life lessons; and my dad, Mr. Joel McPhee Sr., for teaching me how to live; and to my stepmother, Rosalie McPhee. I'd also like to thank my two wonderful sisters, Cheryl McPhee and Carina McPhee Bridgewater, for their love and support through the years. A special thank you to my brother-in-law Trevor, Sr., and to my nephew and niece Trevor, Jr., and Lauren. I'd also like to thank Sherryl Guthrie McPhee, for her support throughout the years and efforts in raising and co-parenting two wonderful daughters. A special thanks to my deceased and very dear uncle, Tony Roach, who served as a surrogate dad, big brother, and best friend. His impact on my life is immeasurable as his spirit and energy will always be with me! Thanks to my many aunts and uncles for all of your support.

A big thanks to my numerous other family members, those past and present including my ancestors on whose shoulders I stand.

In addition to the individuals who worked directly on the book project are other individuals who have contributed in some way to my professional and personal journey. They include advisors and friends such as Dr. Richard Williams; Roy Hollman; Dr. Leon Higgs; John Waddy, Esq.; Michael Ozier, Esq.; Jordan Miller; and others. Other individuals I'd like to recognize include Jean Davis, David Carroll, Elizabeth Williams, Tom Wurtz and Lisa Brinkley. Thanks also for the support given by many dear friends throughout the years and during the writing of this book.

A special thanks to the close family and friends who have supported me through the years, including those in Nassau and Freeport, Bahamas, and those in Rochester, New York, and Columbus, Ohio.

Introduction

Mastering the Complexities of a New Age

On a cold and silent January morning I jolted awake. Startled, I sat up and peered through my bedroom window. The darkness engulfed everything, save the light dusting of snow blanketing the treetops and frigid ground below. It was still, and the solitude of the early morning hour seemed deafening—so deafening, those moments reverberate ever so loudly to this very day.

What time was it? As I glanced at my phone lying on the nightstand next to the bed, I saw that it was only 3:00 A.M. Though exhausted from a long week, I was wide awake. I'm not certain what woke me up so suddenly, but my mind was racing at a feverish pitch as a clear image came into full view.

Reflecting on what I saw, I stumbled out of bed, sprang to my feet, and rushed to the dining room table. As a deluge of thoughts poured through my head, I began to furiously map a framework of an idea. Unbeknownst to me, what I saw on that fateful January morning would eventually become the very foundation of *Mastering Strategic Risk*.

* * *

In contemplating my epiphany, I wonder: Where did it come from? How did these concepts come to me, and why did they come with such clarity? I never, prior to that day, consciously thought of the concepts, let alone aspired to write a book. Only after several months of prodding from a good friend did I take the agonizing step of putting pen to paper. I've been writing ever since.

What I do realize is that I was in a state of flux. I was one year removed from a rewarding career at a top financial institution, and carefully parsing through career alternatives. I also deeply desired to understand the enormous change occurring not only in my world but in the world around me. During this time the markets were in turmoil as organizations everywhere contended to survive amidst withering circumstances.

It was January 2009, and since the summer of 2007 the entire planet had been experiencing tremendous change. There was the collapse of the real estate markets, a debilitating credit crisis, government bailouts of the auto and banking industries, and a crippling global recession. Accompanying these conditions were a litany of corporate failures, from Washington Mutual to Lehman Brothers, Blockbuster, AIG's near collapse, and WorldCom, to name a few.

I also observed firsthand how Wachovia, a company I had grown to deeply admire, ascended quickly to the top of the banking industry, only to experience an equally rapid decline. The state of the economy, when coupled with our geopolitical tensions and environmental and social conditions, also signaled that we were living in unprecedented times.

In observing this sea of change, a common theme emerged. As a civilization we are challenged in managing our most critical systems, and even more so organizational systems. Whether it is on Wall Street or Chicago, in New Delhi or Shanghai, we contend mightily to manage a corporate agenda held captive to an increasingly complex and dynamic world.

As a result, I wanted to know how we could manage organizations more effectively. And if we couldn't, what would it mean for the future of the markets and our wonderful planet? Now five years removed from that fateful January morning, we still live amidst significant uncertainty and face formidable challenges as we combat a lingering global recession.

Over the past 20 years we've also witnessed the failure of numerous organizations as they careened out of control due to the breakdown of fundamental management practices. Examples include the story of Enron and how the failure of critical governance mechanisms led to its eventual demise. Or consider how BP's catastrophic *Deep Horizon* spill emanated from its fractious risk management system.

Think of how over the past 12 years banks have failed to learn from the lessons of others, as evidenced by the enormous trading losses they still experience. In 1999 a rogue trader single-handedly took down the United Kingdom's most storied investment bank, amassing close to $1.4 billion in trading losses. Then, over a decade later, UBS experienced $2 billion in trading losses due to a rogue trader's activities.

Despite these painful lessons, only two years ago industry darling JPMorgan Chase racked up over $5 billion and counting in trading losses. It was later discovered that these substantial losses were all due to the bank's failure to activate critical trading controls. To date, the company is still challenged in managing the risks that span its sales and trading activities.

The many examples from our most recent past point to similar yet fundamental challenges facing organizations across industry types. And while we spiral hastily toward the future, we are greatly in need of change.

On the following pages, I will provide you with new information to give you a fresh perspective into the challenges organizations face in this new century. This insight will arm you with the knowledge required to effectively manage the most critical forces that dictate performance in organizations.

For close to 20 years, I have been a leader in large, complex organizations. During this time I've either led or been a part of key management teams charged with addressing some of the most critical challenges facing these organizations. Whether it is in the area of the global sourcing of resources (offshoring), large-scale operational efficiency efforts, key disaster recovery and business resumption activities, or helping to shape the strategic vision of a company's culture, these unique experiences have provided me with the opportunity to understand the critical drivers that underpin corporate performance.

The fundamental components on which this book is based are concepts that are well understood when considered individually in the context of companies and the key drivers of performance. What makes the approach in *Mastering Strategic Risk* unique is that it extracts patterns and realities in natural systems and applies them to organizational systems. These realities dictate performance in both nature and organizations. They illuminate how the elements and forces in nature are no different than those found in organizations or for that matter the world we've created for ourselves.

The intent of this new approach is to provide readers with a compelling guide. It is a new model that outlines how key activities and functions should come together to provide a holistic governance framework. In addition to introducing a new framework, *Mastering Strategic Risk* underscores how integrated and connected we are, not only in our commercial and social lives, but in the activities and realities that transcend our traditional view of our world.

It is also my hope that you will be inspired by these new learnings, applying them in navigating your organization through the risks and uncertainties of an unforgiving marketplace. Throughout these pages I've also distilled what I've learned and observed through the years to unveil a new framework in which to govern companies. And while there are many lessons to glean from the mistakes of the past, at such a critical time, there is none more important than for us to move forward with a renewed intent, to consciously shape our world into the type of planet we've deeply desired it to be.

Ultimately, I guess I am a teacher at heart; after all, I do come from a family with a rich teaching tradition. It is in this spirit that I share with you *Mastering Strategic Risk*. Whether you are a leader in a large or small organization, manage shared services or customer facing function, or simply desire to understand the key elements and forces that drive performance in organizations, this is the book for you. It is my hope that armed with this new insight you will thrive in these uncertain times.

CHAPTER 1

The Round World, the Square Pegs: Redesigning Organizations to Manage the Risks of a Different World

The markets are raging! They roar tumultuously toward an uncertain end. Meanwhile, the fates of billions hang in the balance, as we look to the future with fear and trepidation. The truth is that we've created a monster, as a beleaguered and mismanaged corporate agenda continues to wreak havoc on cities, sovereign governments, and communities everywhere. There is no doubt that the turbulence we are experiencing was brought on by our very own miscreations; however, the question remains: How do we move confidently toward the future while ensuring we do not repeat the mistakes of the past?

RIGHTING THE SHIP: MANAGING THE COMPLEXITIES OF A NEW AGE

While we forge steadily toward a future of unlimited possibilities, at the center of these turbulent yet fascinating times sits the corporation. The commercial corporation has been in existence since the seventeenth century, yet, despite its storied history, still struggles to effectively govern its varied activities. Furthermore, the corporation of the twenty-first century is like none other, for it has become a critical aspect of almost every facet of life on our planet.

It is truly the most powerful and ubiquitous force in an unrelenting, high-stakes global marketplace. Think of the many ways corporations play a pivotal role in our society, mainstream culture, and economic lives. Think of the role they play in your very own community.

To make matters worse, government has often needed to step in to provide much-needed oversight of corporate activities. There was the savings-and-loan (S&L) crisis of the 1990s, Sarbanes-Oxley, and now recently enacted

Dodd-Frank legislation that was put in place on the heels of the 2008 credit meltdown. While often government intervention is necessary in order to protect the system, it is often reactive and done in order to avert a crisis. Although we must be responsive to a national crisis, shouldn't we find it indefensible that we've grown accustomed to addressing systemic issues from a reactive, knee-jerk posture?

As our beloved guardians at the gate work tirelessly to piece together overnight solutions to address systemic issues, is this reactionary posture the right approach? Moreover, the public outcry for swift and decisive action during a crisis often contradicts and outweighs the need to exercise prudence and good judgment. Government has a formidable role in providing oversight of commercial activities; however, we are at a point in this country where the regulatory agenda has become overly burdensome.

During the past few decades, we've experienced a crescendo in the volume and intensity of regulatory oversight. As we move hastily into the twenty-first century we will experience even greater regulatory oversight. From Sarbanes-Oxley to the Basel Accords, from Gramm-Leach-Bliley to Dodd-Frank, the regulatory agenda continues with no end in sight. Think of the tremendous costs these requirements have added to corporate bottom lines.

To make matters worse, these costs are ultimately borne by you and me, the end user and consumer. These efforts, though well intended, will eventually cause the system to buckle under the intense burden of regulatory adherence.

Consider the world in which we now live and how, during the past decade, we've experienced such significant change. We live in unique and unparalleled times. Think of how just recently the credit markets were in a tailspin, ushering in an unrelenting and debilitating recession. Of how the auto and financial services industries were on life support, and how the saber rattling between nations, tribes, and people even today continues at fever pitch. When we consider the state of the environment, along with deteriorating health and social conditions across the planet, we attempt mightily to manage the risks and complexities of an ever-changing world.

We also sit at the most critical juncture in Earth's history: On one hand lies a future of unparalleled promise; on the other, a world filled with tremendous uncertainty. However, the truth is that we can no longer count on the old ways of managing our most critical systems; we must look to new models by which to govern a new age.

In addition to these formidable challenges, corporations continue to struggle to keep pace with an ever-changing world. As change continues at an unprecedented pace, the marketplace will continue to become even more dynamic and volatile. Coupled with this is how quickly we've moved into a truly global marketplace. As the Internet and technology have removed geographical boundaries and business has become ubiquitous, many corporations now serve and manage a global footprint. This reality is placing additional strain on corporate agendas and resources as the governance of activities has become more complex, integrated, and dispersed.

The time has come for organizations to change. Companies must change the manner in which they govern internal activities, for the cost is too high for society to bear. Regardless of how ubiquitous and powerful the corporation has become, it has failed to regulate itself. It's time for corporations to take control of their destinies by transforming within. This change must occur from inside their hallowed walls, rather than being mandated from the external forces of government regulation and political influence. Yes, the time has come for stronger self-regulation. It's time to rethink business!

THE UNTOLD STORY OF WACHOVIA'S DEMISE: THE RISE AND FALL OF AN INDUSTRY GIANT

It was Friday, September 26, 2008, around 11:00 in the evening. It was a clear and cool autumn evening. As I made my way home after entertaining a few out-of-town business guests, my mind began to drift slowly, far away into the distance. I was in a fog! The events of earlier that day created a dark cloud of despair, and a deep sense of anxiety loomed over my head. To make matters worse, a state trooper had just pulled behind me and turned on his lights. After finally realizing what was occurring, I slowly pulled over to the side of the highway and anxiously waited. What could I have possibly done wrong? Why was I being pulled over? The tension and anxiety began to build!

After what seemed like an eternity, I was startled by a pointed tap on the glass. As I rolled down my window, I was greeted by the trooper. With a surprised look on his face, the trooper asked, "Are you okay, sir?" I replied, "Yes, I am." He then asked, "Are you sure?" In a frustrated and irritated tone, I answered, "Yes, I am, I'm sure, why? What did I do?"

"Well, I've been following you for a few miles and you have been swerving repeatedly to the right, as if you were about to drive off of the highway. I'm going to have to give you a few field sobriety tests," the trooper said. I ended up passing the tests; however, what dawned on me that very moment was how emotionally immersed I had become with the events of the day—so much so that I became overrun with an overwhelming sense of apprehension and fear.

It was that fateful day when the proverbial writing had been written on the wall, as the day's events signaled the coming demise of Wachovia. That Friday was a crazy day, as I had become deluged with myriad phone calls, conversations, and e-mails concerning the fate of Wachovia. These conversations were with former colleagues, employees, and others who were associated with the bank. Many of them still played significant roles at the bank. We were all anxious.

Those of us who were no longer at Wachovia had similar concerns. We all owned company stock and stock options, and were concerned about our pension. Those who remained were concerned about whether they would have to pack up their boxes in the next few days and be required to leave. We were all worried about whether Wachovia would survive through the weekend as conditions regarding the bank's financial status were rapidly deteriorating.

This was the Friday right on the heels of the federal government's intervening to save Washington Mutual by seizing it and arranging the sale of most of its operations to JPMorgan Chase. As news of this transaction spread and as the market was in a tailspin due to instability as a result of the credit crisis, questions began to arise about Wachovia's stability and liquidity. And remember, Lehman Brothers had just failed a few weeks earlier. On that Friday, Wachovia's stock was in a free fall.

Rumors that day began to emerge regarding a silent run on Wachovia's deposits. We would later discover that these rumors were well founded, as many of Wachovia's commercial customers began to draw down their balances to below the $100,000 limit that the Federal Deposit Insurance Corporation (FDIC) insured. Approximately $5 billion in deposits was lost that day. There were also rumors that Wachovia was in the midst of talks with Citigroup and Wells Fargo.

The concerns were so serious that many wondered if Wachovia would make it through the weekend. These concerns prompted FDIC Chair Sheila Bair to declare that Wachovia was "systemically important to the health of the economy and therefore could not be allowed to fail." This was no routine announcement, for it was the first time that the FDIC had made this determination since the 1991 passage of a law that allowed the FDIC to handle large bank failures on very little notice. To confirm the state of emergency concerning Wachovia, on the evening of September 28, Blair called Wachovia's then-CEO, Brian Steele, and informed him that the FDIC would be auctioning off Wachovia's assets.

Eventually, Wachovia would be purchased by Wells Fargo, with most of its banking operations intact. Although Wachovia technically survived through Wells Fargo's purchase, its overnight failure evidenced one of the most significant events in banking history.

A Legacy to Be Proud Of

"Come to the mountain called First Union, or if you prefer, the mountain will come to you"! These were the words that bellowed from a deep and enchanting voice in First Union's newly released commercial. The commercial was especially created to position the bank's powerful new brand. It was a branding approach that would serve as a key plank of First Union's strategy to becoming a national player.

CEO Ed Crutchfield desired to quickly build his branch banking network into a power national franchise. And it was his carefully positioned branding effort, coupled with an aggressive acquisition spree, that would serve as the launching pad in its new chapter.

It was the fall of 1998, and I first saw the commercial as a new recruit during the first hour of my orientation into the Finance division. The leaders managing the orientation were proud of the new ad and, more important, First Union's new strategic direction. The entire company was excited, as it was on the heels of two significant acquisitions, both signaling that the best was yet to come. You could feel the energy in the air while interacting with employees in different pockets of the organization. There was no doubt our future was bright!

Three years later First Union would purchase Wachovia, and the once fledgling interstate banking operation would blossom into a financial services powerhouse!

At its height, Wachovia was one of the largest financial services institutions in the United States, amassing a banking empire that stretched from New York to California. Its banking franchise extended to every major market from Miami to New York and continued throughout the Midwest, South, and all the way to the Pacific Coast. In addition to its extensive network of branch banking operations, Wachovia was well positioned in each major market it served.

Its banking footprint served coveted metropolitan markets such as Philadelphia; Washington, D.C.; New York; New Jersey; Atlanta; and South Florida, to name a few. Wachovia did not merely maintain a presence in these markets but it dominated these major metropolitan centers, often ranking as the number one or two bank.

Wachovia was also a great place to work, and my colleagues and I enjoyed working for such a fine organization. During those glory years, Wachovia had garnered top industry accolades and awards for being a great place to work. There were formidable challenges that we overcame during those years, but Wachovia was on a tear, as we were in the midst of tremendous growth and success. Throughout its storied history, Wachovia had become known as a merger-and-acquisition juggernaut, as over time this strategy served as the cornerstone for its growth. From the early First Union days, its renowned CEO, Ed Crutchfield—or Fast Eddie, as Wall Street would call him—went on an acquisition spree and snatched up more than 70 deals in a span of 10 years. He was a force to be reckoned with as his spirited will served as the driving force behind First Union's success. Within that period, he took Charlotte, North Carolina's, third-largest bank and transformed it into the nation's sixth largest bank, amassing close to $260 billion in assets in 1998.

It was through the efforts of Ed Crutchfield and Bank of America's legendary leader Hugh McColl that Charlotte, North Carolina, developed into a global banking center. After the landmark 1985 Supreme Court ruling upholding regional interstate banking, their visionary and aggressive efforts served as the catalyst for Charlotte's emergence onto the national banking scene.

Prior to retirement, Crutchfield selected Ken Thompson to become his handpicked successor. Thompson, as First Union's newly crowned CEO, would follow in his mentor's footsteps, orchestrating some of the largest deals in banking during this time. From 2001 to 2007, First Union quickly grew its banking footprint.

In April 2001 it announced a historic merger with in-state rival Wachovia bank. First Union would shed its name in place of the more favorable Wachovia brand. This was a watershed event for both banks, as it laid the foundation for a formidable financial services organization that would soon be catapulted toward the very top of the industry.

The historic merger of Wachovia and First Union was followed by a slew of acquisitions. In 2003 it purchased Prudential Securities, which was quickly followed by the 2004 acquisition of Birmingham-based South Trust Bank. These transactions were followed up by two other significant deals: first the September 2005 purchase of auto finance leader WestCorp, which was followed by the May 2007 acquisition of Golden West Financial. Also in May 2007 Wachovia purchased brokerage industry powerhouse A. G. Edwards.

Wachovia's meteoric rise, fueled by these transactions, quickly cemented its position as a banking industry leader. It garnered Thompson the coveted Banker of the Year Award in 2005 along with numerous other industry awards, and Wachovia was recognized as Bank of the Year by *BusinessWeek* in 2002. By the end of 2007 Wachovia had become the darling of the industry. It had become the nation's fourth-largest bank by asset size, with deposits exceeding $700 billion; boasted one of the nation's largest brokerage companies, with more than 18,000 registered representatives; and now possessed a banking footprint that stretched from sea to shining sea. Wachovia had also developed a stellar track record of delivering outstanding customer service. It was recognized as the top-rated bank in customer service by the American Customer Satisfaction Index (ACSI), a survey of consumer satisfaction conducted by the University of Michigan Business School, for five straight years.

However, things were not all well with Wachovia, as the debilitating credit crisis would soon reveal.

What Went Wrong

What happened? How could such a financial services powerhouse be brought to its knees so quickly? Yes, the credit crisis significantly impacted Wachovia, but was there more to this story? Indeed, there was!

Two fundamental things went wrong at Wachovia, and one would eventually build on the other. The first was Wachovia's inability to organically grow its core banking business, and the second was its failure to follow its own internal merger due diligence process. However, the pivotal misstep that served as the primary catalyst of Wachovia's sudden demise in 2008 was ironically tied to its rigorous due diligence process in acquiring banking franchises it purchased.

Wachovia bought mortgage giant Golden West at the peak of the U.S. housing boom. As the course of events would later unfold, the timing of this purchase, coupled with Golden West's concentration in mortgages and the quality of its portfolio, would prove to be the cause of Wachovia's final demise. However, Thompson viewed Golden West as a huge prize, as it would not only provide him with a more formidable retail and secondary mortgage business but bring him what he coveted most: a truly national footprint.

The Golden West acquisition gave him a strong presence in the West, and most important, California, a state that provided a thriving and robust economic opportunity for financial services. Although the timing of this acquisition was not the best, there were other, more fundamental core business issues lurking behind the scenes. I might add that these issues are no different than those that arise at other companies regardless of industry.

The catalyst behind Wachovia's final demise had to do with simple management decisions and the failure to manage critical processes appropriately. The Wachovia story is one that could be told at many organizations, as it highlights the criticality of ensuring that fundamental processes are followed, even for the most routine of activities.

It is no secret that Wachovia's top brass coveted California and desperately desired to expand west. It was a strategic imperative! So when the opportunity arose to acquire Golden West, Wachovia hastily seized the moment. It was later revealed that Thompson purchased Golden West even though his board of directors was not supportive of the deal. However, because of his overzealous desire, the due diligence process in evaluating Golden West's assets was less than desirable.

Although Wachovia had built up a strong culture and industry-leading merger and integration capabilities, it failed to follow through in carefully assessing Golden West's mortgage portfolio. Even more fundamental than the failure to thoroughly assess Golden West's mortgage portfolio, Wachovia was challenged in its ability to grow organically. This was no secret, as internally we tried desperately to organically grow and build our existing business.

This challenge to organically grow came from the inability to cross-sell products and services to existing customers and garner a larger portion of our customers' coveted "wallet share," which, ironically, Wachovia's successor, Wells Fargo, is a master at doing. Therefore, over the course of several years, Wachovia grew through an aggressive campaign of acquisition and merger.

This is a critical point in that although growth through merger is a formidable strategy, it must be balanced in business by an organization's ability to leverage its internal assets to fuel growth. Growth in business must be balanced. Further, an overreliance on acquiring growth, regardless of the short-term results, will eventually take away an organization's ability to build other critical core capabilities.

A SYMPTOM OF A MUCH LARGER CHALLENGE

What happened at Wachovia is no different from what has occurred at other high-flying corporations over the past few decades. There was Enron, Lehman, AIG, Burger King, Pan Am, and Blockbuster, to name a few. Although some of these organizations are still a part of our commercial landscape, there are still important lessons to learn from their missteps (I will highlight several of these organizations in Chapters 2 and 3). We also have lessons from the systemic crisis of the S&L failure of the 1990s as well as the mortgage crisis of 2007 to learn.

In observing the fall and eventual missteps of these organizations and our systemic failures, they all were initiated from within. They centered on some very fundamental risk and business themes. These fundamental themes include the failure of internal governance processes, the inability to keep pace with competitors and marketplace trends and realities, and failure to balance critical business activities.

We are moving into an era where we can no longer afford to withstand the type of systemic failures we've experienced over the past few decades. We live in a time of unprecedented opportunities. However, with these opportunities comes intense pressure on business to move and operate with great prudence, agility, and speed. Think about what has transpired over the past 25 years and how the Internet and technology have transformed our personal lives and the marketplace.

These changes—and the fact that because of technology we live in a truly global community—have provided unparalleled opportunities. Despite these opportunities, business and the corporation must respond in kind to the new paradigm. No longer can the corporation afford to manage its structure and govern its activities in the same manner it has for the past 50 or so years.

Across industries, organizations of all types, shapes, and sizes do respond to change with success. We find pockets of success that span industries, as very often we can find best practices that propel these organizations to the very top of their industry class. I also realize that, as we speak, many corporations are experiencing record earnings and years of success.

We also find that in times of austerity or market turmoil, organizations struggle to find their footing, often scrambling to implement some efficiency or new revenue initiative. The same can be said in times of prosperity, as history has shown that organizations frequently become victims of their own success and fail to consistently apply a certain discipline and rigor to their internal activities.

I know from my own experience at Wachovia how we struggled to maintain a culture that consistently applied routine processes. In times of prosperity we would spend little time thinking about efficiencies or ways to reduce expenses; however, whenever we predicted a quarterly earnings shortfall or it was forecasted that we had a difficult year ahead, the call would go out for everyone to contribute their portion to "the expense reduction pool." Or from time to time the CEO would announce a major enterprise-wide expense reduction initiative whose objective was to provide a one-time reduction to expenses, but also signal to the street how serious we were in fostering an environment of efficiency and expense control.

To implement the initiative, he would place a key lieutenant or rising corporate star to "run herd" over the effort. However, these valiant efforts occurred infrequently, and as soon as we completed the exercise and all the contributions were counted, we would settle into the old ways of doing things. And, quite often, many of us would work very hard to protect our very own sacred cows. Observing these efforts firsthand made me wonder: Shouldn't specific types of activities be an inherent part of an organization's DNA or culture? Wouldn't good corporate management ensure that an organization, division by division, has instilled in it a process that would continually seek and evaluate organizational efficiencies? I will provide more commentary on the importance of organizational efficiency in Chapter 4.

Even industry banking leader Wells Fargo, Wachovia's successor, has trouble fostering a culture of efficiency. In 2011, CEO John Stumph announced a significant cross-enterprise expense reduction effort. Called Project Compass, Wells Fargo hoped the program will drive out $1 billion in expenses from its bottom line within 12 months.

The company has mastered several key business levers, but shouldn't Wells Fargo, like other corporations, be adept at managing other critical levers or organizational disciplines consistently, rather than a onetime effort? Can't we observe that pattern here again? We are in a period of austerity—especially banks, as marketplace dynamics and the yield curve have placed intense pressure on banks to grow earnings. As growth is difficult in this environment, cutting costs and reducing expenses is a natural lever. However, shouldn't these practices be embedded in organizations?

THE BURNING PLATFORM: WHY THE NEED FOR CHANGE

The need to change the way organizations manage their activities is being driven by several factors. These include technology, how interdependent and connected we've become, globalization, the speed of transactions, and complexity. These factors are all tied to the tremendous change we are experiencing in our world.

Think about how interdependent we've become regarding global investment, and how the debts of many foreign nations affect the global marketplace. Consider how individuals, corporations, and sovereign nations alike are investing in corporations and interests across our planet. Or even think about how many of the top-performing corporations have come to depend on revenue and efforts from operations in all corners of the globe.

Along with this dependency on global operations and revenue comes the need to manage and coordinate resources and activities across several continents and time zones. Even if an organization operates solely domestically, the increasing pace of activity is mind-boggling, as technology and the Internet have enabled us to communicate and transact business at lightning speeds. The speed and ubiquity of business have added complexity to internal operations, imposing a greater need to ensure that internal activities and resources are carefully coordinated, consumed, and aligned.

As great an impact as technology is having on business, it is having more of an impact on us as individuals. Technology has affected our lives and transformed our behaviors in many ways. Think of all of the ways technology has transformed the way we interact, transact business, and behave: texting, the iPhone, navigation systems, working remotely, the ability to download movies and music to handheld devices, as well as buying goods and services online. Technology's impact on our lives hasn't even reached a crescendo; technology will continue to transform our lives at a dizzying pace, in ways we cannot imagine.

These factors all indicate that we are leveraging square pegs to address the needs of a round-hole world!

LEVERAGING THE POWER OF PEOPLE

Our new era also calls for a new way to leverage and lead employees, as the paradigms of the past no longer fit the realities of today. Technology has transformed our lives and will be a key differentiator for those organizations that leverage it to empower their people. Think of the volumes of information now available to us, all at the push of a button; how through our laptops we are privy to a world without boundaries.

Leveraging employees, who are at the epicenter of delivering value to customers and shareholders, will become more of a competitive advantage as technological capabilities continue to advance. Consider the specialized and in-depth knowledge employees have of critical customer preferences, behaviors, and expectations. This also holds true as they have an intimate understanding of how core processes and internal operations really work. Unleashing these critical resources through the power of technology will drive incremental value.

As the marketplace, and more specifically, competitors, access and utilize talent from around the world, building a culture that promotes learning and the building of new capabilities will help to ensure globalization. Also, the battle to recruit and retain the best and most talented resources will continue to intensify, as globalization has provided access to new pools of resources.

Engaging employees and connecting with them is even more important in this new age. This is of paramount importance in the twenty-first century as a typical employee's "mindshare" is bombarded with a host of distractions. Think of the limited "bandwidth" we face, as each day our lives are filled with a confluence of texting, tweeting, and e-mailing. This is not to mention how easily we become distracted by LinkedIn and Facebook, or for that matter easy access to fascinating online headlines and articles. These realities underscore the importance of employee engagement and ensuring that they connect with an organization's mission and core values.

However, these opportunities all hinge on one of the oldest and most basic factors: trust. Enabling employees and eventually empowering them can be realized only through the building of trust. Providing employees with the tools to make important decisions is only a part of the answer. Allowing them to make the important decisions will eventually result in true empowerment.

The world we live in today—and tomorrow—will no longer be forgiving of corporations' missteps and reliance on antiquated systems of internal governance. In today's marketplace, organizations can quickly slip into obscurity or wreak havoc on us all; we have seen how individual corporate miscues can easily add up to systemic chaos. The time has come for business to adopt new ways of ordering and governing internal activities in a manner that keeps pace with complexities and demands of the times.

These new principles or activities should be centered on adopting more holistic models for managing strategic risk. This would assist in unleashing organizational creativity and innovation, and fostering strong organizational governance structures and systems of accountability. Undisciplined, fragmented and reactive management of external market forces and internal demands are inadequate to meet the demands of the twenty-first century. Further, unwinding and measuring risk after a catastrophic or major event is far too late. "The horse will have already left the stable" at that point. Corporations must adopt more holistic management practices to govern themselves. But where can we find the answers to address these very simple—yet at the same time complex—answers? Today, I propose that we look to nature, for it is the space where mankind has looked to model our wonderful world for thousands of years.

A WORLD OF PATTERNS: DOES NATURE HOLD THE ANSWERS?

We live in a world consisting of a kaleidoscope of patterns. These patterns often possess critical cues as to how life on our planet functions, from the patterns in nature, mathematics, and science to the patterns that are responsible for the way humans live and process information. We are a part of an existence that is governed by myriad intricate and amazing processes, systems, subsystems, and interdependencies.

These patterns and themes play a pivotal role in the basic design of the planet and are at the core of how our world works. No matter how complex and intricate our natural world is, its basic structure and the way it is ordered are simple.

Let's consider a very simple example. Think of the anatomical makeup of living creatures. Most creatures share similar functions and systems, including reproductive, skeletal, muscular, and respiratory systems. These common systems or elements span a wide array of creatures, including mammals, reptiles, and amphibians. This includes animals such as birds, fish, frogs, snakes turtles and include us human beings. Although there is variation in the manner in which these common systems work, they all follow a similar pattern that spans each class of creature.

These patterns even transcend the animal kingdom and can be found in the plant world, as well. All plants possess similar processes and systems that serve as the foundation of how they operate, including their reproductive system, or even fundamental elements that serve the same functions as animals' skeletal and respiratory systems.

It is critical to identify and track these patterns and themes because they are at the core of how our natural world works, and they can provide us with models of how to structure our man-made world. Following patterns and themes in nature is not new; throughout time, man has looked to nature in order to design objects for his own use. Think of the airplane and the bird, the camera and the eye, ball joints and the shoulder joint, radar and bats, and even the pump's relation to the heart. These are just a few examples of the many that exist in our world.

Leonardo da Vinci, who to this day is considered one of the greatest minds in history, took lessons from nature. He is credited with inventing and pioneering work in many areas. Da Vinci is considered the father of the science of embryology and was the first to make detailed study of the human fetus. He also designed early versions of the airplane, military tank, helicopter, and submarine equipment. Even before Charles Darwin, da Vinci devised a theory that foreshadowed that of evolution. Da Vinci mastered and explored diverse and complicated subjects such as engineering, archeology, botany, and anatomy. The secret behind da Vinci's great genius was that he was a student of nature. Da Vinci believed that nature held all the answers on how to build and design our world. As a child and young man, da Vinci strove to understand in great detail how nature worked. He mimicked nature and, as such, was a pioneer in almost every field. Da Vinci saw subjects not as disjointed but as interconnected and inseparable.

In this spirit, and following what man has leveraged over thousands of years, I believe there is also a pattern in our natural world that will assist us in this new day. This pattern will effectively assist us in managing the most formidable forces that undermine a company's strategic objectives, enabling us to *master strategic risk*. Embedded in all systems in our natural world, this pattern can be applied to systems in the world we have created for ourselves. If we have looked to nature to create most of our man-made world and provide us with many of our modern-day conveniences, why should we not look to it to assist us in structuring how we manage organizations?

REFERENCES

"First Union: Fast Eddie's Future Bank." 1998. *Bloomberg BusinessWeek*, March 22.

Harrington, Jeff. 2003. "Wachovia Picks Branch Growth Over Mega Mergers." *St. Petersburg Times*, November 17.

Horwitz, Jeff. 2009. "Wachovia's End." *American Banker*, November 1.

Serres, Chris. 2011. "Wells Fargo's Next Stage: Cost Cuts." *The Star Tribune*, April 20.

Rothacker, Rick. 2010. "How Steel got the Wachovia Deal Done." *CNN Money*, August 30.

Cowen, R. (1995) History of Life (2nd edition); Blackwell Scientific Publications

Duellman WE and Trueb L (1986) Biology of Amphibians. NewYork: McGraw-Hill.

CHAPTER 2

The Three Elements: Creating, Facilitating, and Supporting Your Competitive Advantage

We live in a world of patterns—both in the natural world and the world we've created for ourselves. Throughout time, there are numerous examples where mankind has leveraged patterns or structures in nature to build many of his modern-day inventions and tools. From the airplane to the camera, from sonar to the ball joint, countless creations came from the careful study of nature. These patterns in nature can assist us understanding the forces that govern the world we've created, and in managing organizations.

A FRAMEWORK TAKEN FROM NATURE

Organizations are no different, for their basic structure and the dynamics that govern them are similar to systems found in nature. However, what makes this new insight into the parallels between organizational systems and natural systems important is that it provides us with new learnings, which can serve as powerful drivers of performance in companies. These performance drivers are at the core of an organization's ability to master strategic risk in a highly complex and dynamic world.

Natural Systems

If we closely observe how systems in our natural world work, there are certain core elements that ensure they operate effectively and with uncanny precision. I've observed a few of these elements only to discover that they are a part of all systems, processes, and living creatures in nature. Consider systems, processes, and the creatures in our natural world. There are essential activities and elements that ensure they grow and maintain themselves throughout their entire process or life cycle.

In the majority of these realities, there are aspects that serve as catalysts and are initiators. Think how there are also elements associated with them that enable or facilitate their activities. It is also apparent that all living creatures, systems, and processes are dependent on structural and supportive elements as well as elements that orchestrate various activities.

These core elements are tightly linked, operating in tandem to provide a holistic approach to drive effective performance in systems. This pattern is composed of three core elements. They are the creative, facilitative, and supportive elements (see Exhibit 2.1). These fundamental elements can be in the form of systems, processes, functions, and activities. I will refer to these three as elements or components throughout the book. Again, these elements exist in all systems, whether in nature or man-made. (In speaking of the man-made world, again, I am referring to everything in our existence that was created by man.)

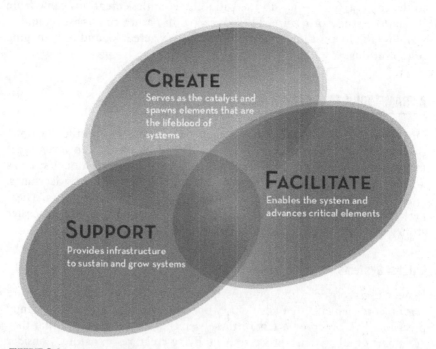

CREATE
Serves as the catalyst and spawns elements that are the lifeblood of systems

FACILITATE
Enables the system and advances critical elements

SUPPORT
Provides infrastructure to sustain and grow systems

EXHIBIT 2.1   The Three Elements

Webster's defines a system as "a regularly interacting or independent group of items forming a unified whole or a group of interacting bodies under the influence of related forces." The Three Elements applies to all systems that grow and/or must be sustained. It is everywhere! As a point of reference, *Webster's* definition of a system also aligns naturally with our understanding of how organizations are structured and operate, wouldn't we agree?

Out of the core elements of create, facilitate, and support, the creative element serves as the catalyst to initiate the entire process. It spawns the critical components that are the lifeblood of the system. Then the facilitate element serves as a conduit. It advances, transports, enables, and facilitates processes. In many instances it acts as a go-between, ensuring that critical elements get where they are needed.

Finally, there is the support element. The support element serves as the foundation of all systems. It provides required infrastructure, governance, and key administrative controls or processes. It supports everything needed to be sustained or grow in a particular system or environment.

Another reality concerning the Three Elements is that each element category contains a subset of the whole; the universal pattern that exists on one level of a system or process is replicated on other levels. Therefore, the pattern is fractal. For example, within the creative component in a complex system like the human body, you will find subsystems that also include the Three Elements (the creative, facilitative, and supportive elements).

Think of the role of systems in our world. Our planet is supported by a collection of millions, if not billions, of subsystems that grow and sustain it. At a macro level, these include systems in nature such as pollination, photosynthesis, ecosystems, and our water cycle. There are subsystems within each system, and the process is replicated all the way to the most fundamental component of life in a particular system or unit.

There are systems and subsystems that play creative, facilitative, and supportive roles. This is another important reality concerning our existence, meaning that the Three Elements are replicated on other levels like a continuous spiral. It's akin to the reality that life exists in the tiniest, most microscopic aspects of our reality on up to the grandest state of existence on the planet. Although many of these processes are complex, I will focus on the most fundamental or rudimentary processes.

Let me begin to explain how the Three Elements works by highlighting an example that you are very familiar with—the human body. A walk-through of the human body in various contexts will help you better understand the various characteristics of the Three Elements and how they work. This is true especially in the context of how it is replicated on different levels of reality.

THE HUMAN BODY AS AN EXAMPLE

As explained earlier, the human body is a system composed of myriad subsystems that possess functions that mirror or follow the Three Elements. These systems can be divided into the same three distinct roles: create, facilitate, and support (see Exhibit 2.2). A few systems that create are the reproductive system, the core system responsible for bringing forth human life, and hematopoiesis, the process in our bone marrow that produces blood. Systems that facilitate include the respiratory and circulatory systems, as they carry and advance essential life-supporting properties throughout the body. Facilitative systems in the body are also critical to enabling certain functions in the body. Finally, there are systems that are supportive in nature such as the skeletal and muscular systems. These systems play a critical role in ensuring that the body is sustained and is physically protected.

It gets even better as we apply the pattern to the human body in more detail. The reality of the Three Elements is that it is replicated continuously down to the tiniest element. First you have the entire body, which is composed of the three components. Then within each system within the body, the model is replicated again. Within each of these systems are subsystems that are made up of the similar components or elements.

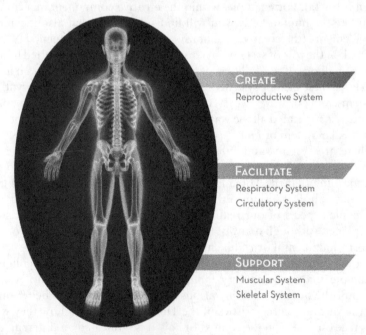

CREATE
Reproductive System

FACILITATE
Respiratory System
Circulatory System

SUPPORT
Muscular System
Skeletal System

EXHIBIT 2.2   Systems of the Human Body
Data Source: University of Buffalo Department of Biological Sciences Website (www
.biology.buffalo.edu/courses/bio531/lecture7.html)

Consider a creative system like the reproductive system. If we examine the system in detail, we observe that the reproductive system also possesses the three primary elements in the ovaries and the process of fertilization, fallopian tubes, and the uterus. The ovaries' primary role is to store the human egg and produce estrogen, the catalyst and critical element needed in female reproduction. The process of fertilization continues the creative process by initiating life through the union of the sperm and egg. The fallopian tubes' primary function is to transport the human egg from the ovary to the uterus and facilitate the process of fertilization. And finally, there is the uterus, which serves in a supportive function. Once the egg has left the ovary, it finally attaches itself to the lining of the uterus. There the uterus's primary role is to nourish the developing fetus prior to birth and to protect it.

If we were to continue to drill further down into the reproductive system, the pattern of the three elements would be replicated all the way down throughout this system to the tiniest element. Yes, the Three Elements are present all the way down to a single cell.

Each cell in your body also has the three components of the Three Elements embedded in it. At its core is the nucleus, which is the cell's creative component. It is the where DNA replication and other creative processes occur. A component or element of the cell that plays a facilitative role is its nuclear pore complexes. It facilitates the transport of critical substances from different compartments of the cell. This occurs through a vast network of transport cycles and receptors. Finally, the cell's plasma membrane and cytoskeleton play supportive roles. They protect the cell from its surrounding environment and help the cell maintain its shape.

While each of the core functions in a cell possess creative, facilitative, and supportive processes and activities, each has a primary function. This pattern is replicated to the nth degree through all life on our planet. It is important to have a solid understanding of how the Three Elements works in order to truly recognize its power and influence as it applies to our lives and to life in the world around us.

Think of how the Three Elements is inherently embedded in critical corporate activities, and how they are essential to internal operations. How organizational activities such as research and development, marketing, and cross-selling efforts, and back-office operations are at the epicenter of an organization's success. Let's take an additional look at another example from the body, the nervous system.

The Nervous System

Consider how the Three Elements correlate to the comprehensive nervous system. The brain, which is a part of the central nervous system (a subset of the nervous system), is the creative element or organ as it initiates or is the catalyst for activity in this system. Facilitative elements or components of the nervous system include the peripheral nervous system (PNS) and neurons. The PNS acts as a conduit in carrying impulses to and from the central nervous system, while neurons send signals throughout this system.

Supportive elements include the spinal column, which protects the spinal cord; the skull, which protects the brain; and critical membranes and meninges, which are essential to protecting the brain, spinal cord, and other components. As part of the PNS, the somatic and autonomic systems serve in a supportive capacity as they control or administer critical muscular and internal organ activities. All of the components, subsystems and parts of the nervous system act in tandem to effectively operate this essential system in our bodies.

Governance and the Body: The Cell Cycle and Temperature

To examine the pattern from a different angle, think of supportive elements in our body and how they "govern" or control important functions. These governance functions, although different than the infrastructural ones mentioned earlier, also play critical roles in support of our bodies. These elements order the flow and timing of certain processes essential to life. Staying with the cell theme, let's look at the important cell cycle.

The cell cycle and the process of cell division is one of the most critical in the human body. This important process is governed by rigid rules that ensure an orderly and carefully sequenced flow of events. During the development of a cell, various checkpoints are in place to ensure that each stage of the cycle of development is fully complete prior to the next phase beginning. This process also requires that a cell's DNA is intact and not damaged before it is divided.

These checkpoints are critical to ensure the development of healthy cells in our bodies. If there were a breakdown in this intricate checkpoint or governance process, cells in the body would divide in an uncontrolled manner. And although there is a process to repair damaged DNA in cells, this uncontrolled division of cells ultimately leads to diseases like cancer.

Or consider how our bodies regulate and "govern" temperature through numerous feedback mechanisms. These important mechanisms operate through the hypothalamus. As the body temperature rises and falls at various levels, these mechanisms are triggered to cause a number of responses to regulate temperature. These responses can include shivering, which increases heat production in our muscles; secretion of certain hormones to increase heat production; or the cessation of sweating to name a few.

These processes and functions ensure that our bodies are in a state of continual growth and sustainment. As our bodies are designed to foster and cultivate an environment that effectively supports us, so it must be with the culture of an organization in fostering the growth and sustainment of its employees and internal activities.

The Three Elements is also found in systems that sustain the natural world. It is found in processes such as pollination, the water cycle, and others. It is even found in ecosystems.

ECOSYSTEMS

As with the human body, ecosystems also possess a similar pattern as they are composed of the three elements (see Exhibit 2.3). The beginning of the process or system is kicked off by producers. They are the catalyst, as they create what becomes the lifeblood of the system. Producers, such as plants, provide food for the system. This is a critical role in providing energy to the entire system. The facilitate element is performed by consumers, such as plant-eating animals, which consume what is created by producers. They facilitate the process of energy transfer by passing on what they consume to the third component, decomposers, which play the support role.

Decomposers support the entire system by breaking down matter from the consumers (such as waste or a consumer's dead body) and releasing them

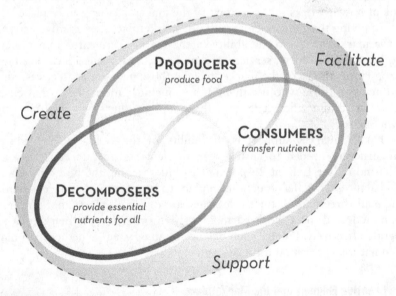

EXHIBIT 2.3   Ecosystems
Data Source: The University of Michigan Global Change Website (www.globalchange .umich.edu/globalchange1/current/lectures/kling/ecosystem/ecosystem.html)

back into the system. The materials released by decomposers are nutrients for plants (producers), which serve to initiate the cycle again by performing the creative aspect of the entire cycle.

Ecosystems illuminate an important aspect of the model in that the entire process must continually repeat itself in order for the system to operate effectively. The entire system would die if it were stopped after one cycle without returning nutrients to producers to begin the cycle again. There must also be balance within all ecosystems. If consumers extract too much from the creators (overgraze a field), this harms the entire system. These features of the model will be discussed in detail later.

Organizations share the same fundamental elements and components as found in our bodies and systems in nature. They have functions and activities that are creative, such as product development and innovation; facilitative, such as sales and brokering; and supportive, such as governance or technology. Just like in our bodies, in companies these functions and activities serve as the foundation of its sustainment and growth.

THE THREE ELEMENTS AND OUR MARKETPLACE

To understand how the Three Elements applies to organizations, let's first look at how it works in the context of the much broader marketplace.

Applying the Three Elements to our marketplace, the creative activities in the market speak to the ability of the market to create, innovate, and produce new products, services, technologies, and sciences. Market facilitation is the ability of the market to take those new goods, services, ideas, and items to those who use them. It also includes mechanisms that ensure the effective and efficient flow of those new products, services and other components.

Finally, market support is the ability of the system to provide the infrastructure needed to ensure that all elements operate effectively and in harmony (see Exhibit 2.4). It also includes having the necessary checks and balances as well as functions in place to support marketplace activities. While all three play distinct roles, they are of equal importance, are interconnected, and must work harmoniously in order for the marketplace to operate effectively. Indeed, such balance in any system, whether man-made or in nature, is essential for its overall viability.

The Creative Element and the Marketplace

As in systems in nature, the creative element is the lifeblood and primary initiator of activities in commerce. This is evident in all man-made systems, as

Create Market	Facilitate Market	Support Market
Catalyst	*Enables*	*Supports*
Research	Sales/Trading	Regulatory Framework
Development	Import/Export	Legal System
Exploration	Financial Markets	Educational System
Innovation	Technology	Military
Invention	Taxes	Infrastructure
Creative Arts	Venture Capital	Government
high risk		*low risk*
	CREATIVITY	
high reward		*low reward*

EXHIBIT 2.4   Marketplace Activities

our lives, both commercial and personal, are shaped by innovation and creativity. Everything in our man-made existence emanates from the idea! Ideas from all corners of the world spawn new realities and flood our existence with meaning. Hence, it is the creative element in systems that drives performance and greatly influences what is generally needed for growth and sustainment.

Facilitative and supportive elements in systems follow and enable and provide the infrastructure for what has been spawned by the creative process. In commerce, the creative element is the catalyst for new industries, professions, technologies, and requirements. This applies to many new and transformative innovations such as the smart grid, digital technology, and the computer, to name a few.

For example, think of the impact that the smart grid and new green technologies will have on our lives. The creation of the smart grid—an improved electrical grid for the United States—is creative in the context of the Three Elements model. This new way of leveraging technology to make our energy systems more efficient and cost effective is a product of creativity and innovation.

Through this innovation, we are spawning new commerce, jobs, and a host of supporting services. However, smart grid technology also has characteristics that are facilitative and supportive, just as do all creative functions or elements in nature. Ultimately, the smart grid will account for trillions of dollars in our global marketplace and spawn myriad opportunities across the planet. Cisco Inc. views the Internet Smart Grid as a $100 billion market opportunity.

In a May 2009 interview, Marie Hattar, vice president of marketing in its Network Solutions Group stated, "Our expectation is that this network will be 100 or 1,000 times larger than the Internet. If you think about it, some homes have Internet access, but some don't. Everyone has electricity access—all of those homes could potentially be connected."

Another example of the creative element in business is the ubiquitous credit card. The general-purpose credit card was introduced by Bank of America in 1966, although versions of credit cards existed before then. Think of how much commerce and how many products and services have been born out of this one innovation. We have created an entire industry from this product of innovation.

Yes, at the core of the marketplace and society is creativity and the idea. Think of the nineteenth and twentieth centuries and all of the amazing things that came out of this period; from the automobile to the airplane, from the combustible engine to the computer, from the telephone to camera. All of these inventions have contributed significantly to the advancement and quality of mankind.

It is important to provide a more expansive view and understanding of the role of the creative element before I apply it to organizations, for it helps to underscore how pervasive and critical it is in the much broader marketplace and our daily lives.

Continuous Creativity   Creativity is a continuous process. It is an inherent aspect of how life is ordered. As in all systems of nature, whether it is the continuous cell development in the human body or processes in systems in nature such as photosynthesis, creativity is cyclical and continuous. In the marketplace, the continuous process of creativity ensures growth and sustainment.

The Austrian American economist and political scientist Joseph Schumpeter popularized the theory dubbed "Creative Destruction," in which he described an evolutionary and continuous process of creativity. It was a reality in capitalism he viewed as necessary to fuel production and growth:

> *Capitalism, then, is by nature a form or method of economic change and not only never is but never can be stationary. And this evolutionary character of the capitalist process is not merely due to the fact that economic life goes on in a social and natural environment which changes and by its change alters the data of economic action; this fact is important and these changes (wars, revolutions and so on) often condition industrial change, but they are not its prime movers. Nor is this evolutionary character due to a quasi-automatic increase in population and capital or to the vagaries of monetary systems, of which exactly the same thing holds true. The*

fundamental impulse that sets and keeps the capitalist engine in motion comes from the new consumers' goods, the new methods of production or transportation, the new markets, the new forms of industrial organization that capitalist enterprise creates.[1]

Schumpeter believed that the pursuit of self-interest and improvement also influenced this continuous cycle. The shifting of resources and inputs in declining sectors to those sectors and areas that were expanding also created a natural destruction of the old ones.

Though the primary focus of Schumpeter's theory is on how through the introduction of new products, services, and markets old ones are undoubtedly destroyed. However, a salient point to draw from in his approach is the cyclical nature of the marketplace—how changes in market components such as enhanced productivity, human behavior, and technological advancement influence the evolutionary dynamic of capitalistic economies. This underscores how the creative element in systems is not only cyclical but also continuous.

Facilitation and Our Marketplace   The facilitative aspects of our marketplace are the conduit through which goods and services flows. Goods, services, and products reach consumers in many ways, such as through small businesses, real estate agents, stockbrokers, marketing, advertising, mortgage brokers, and so on. There are other aspects of market facilitating related to dealing or transacting that complement the market-creating products and services. These types of transactions can have a significant impact on a particular industry, even in times of economic challenges. An example of this is that of professional sports and advertising.

I consider advertising and marketing a facilitative function; however, there are creative aspects to facilitation as we see in the next example. In professional sports, the catalyst or creative aspect rests with the product or players who produce the sporting event. Marketing and advertising is the facilitative element because it advances and promotes the product, the sporting event. Remember the pattern in systems here, as each of the elements has embedded in it the whole model.

During the past five years, we've experienced one of the most severe recessions of the past century. Over 10 million Americans lost their jobs, although the job market is currently experiencing some growth. Additionally, many businesses have filed for bankruptcy and corporations continue to tighten their belts due to the need to slash expenses and reduce costs.

As the market contracted, you might think that it had a major impact on professional sports. If you have watched most professional sporting events on television during these past few years, you can see that in many venues attendance has significantly declined. Earlier during the recession, many corporations pulled their sponsorships of teams across the sporting world in order to save precious marketing dollars. Nevertheless, despite all of these major forces impacting professional sports, how is it that we continue to see a slew of athletes sign and receive record-breaking contracts and their teams experience tremendous growth?

The NFL itself has experienced steady growth in revenue during this time period, as well as other sporting leagues and events such as college football through the NCAA and its Bowl Championship Series (BCS). While corporations have cut back their sponsorship and attendance had been far below average, how are teams able to open up their rich coffers and sign athletes to history-making contracts? When we apply old economy rules, this doesn't make sense. However, in applying the new rules, it makes perfect sense.

In today's sports and entertainment world, lucrative television and licensing deals are negotiated by teams. They are no longer restricted to ticket sales as their only source of direct revenue. They have revenue pouring in from their television and merchandising deals. This enables them, even in tough economic times, to turn a profit. While many in the general population have personally felt the economic slowdown of the past several years, they still could participate and enjoy their favorite team or athlete in their living rooms.

This further demonstrates the many facets of the facilitative elements and the beauty of our free market system. Through advertising, companies wish to ultimately reach prospective customers. Because there is a limited amount of airtime allocated for each event, depending on how popular it is, advertisers will pay handsome dollars for these spots. Professional teams are then able to sign long-term agreements with the media and television conglomerates that air these events. Therefore, these organizations continue to make money and pay their athletes large sums, despite poor economic conditions.

Support and Our Marketplace　　There are many facets to supporting the overall marketplace. They include systems, processes, and infrastructure that support the creative and facilitative activities in the market. For example, a critical part of our marketplace is our regulatory framework. As goods and services are distributed to the consumer, functions such as the Food and Drug Administration or the Securities and Exchange Commission are necessary to protect the end user. Infrastructure—such as child labor laws, workplace standards, and simple traffic laws—is necessary to affect the appropriate functioning and balance in the marketplace.

Infrastructure also includes critical technology and telecommunication assets, as well as roads, highways, and utilities. The many skills and roles that individuals play are also critical to ensuring a properly functioning marketplace such as accountants, doctors, lawyers, analysts, teachers, technicians, and laborers. All of these functions are necessary to ensuring the support of an effective and smooth flowing marketplace.

THE THREE ELEMENTS AND THE AUTO INDUSTRY

The auto industry offers an example of how the Three Elements works in our marketplace. The creation of any new automobile model or type is a product of innovation and, depending on the make and model, services a particular market segment. For example, think of how in 1984 the launch of Chrysler's newly designed minivan was the primary catalyst for its historic comeback. This newly designed and functioning automobile immediately took the place of the family station wagon.

On a broader scale, the introduction of the sport utility vehicle (SUV) in the mid-1990s propelled all three domestic automakers to record profits. Through introducing and promoting a new body style and type of vehicle, automakers were able to bolster revenue through SUV sales. Now, however, SUVs are dragging down sales of auto companies due to the economy and high gas prices. During the create portion of the cycle, the production of an automobile spawns many activities, including the mass production of new vehicles and the manufacturing of other components and parts that comprise a car.

Think of the many jobs that are created in the building of an actual automobile and all of the related components such as the battery, alternator, tires, engine, seats, upholstery, carpet, and transmission. Is it any wonder that we've gone to such great lengths to save our domestic auto industry?

Now consider how this product of innovation, the car, gets to you, the end user, through the facilitate function. Automobiles are distributed through a very sophisticated yet simple network of market-making conduits, namely, dealerships. These dealerships are usually independently affiliated with the creators of those cars, the car manufacturers. Dealerships are the conduit through which most automobiles flow to consumers.

The final component in this example is that of market support. If a car could not be supported or maintained, think of how much less useful it would be. Can you imagine millions of people doing all of the maintenance and repairs on their own cars? It would be costly, time consuming, and incredibly burdensome for all of us.

In this example, there are three basic forms of marketplace support for the auto industry. There is the support offered by auto dealers in the form of their service departments. Those support services are also offered by independent franchises such as Firestone, Jiffy Lube, and Midas. Finally, there are privately owned and operated automobile maintenance shops.

The three types of automobile servicing businesses are the backbone of the overall industry and generate significant revenue. In fact, if you asked a dealership that also offers maintenance services, they would tell you that a significant part of the dealership's revenue stream comes from this aspect of the business.

These services can be further broken down into businesses that offer auto servicing and maintenance versus those that offer body shop services. Regardless of where these functions play in the model as applied to the auto industry, each is a critical component and is vital to the effective functioning of the whole. This model, as it applies to the auto industry, can also be applied to other industries.

THE THREE ELEMENTS AND ORGANIZATIONS

In today's unrelenting marketplace, organizations are challenged in finding their competitive footing. Whether it is in the ability to continuously create new products and services or ensure the effective management of critical resources or ways in which to advance critical products and services to the marketplace, these challenges are at the core of managing strategic risk and drive performance.

Consider a company with a strong legacy of performance: Motorola, Inc. Through its rich history of introducing innovative products to the marketplace, it experienced tremendous success. However, like many others, Motorola ultimately failed, as it was challenged in managing critical elements fundamental to an organization's success.

The Motorola Story

For close to 80 years Motorola, Inc. was a pioneer of innovation in the United States. Its long history of creating leading-edge technology innovations has had a major impact on both the semiconductor and communications industries. Founded in Chicago in 1928, few American companies rival the storied history of innovation and creativity of Motorola, Inc.

Once an industry leader in cutting-edge technology, Motorola pioneered the development of the transistor radio, in 1958 developed the first two-way radio for NASA, built the first rectangular television, invented Six Sigma, and in 1983 was the first to introduce the commercial cell phone. In 1930, Motorola created and installed the first car radio, and during World War II, its Handie Walkie-Talkie enabled American troops to communicate more effectively on the battlefield. This portable two-way radio invention is considered the predecessor to today's cell phone. Motorola is also credited with developing the first global satellite communications network.

Motorola created the first cellular phone, which at that time weighed four pounds and allowed one hour of talk time. By 1994, it had cornered 60 percent of the U.S. wireless market, and between 1993 and 1995 averaged 27 percent in growth. By 2002, Motorola had become the second-largest cell phone manufacturer in the world. However, it quickly saw its U.S. market share in cell phones drop from 18.4 percent in 2007 to 6 percent by 2009. Despite its rich tradition and track record of innovation, Motorola steadily lost its market share.

One of Motorola's missteps is that it failed to continue its rich tradition of innovation! Although Motorola led its competitors in the global analog cell phone market, it was slow to embrace digital technology. It was ill prepared for digital technology as it hit the market.

Its top executives and a core of leading engineers also believed customers were satisfied with analog phones. Over time, Motorola was outwitted by its competitors, as it was slow to enter the global smartphone market, not entering it until 2010. Its competitors understood emerging user behavior and needs as smartphones enabled customers to easily handle e-mail and data needs.

By 2011, after realizing billions in losses and significant market share, Motorola was divided into two public companies. The first was Motorola Solutions, a data communications and telecom equipment provider, and the second, Motorola Mobility. In May 2012, Google purchased Motorola Mobility for 12 billion dollars.

Motorola's ultimate demise did not occur overnight and was not solely due to its inability to innovate, but was due to several additional missteps along the way. Over time, the company became blinded by its success as its key executives failed to realize the needs of a changing market place. Management's complacency was described at times as bordering on arrogance. Even in its core operations, it had made critical mistakes.

For example, in the 1990s Motorola was dropped by several telecom giants due to its slow response in addressing the poor switching ability of its wireless equipment. This, coupled with internal warring factions, ill-timed strategies, and spotty execution led to its eventual fall. However, Motorola's demise is no different than any others that have occurred over the past few years.

An organization's ability to innovate and create competitive products and services is vital to remaining competitive in an unrelenting marketplace. Creativity serves as the lifeblood in all organizations; without a constant fresh flow, the organization will die.

While creativity is essential there are other activities that serve as the foundation of organizational success over time. They include a company's administrative and structural elements as well as activities that enable and

	CREATIVE	FACILITATIVE	SUPPORTIVE
ACTIVITIES AND FUNCTIONS	Research and Development	Sales	Governance
		Marketing and Advertising	Administration and Management
	New Products and Services		Operations
		Trading	
	Innovation		Data
		Procurement and Supply Chain	Technology Infrastructure
	Strategy		Customer Service
		The Internet	
			Risk Management and Compliance
			Legal, Finance, and Human Resources

EXHIBIT 2.5   Organizational Activities and the Three Elements

advance critical products and services. These activities are vital to a company's ability to manage internal operations, their customer, and external market forces. They are essential to mastering strategic risk.

Aligning the Three Elements with Corporate Activities

The components of the Three Elements apply to organizations, both private and public. Organizations are systems and, as such, must be managed in a manner that ensures the efficient and effective operations of its activities. It's no wonder that when we observe the key activities in corporations, they naturally align with the Three Elements (see Exhibit 2.5).

THE CREATIVE ELEMENT IN ORGANIZATIONS

Success in companies originates with the creative element—the initiator and the pivotal player in all systems. Without creativity and innovation, a corporation cannot experience sustainable growth over time. It is paramount to long-term success. The ability to create and introduce new products and services to the marketplace spawns new opportunities for revenue.

Whole new departments and requirements in corporations are a result of creativity and innovation, whether it is a sports shoe company introducing a new line of shoes, a financial services organization introducing an innovative new banking product and services, or even a technology company introducing a new application or technology to customers. Creativity and innovation—whether it is developed internally or adopted by an organization and leveraged for its customer base—is a critical part of ensuring its growth and sustainment.

Facilitation

Facilitation serves as the conduit in corporations. These functions include brokering, marketing, communications, procurement, and sales. They not only ensure that new products and services are delivered to customers but are the primary player in furthering growth and sustainment. While the creative element produces new elements, the facilitation element is the mechanism that carries it forward.

Facilitation in corporations can also take the form of functions such as procurement in that it furthers growth and sustainment by creating opportunities to reduce the costs and expense in delivering products and services. It also includes tools such as the Internet, as this new phenomenon has been a powerful enabler of commerce.

Support

The supportive element is the foundation in corporations. It serves to provide the critical infrastructure needed for growth and sustainment. These are functions or activities such as an organization's structure and internal processes, policies and procedures, and functions such as information technology (IT) and legal—the list is endless.

A critical support reality that is fundamental to corporate success is organizational culture. Although organizational culture may not be as tangible as the physical elements that are necessary to support organizational activities, it is nevertheless a very real determiner of how well a corporation performs. Building and fostering the right organizational culture is as critical to corporate performance as the importance of our body's maintaining the right internal environment to ensure that our internal processes and systems operate effectively. Consider the critical functions in the body that controls and governs the important cell cycle process.

The criticality of the support element also reinforces the holistic nature of the Three Elements, for the success or failure of any one component is tied to the performance of the entire system. When a corporation's critical support components are broken down or missing, it harms the company's overall performance. However, if support components are working as they should, they go a long way in supporting the overall sustainment and growth of the organization.

INFORMATION TECHNOLOGY AS AN EXAMPLE

An IT department in a typical corporation stands on its own as a support function to the corporation as a whole. If we follow the pattern there will be the Three Elements that comprise the IT department (create, facilitate, and support). The primary role of technology in organizations is to support underlying business activities.

The IT department is one of the most critical support elements in the system that is a corporation. As with most systems, there are subsystems. Through an assemblage of different components and parts this critical function serves as a company's backbone. There is a creative function such as a system designer, a facilitative function in the network, and finally a support function such as information security. A system designer or engineer plays a creative role in the IT process in that it creates models that serve as the basis for determining the best use of a system. The model selected is then tested; however, the system designer also then creates coding charts to be used as a guide to develop the software by programmers. This process also entails taking the technical specifications and requirements to create the system.

The network function within technology is primarily a facilitate role. It is responsible for linking computers and devices for communication and to share critical resources and information. When you think of technology devices such as modems, switches, and routers, they are at the core of the networking function in technology.

Finally, you have a support function such as information security. Its primary role is supportive in nature, as its primary objective is to protect the organization's critical assets—those related to the physical protection of technology assets as well as critical electronic assets which include financial, consumer, and proprietary information.

As with all systems in nature, this pattern—the presence of the three components of the Three Elements in corporations—would repeat itself all the way to the most fundamental business units within the technology organization. The first would be applied at the division level as laid out earlier, but then apply it to a function within the division such as to the systems engineering, network, or information security groups.

EVERYTHING OLD IS NEW AGAIN

The Three Elements represents ancient insight appearing in a timely manner to address the challenges we face today. These challenges span the entire spectrum of issues that exist on an organizational and even global level. It is clear that, no matter how sophisticated our world becomes, there is ancient yet simple wisdom that is relevant in a modern world. The type of knowledge I speak of has been passed down through the ages and is deeply rooted in the flow of life and natural order of our world. There's nothing new under the sun.

These ancient treasures are quite simply universal truths. They have been here since the beginning of time and will continue on into the future far beyond our time on this planet. Examples include the wisdom found in ancient writings such as Sun Tzu's *The Art of War* and Lao Tzu's *Tao Te Ching*. Both of these ancient passages were written between the years of 700 and 300 B.C. and can be applied to our daily lives in many different contexts.

The *Tao Te Ching* is an ancient Chinese book of wisdom attributed to the great Chinese scholar Lao Tzu, although historians still debate whether he was the author. It is believed to have been written during the early third or late fourth century B.C. The *Tao Te Ching* provides the foundation for the Chinese religion of Taoism, which is the cornerstone of Chinese thought.

In Taoism, there is one undivided truth at the root of all things in life. For example, in Taoism man is a micro replication of the universe, and the human body is connected to the five Chinese elements: fire, wood, water, metal, and earth.

Though written more than 2,000 years ago, the *Tao Te Ching* contains ancient enlightenment that still is relevant in our modern world. Its passages are rich and point us to a deeper meaning of our existence. Another aspect of the *Tao* is that the wisdom shared is practical and can be applied to one's daily life.

Throughout the centuries, many people have also applied *The Art of War* to their lives. If you peruse the bookshelves of corporate climbers, you often will find a copy of this ancient treasure nestled between their favorite books on organizational culture and corporate success. Although *The Art of War* can be applied in a much broader context, It generally is used as a tool to assist businesspeople to navigate their way through daily challenges and corporate politics.

The *Tao Te Ching*, *The Art of War*, and other ancient texts transcend time and will always enrich the lives of those who study them. The Three Elements is similar in that it sheds light on a reality that is timeless. Yes, we've experienced significant advances in civilization through amazing capabilities provided to us through science and technology. However, as much as things change, they remain the same.

Regardless of the significant advancements in our capabilities, the most fundamental building blocks of this existence will always remain the same. Life on this planet has and will always be dictated by people, processes, and, ultimately, systems. And there is no greater example of where to apply these fundamental requirements than in organizational systems.

SUMMARY

It's time to get back to basics. Again, consider how complex and intricate the processes and systems in nature can be. Think how amazing and complex the human body is, or, for that matter, any system in nature. They account for myriad variables, possibilities, and outcomes.

Are the institutions and systems we created for ourselves more complex and advanced than those found in nature? For some reason we believe we are too advanced for simple yet time-proven solutions for the answers to our challenges. It's as if we often associate simplicity with ineffectiveness. This is far from the truth.

Let's remember that we showed up in this world with the Earth already in place. Our world was not the brainchild of some human being, but some other, to date unexplainable, phenomenon created it. So we must look to that world for some of the fundamental solutions to our most complex challenges.

Leveraging the Three Elements in organizations provides a unique opportunity to mastering an organization's strategic risk. When referencing an organization's strategic risk, I speak of those internal and external realities that pose the greatest threat to a company's ability to achieve its strategic objectives. They run the gamut and include effectively managing and accounting for internal operations, competitors, meeting customer expectations and demands, governance, the external marketplace and its employees.

While these activities are not new to organizations and their internal capabilities, applying them with intent and rigor will yield more consistent and predictable results.

QUESTIONS

1. What activities and functions in your organization are areas that create products or services or produce certain output that is of value to your customer?
2. Are there areas outside those traditional creative functions that should be explored?
3. Is there a discipline or defined process in your organization that ensures that you continue to introduce and develop new products and services?
4. If there is a process or discipline, can it be improved?
5. Identify the most critical facilitative activities and functions in your organization.

6. Where and what are they and how can you leverage them more effectively to create new products and services?
7. What of supportive activities? Are there opportunities to exploit new growth opportunities in these areas?

NOTE

1. Joseph Schumpeter, *Capitalism, Socialism and Democracy* (New York: Harper, 1975 [orig. pub. 1942]), 82–85.

REFERENCES

Cardenas, Felipe. 2003. "Motorola's 75 Years Are a History of Technical Evolution." *Caribbean Business*, October 2, 33.

Crocket, Roger O., and Peter Elstrom. 1998. "How Motorola Lost Its Way." *BusinessWeek*, May 4, 140–148.

Franklin Institute. "The Human Heart, Resource for Science Learning."

Genetics Home Reference, a service of the U.S. National Library of Medicine. 2012. "Your Guide to Understanding Genetic Conditions." August 20.

Gubman, Ed. 2006. "When Innovation Becomes Efficiency: Motorola's Global Supply Chain Initiative." *Human Resources Planning*, July 1, 23–24.

LaMonica, Martin. 2009. "CISCO: Smart Grid Will Eclipse Size of Internet." *CNET News Green Tech*, May 18.

"Mr. G's Environmental Systems." 2012. *NeoEase*, February 5.

National Center for Biotechnology Information. 2003. "A Science Primer: A Basic Introduction to the Science Underlying NCBI Resources," February 10.

Nicholas, Tom. 2003. "Why Schumpeter Was Right: Innovation, Market Power, and Creative Destruction in 1920s America." *Journal of Economic History* 63, no. 4 (December): 1023–1058.

Solow, Robert. 2007. "Heavy Thinker," review of *Prophet of Innovation: Joseph Schumpeter and Creative Destruction*, by Thomas K. McCraw. *New Republic*, May 21, 48–50.

University of Arizona. 2004. The Biology Project, Department of Biochemistry and Molecular Bio Physics. April 1997, rev. August.

CHAPTER 3

The Three Forces: Mastering Strategic Risk with Repetition, Balance, and Movement

L ife marches to the cadence of a harmonious existence. This reality orders the flow of all living systems and influences their proper functioning. Performance in systems, both man-made and in nature, holds sway to three primary forces; movement, repetition, and balance. This phenomenon rules our world!

ANTICIPATING CHANGE: TOYOTA

Realizing the coming change in demographics of the U.S. population, in the late 1980s Toyota embarked on an ambitious journey to become the number one car seller to the Hispanic market. Today, as a result of its carefully orchestrated strategy, the car company is the most popular car brand among American Hispanics. If we look at the eye opening data, you can see why Toyota's big bet paid off.

However, Toyota's pursuit of this emerging market is more impressive when we consider that its pursuit of this burgeoning group occurred at a time when few companies saw the enormous opportunity ahead. The audacious bet Toyota made anticipated the sweeping change that would result in a major shift to our socioeconomic landscape. This shift has created an economic opportunity that companies today, across industries, are scrambling to seize. Early on, Toyota paid attention to the emerging Hispanic/Latino community's buying potential. It paid careful attention to the data that showed strong population growth trends.

Between the years 2000 and 2009 the Hispanic community made up at least 50 percent of U.S. population growth. As of 2013 Hispanics made up 17 percent of the nation's population. Today, the Hispanic population is the fastest-growing ethnic group in the nation. What's even more startling is that between the late 1990s and 2007 there was a 126 percent increase in U.S. Hispanic households making more than $100,000 per year. This intense economic growth has increased the purchasing power of this community from $862 billion in 2007 to $1.2 trillion in 2012.

The data relating to the auto industry and the Hispanic community are even more compelling. From 1994 to 2005 the Hispanic community's spending on new vehicles went from $9.8 billion to $22 billion. While in 2005 the national number for new car growth was at an anemic 1.9 percent, the Hispanic community increased its new car purchases that year by 9.2 percent. It accounts for over 10 percent of new vehicles registrations in the United States today.

However, the awareness of how significant Hispanic consumers have become to our nation's economic picture became even clearer in 2002. This is when the census figures showed that Hispanics had become the largest minority in the United States. It wasn't until after the release of this information that companies began to pay careful attention to the Hispanic community, launching special marketing efforts aimed at luring Hispanic consumers.

Marketing to this group also changed as advertisers realized that there needed to be more effective ways to reach this community. It could not be a one-size-fits-all strategy, as this community possesses many different facets that distinguish its various subcultures. This meant that companies interested in capturing this coveted market were now required to design more sophisticated strategies that reached specific segments of this community.

For example, the fact that approximately 60 percent of Hispanics who live in America are born in the United States needed to be addressed, as this emerging group within the community tends not to view Spanish media. Marketing experts realized that Hispanic children born in the United States were also young, upwardly mobile, tech-savvy, and favor popular American shows. This group was also either bilingual or has a preference for communication in English. However, they were typically ignored by many brands.

From 1999 to 2003 Toyota increased sales to the Hispanic market by 50 percent, as compared to 26 percent by the rest of the Industry. Finally, in 2004, after aggressively campaigning to capture the Hispanic market, Toyota became the most popular car brand among this community.

However, Toyota's big breakthrough came when during the 2006 Super Bowl half-time show, it aired an ad that showcased the new Camry Hybrid. The Toyota commercial was a major milestone. Today, Toyota continues to be the most popular car brand among Latinos. For example, it sells more than half the hybrids bought by Hispanics.

There are other tactics Toyota employs to drive its strategy. One of the strategies entails sponsoring important Latin and Hispanic community events. For example, in September 2012, Toyota was the presenting sponsor of Fiesta DC, the largest Latino festival in the DC area. The event brought together social media and technology influencers, community leaders, educators, and governmental officials. This was important, as it demonstrated the company's commitment to the Hispanic community by tying into an important cultural activity. Tellingly, Toyota was the only automotive sponsor.

Although Nissan and Hyundai have experienced success with this market, Toyota's efforts and carefully executed plan have propelled it to the top of this market. Toyota understands how to reach and effectively market to this market. It executes its strategy by keeping abreast of the important segments in this community and by embracing change.

THREE FORCES THAT DICTATE PERFORMANCE IN SYSTEMS

Performance in all systems is dictated by movement, repetition, and balance. As with the Three Elements—create, facilitate, and support—these forces are present in all systems that must either grow or be sustained. They exist in both natural and man-made systems. In today's dynamic marketplace companies must account for these forces to master strategic risk.

Movement refers to the process of moving or, more important, a change in place or position. This movement can take many forms, physical or nonphysical, and may or may not be apparent in the world around us. Movement and change can refer to the images, sounds, and other nonphysical stimuli that we experience.

In order for any system to operate effectively, it must be in a constant state of equilibrium. In this context, balance means that every element must work collectively and harmoniously to ensure that underlying processes perform optimally and are carefully allocated. Every element or key component—whether it is the creative, facilitative, or supportive function—must operate as a distinct entity unto itself while being interdependent on the others.

Another reality is that all systems possess repetitive processes. This is how systems function in order to ensure optimum performance. Key processes and subprocesses are repeated in order to sustain, grow, and advance the entire system. In systems, if critical processes are not cyclical or repetitive, there can be no growth or sustainment.

Movement, repetition, and balance are the primary drivers and influencers of systems both in nature and our man-made world.

MOVEMENT AND CHANGE IN NATURE

Of the Three Forces that affect systems, none other is as influential as movement. While repetition and balance are of equal importance, movement shapes the rules that govern life in nature and the world we have created for ourselves. In fact, movement is one of the most important forces in existence. John F. Kennedy once said, "Change is the law of life, and those who look only to the past or present are certain to miss the future."

Every living thing in our natural world shares two things in common: they must grow, and this growth depends on being sustained by the outside world. Whether it be plant life or animals, all creatures, and all systems and processes in nature, have this in common—they all must grow and be sustained. And both of these processes require movement.

At the heart of all processes in nature is movement, as it is the primary force that ensures that the world around us operates with precision and great effect. Consider the important and critical processes in our world and how movement is at the core of how they work; from the changing of the seasons to pollination, from evaporation to fertilization.

Think of the migration of creatures and insects during pivotal times of the year to ensure their survival. We live in a constantly changing, shifting, and moving physical world, as all inhabitants of our planet are governed by the force of movement.

We can experience much of the movement through our senses, while other movement is not as apparent to us. Think about the blood that at this very moment is flowing through your veins. You know it is flowing, yet you generally do not feel it traverse continuously and in great volumes throughout your entire body. Movement is constant and is a part of the reality of even lower levels of life in all living things, such as the millions of cells and organisms constantly moving through our bodies. Both types of movement—apparent and hidden—are critical to our lives.

The dynamics of a constantly changing world require a corresponding response in all living things that experience this change. Think of the cells in the human body. As a foreign or unfamiliar element enters into our bodies, this change that occurs due to movement triggers a corresponding reaction within us. What naturally occurs is that the body and critical systems that protect and sustain it kick in to ensure that our internal systems respond in the appropriate manner to keep us in balance.

Movement and Change in the World We've Created

Movement, along with the ensuing change that results from it, has a tremendous impact on us and the world we've created. Our world is continually shifting, moving, growing, and evolving. Everything in our world is in a state of constant change, from the physical Earth itself to everything living and existing on it.

Contemplate the movement and corresponding change occurring across the globe and how these subtle and often significant shifts impact all forms of life. These changes are as varied as the environment, health, or social and economic forces that shape our day-to-day lives. Think of the tremendous social and political change that has swept through the Middle East in the past few years. Millions of citizens across that region are calling for change in the form of new freedoms and democracy.

The catalyst of these events has been movement and change. A now-wired world, especially through the Internet, has altered and shifted people's understanding of the world around them. It has truly transformed their concept of reality and of what is possible!

Conversely, think of what happens when there is little change or move-ment, especially as it relates to us as human beings. We are inherently designed to move and experience changes physically, emotionally, intellec-tually, and socially. Better yet, think about what would happen should the natural world around us cease to operate and function in the rhythm and cadence it has throughout history.

What would become of our planet and all life on it? Where there is no movement or change, there is no growth, which leads to stagnation and ultimately death. There are many examples in business of how the lack of movement and change has negatively affected a business or an industry.

Another example of movement and change is evidenced by the significant influence of a powerful tool in our lives. This tool I speak of is the television. Although there are many challenges relating to the television, in my mind it is one of the most powerful forces of transformation in our world today.

Think about the billions of people around the globe who have access to a television, and how the images displayed on the television have such a power-ful and transformative impact on us all. These images transport us to places unimagined and unreachable. Viewing the images can ignite in us the desire to forge ahead and achieve things that transcend our current station in life. This is also the power behind books, allowing readers to go places far beyond their current reality. Again, by being exposed to new ideas, concepts, and experiences, our reality changes. These new realities serve as the catalyst for new aspirations.

When a system does not have movement and change, it operates like a closed form of government such as communism. Any closed society or country cannot succeed by standing still in a world that is constantly shifting, moving, and evolving. Even as a society or country closes itself, this action alone runs contrary to the reality flowing within its boundaries.

Movement, change, and development are core to the forces that influence and dictate life within it. All types of systems—including governments—are inextricably tied to these realities and must respond on many fronts to a world that changes on many levels. Additionally, the foundation of any country is its people; without their exposure to new ideas and information, they become stagnant, making it difficult for them to grow. When a country's people are not continually moving, growing, and hence experiencing change, they are not receiving the stimulation needed to truly advance.

This is also present in organizations, as often we may work for a leader who micromanages the activities of his or her employees. Micromanagement not only stifles progress in organizations or groups but also inhibits growth in individuals. A manager, leader, or employee who has been given certain responsibilities and is not able to execute them due to a manager's insisting on making all the decisions cannot grow or thrive as an individual or leader. Being provided opportunities to make decisions in various contexts enables individuals to be confronted with new experiences and learnings. This new opportunity opens a new world for individuals, providing them with growth and enrichment.

This dynamic also transcends systems of government and can be applied to communities or groups of people representing a host of characteristics. It can be applied to a group in either a socioeconomic, cultural, or ethnic context, for example, communities in Appalachia or ethnic groups in our society that face formidable challenges.

When a group exists outside the flow of fresh and emerging ideas, knowledge, know-how, resources, and even people, it becomes stagnant. Over time, this stagnation and the failure to infuse a new lifeblood, if you will, into the community will have significant consequences. These consequences emerge in the form of systemic patterns and issues that negatively affect the group or community in various ways—health, economic, lifestyle, educational, and even social.

They may be due to the lack of resources to obtain fresh water and healthy food. Or it may be an inability to acquire critical and new medical treatments, resources, and information. Or the community may not have access to important information that can improve the economic conditions it finds itself in. While there are certain groups who have with intent extracted themselves from systems we have created, this holds true for groups that are a part of and live within our system.

Eventually, a closed group or community will buckle under the weight of these systemic forces. Think about the issues that plague poverty-stricken communities within our country like Appalachia and any large inner-city community. Think about what is occurring in the world beyond our borders, as millions of our fellow human beings fight to exist as a result of being outside the flow of crucial information and resources.

An example that comes to mind is the staggering devastation facing Africa as the result of HIV, famine, and the lack of clean water. The lives of millions of our fellow human beings remain under siege as they struggle daily to simply survive. There are many reasons why this occurs; however, these situations highlight the importance of movement and the need for all human beings to exist and live within the flow of critical resources and vital information.

Balance in Nature

Balance is an essential part of everything that exists in our world. It is a critical part of every system in nature and our man-made world. Balance is also an integral element that keeps everything in our world performing optimally. It is quite simply a very real and important part of our natural world as everything in nature performs harmoniously and with precision to ensure balance.

Think about your own body, our critical water cycle in nature, and ecosystems. All components are ordered in a manner to ensure that they provide equilibrium to the underlying system they support.

How about the water cycle in nature? All of the processes within this system or cycle—evaporation, condensation, and precipitation—are both independent and dependent on each other. They all act harmoniously to ensure that one of the planet's most critical processes operates effectively. When these processes in the water cycle are not in balance, the planet experiences myriad challenges, such as drought, floods, and erosion. These problems can harm the crops we grow and the critical ecosystems that support plant and animal life in many environments.

Consider the realities of our man-made world—every system that man creates must be balanced. These systems include machines, organizations, and even our national government and economy. All of these man-made devices or entities require balance. Think about your car or an airplane, or even the simple yet precise inner workings of a fish tank or washing machine. They all must possess balance in order to operate.

Balance is also critical in organizations, as it is necessary to manage the pace, volume, and scale of activities. Often, corporations must carefully sequence and prioritize activities to ensure that internal operations run smoothly. Walking this tightrope is no easy task, as quite often there are competing priorities that require immediate attention and resources.

Repetition in Nature

There is not much to say concerning repetition, for it is such an integral part of our daily lives. It sustains life on this planet. Repetition is a vital part of life in nature, as it is in the world we've created. Ralph Waldo Emerson once said, "Nature is an endless combination and repetition of a very few laws. She hums the old well-known air through innumerable variations."

There is a transformative nature to repetition—it is quite simply one of the most powerful realities we have in this world. As with the other elements and forces, without repetition many of the critical systems and processes that sustain life on our planet would cease. We simply can't live without a world of repetition.

Quite often, we experience repetition in the form of cycles. Repetition in the form of cycles is so highly immersed into our daily lives that we take its tremendous importance for granted. The concept of being cyclical is also rooted in movement; however, the distinguishing aspect of the concept of repetition is that it describes activity that is continuous. It represents a complete round or series of activity.

Consider its role in the body and how all processes are repetitive, how simple and mundane cycles of activity are essential to the body's proper functioning. From the development and replication of cells in the cell cycle to the systems such as the respiratory and circulatory systems and myriad others, repetition is seamlessly interwoven into the core aspects of our lives and dominates how processes work.

Something miraculous occurs when a process is continuously repeated. This is true in many contexts. Not only is it prevalent in nature but also when it comes to learning or mastering a particular skill. When we are attempting to learn new information, we rely on repetition to memorize and truly understand the concepts. Think through the power of repetition when it comes to learning a new sport, practicing a musical instrument, or learning new mathematical formulas.

Repetition is also a vital force in business and organizations, whether it is in leveraging best practices to enhance internal operations, such as with capabilities such as Six Sigma, or how it comes into play when considering its importance to manufacturing and the assembly line.

MOVEMENT, BALANCE, AND REPETITION IN OUR MARKETPLACE

Movement and change are experienced in the prevailing marketplace through various shifts in our social, economic, and governmental landscape. Whether it is in the change we experience in the form of new social and economic paradigms to shifts associated with technology and politics, these types of changes leave an enduring impression on our lives. These are the type of monumental imprints that shape the course of history!

In the mid-1990s, during my days in the retail banking brokerage industry, there was tremendous excitement on what institutions viewed as an unprecedented economic opportunity. This watershed event, centered on what was viewed as the greatest transfer of wealth in the history of the world, would result in a economic boon for financial institutions. The transfer of wealth—which, by the way, we are in the midst of—would see the Depression-era generation transfer trillions of dollars to Baby Boomers. Although estimates vary, this transfer is calculated to be in excess of $20 trillion and will continue through the next 20 years.

Considering this significant opportunity at hand, many institutions quickly scrambled to position themselves to be prepared to capture these assets. The types of organizations ran the gamut from mammoth insurance carriers and bread-and-butter banking franchises to traditional investment and brokerage houses. Organizations that did not anticipate this eminent shift were ill-prepared to reap the financial rewards this event brought.

There are other types of major shifts and change in our society that, over time, shape our national story. One that comes to mind is the Industrial Revolution, which triggered America's shift from an agricultural to industrialized nation. The Industrial Revolution, although serving as the catalyst for significant economic growth in the twentieth century, helped to shape the social landscape of our nation.

The explosion in growth in the manufacturing sector and the need to fill essential factory jobs created a tremendous need for labor. This event prompted millions of Americans to move from small rural towns and communities to urban centers. The mass exodus occurred at the turn of the twentieth century, from the late 1800s to the early 1900s. However, along with this increase in the number of factory jobs appeared a new urban lifestyle that transformed people's lives.

Supporting this mass migration was that in the nineteenth century significant technological advances occurred in transportation. This was evident by the development and building of streetcars, trolleys, and railroads. The emergence of new transportation options caused city boundaries to expand, providing individuals with several alternatives to travel with greater ease over longer distances.

Eventually, these advances in transportation and the explosion of growth in urban centers became the precursor to what we now know as the "suburbs." Suburban life created a higher standard of living for many. And as we have witnessed over the past 80 years, suburban life has not only changed our standard of living but has also significantly impacted our lives in many ways.

Balance in the Marketplace

Balance in the marketplace can be observed best through the various mechanisms our federal government leverages to manage the economy, for example, its efforts to manage trade and its fiscal and monitary policies aimed at
ensuring a healthy marketplace. A lack of balance can also rear its ugly head
in the failure of industry to regulate itself.

Think of our most recent real estate fallout and the 2008 credit crisis.
Although many factors led to these events, which ushered in the recession,
the role of balance was front and center. There were many signs that pointed
to a looming disaster, but somehow we missed the signs and failed to act.
Consider these facts:

1. By 2002 housing starts were 25 percent above the average growth rate
   of the three years preceding the start of the bubble.
2. There was an oversupply of homes. From 2004 to 2005 the industry
   built 2 million new units. Demographics at that time demonstrated that
   the economy needed only 1.3 million new housing units. Home building
   at that time actually dipped into future demand to support the higher
   levels of production.
3. The significant increase in home building created an oversupply in rental
   housing unit vacancy. During that period, rental housing unit vacancy
   rates were near record levels.
4. An increase in demand for new building led to a steady increase in
   prices. The real estate markets also experienced an excessive flow of
   capital. This increased capital also served as the catalyst for the upward
   or increased move in housing and real estate prices. However, housing
   prices were not in line with fundamentals.

Ultimately, the lack of balance in the system played a pivotal role in
the collapse of the real estate markets. Balance is critical to maintaining
vibrancy in any system.

Repetition in the Marketplace

Repetition in our prevailing economy is evidenced through many realities. It
is a fundamental aspect of economic life. Consider the role of consumption
and its importance to driving the economy. Consumption is a critical part of
our economic system and must be repeated to ensure vibrancy.

Or consider how critical it is for government in its oversight role to
monitor, on a repetitive basis, critical key economic data. Think of the catastrophic fallout of a government that does not repeat its review of the
"vital" data needed to manage its economy and how, through a continuous

and repetitive process of monitoring activity, it can significantly impact the market by taking certain actions.

An example of this is the Federal Open Market Committee (FOMC), which is a part of the Federal Reserve System, and its ability to change interest rates. Meeting eight times a year, or every six weeks, the FOMC may change rates as a result of what it observes in the economy.

CHANGE, BALANCE, AND REPETITION IN ORGANIZATIONS

As in systems of nature, movement and change dictate the performance of companies. In the marketplace, organizations are confronted by many forces and realities that require them to manage movement and change proactively and with speed and agility. These include factors such as customer behavior and trends, natural events, competitors, and innovations and ingenuity, to name a few (see Exhibit 3.1). Change in its many forms is a primary influencer of organizational success.

Because customers are always shifting and changing their behavior, a response in kind by corporations is necessary to meet the new requirements and realities. However, there are also times when it is the idea or the innovation that initiates the change or shift in consumer behavior, such as the impact of the Internet on our shopping habits. The application of change in this context also applies to competitors as external stakeholders and internal ones such as employees and shareholders.

It is easy to understand how the concept of change is tied to customers and the competition. However, for illustrative purposes, let's look at the impact change in nature has on organizations.

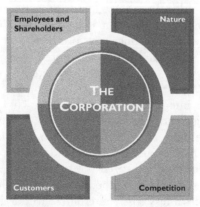

EXHIBIT 3.1   Movement, Change, and the Corporation

Natural events affect companies of all types, whether it is the impact natural events such as hurricanes, tornadoes, or tsunamis have on insurance companies or organizations involved in any business related to natural resources such as those in the oil and gas industry. The impact and reach of these types of disruptions can be experienced by consumers across the globe. Further, due to this risk, organizations across the globe now possess comprehensive disaster recovery and business resumption plans.

Think about the impact changes in nature have on what foods reach our very own dinner table. Droughts, excessive rain, and shifting weather patterns create an imbalance in our food supply, affecting companies in the food industry chain. This reality also applies to companies involved in any business related to natural resources.

Change in our natural environment may impact companies not involved directly in activities tied to the environment. As consumers are affected, so are a number of consumer-related businesses.

Blockbuster and the Impact of New Technology

Often, a corporation does not need to be the first to introduce the idea to consumers or the marketplace; however, it must continually be in the flow of new ideas, innovations, products, and services. Consider the missteps of the former video industry giant Blockbuster as it failed to adapt quickly to leverage emerging technologies and to understand consumer behavior to sustain its business.

For years, Blockbuster dominated the home video entertainment industry, with locations at popular neighborhood traffic posts from coast to coast. However, its failure to keep abreast of consumer behavior and trends by not introducing critical new products and services led to its ultimate demise. Again, change or movement is inextricably linked to the creative element and the need to introduce new products and services. Eventually, companies such as Netflix and Redbox captured enough of the home video entertainment industry to squeeze out Blockbuster.

Founded in 1999, Netflix offers consumers DVD rentals by mail and on-demand through Internet steaming of videos. This gives consumers the ability to rent movies and video games without leaving their homes. This new and innovative delivery system was not only less expensive but also aligned strongly with consumer behaviors and trends.

By the time Blockbuster realized the strategic importance of this new product, it was too late. Even Redbox captured a portion of this market as it offers consumers a less costly alternative to purchasing DVDs. Today Redbox's footprint is extensive. It possesses an enviable network of kiosks at prime retail locations around the country.

Although these actions are too little, too late. Netflix and Redbox have cemented their position with their offerings and now dominate their respective niche product spaces.

Change and Technology

Think about the role of movement and change as it applies to technology, perhaps the most rapidly changing aspects of our lives and work. You can take any of the technology functions, but for the sake of this illustration, let's look at the role of information security in an information technology (IT) department.

Movement and change have a significant impact on the information security function. Because of the tremendous amount of innovation and creativity that occurs in the world outside organizations, information security must stay constantly abreast of new developments, through new tools, software upgrades, and products.

The world of technology is filled with fraud and criminal activity as individuals and crime groups across the globe try to access and retrieve critical data and assets housed in corporate systems. Further, there are individuals who attempt to infect networks and systems with viruses and other costly computer ills.

To effectively manage these issues, information security functions must be within the flow of change and innovation in the marketplace. It must ensure that the latest and most updated software and devices are loaded on systems and assets. The criminals and hackers are constantly thinking of new ways to breach corporate firewalls and protective mechanisms; therefore, this function must always be responding to this movement or constant change.

Balance in Organizations

We all know the importance of balance in organizations, as it impacts so many facets of the corporate agenda. It may be the need to effectively manage the amount of internal change an organization chooses to take on, or ensuring an appropriate mix of products and services offerings for its customers. The importance of balance has long been an acknowledged dynamic that has to be actively accounted for and managed. I will also elaborate more on balance in Chapter 4 by highlighting in some cases the best practices, and in other cases miscues by certain organizations in not effectively managing balance.

Repetition in Organizations

Repetition in organizations has as much to do with an organization's developing and repeating certain practices in order to sustain and grow as it does with ensuring that it builds the right organizational culture. The ability of any organization to institutionalize certain management disciplines and business capabilities will ensure that it is in a continuous state of refinement. Too often, organizations leverage one-time efficiency and revenue exercises as a "silver bullet" to address some immediate challenge. And while it typically achieves its short-term objective, it often fails to capitalize on the opportunity because it does not institutionalize effective capabilities and sound practices.

As with any system in nature, there should be certain operational processes that are on autopilot in an organization. These are ones that transcend the routine processes that center on delivery of product and services to customers but extend deep within the corporation to ensure the effective governance of internal activities.

Change and movement also impact the need to repeat certain processes as we live in a marketplace and world of constant change. These changes introduce new technologies, methodologies, and capabilities, and with these new innovations the opportunity arises to at least examine if not alter the way we do business. However, in the context of efficiency and effectiveness, repetition is most impactful because over time the needs and requirements to perform certain activities shift, creating opportunity to enhance underlying processes.

THE THREE ELEMENTS AND FORCES AND OUR SYSTEM OF GOVERNMENT

Before moving on, it is important to demonstrate how our system of government aligns to the Three Elements and the Three Forces. It is critical to incorporate the role of government after walking through the influence of the three forces on systems. Organizations and the marketplace require a holistic and vibrant environment in which to thrive.

It is also important to show how marketplace and corporate activities are supported. And, of course, there is a natural alignment to government because like any other system—whether man-made or natural—our nation must either grow or be sustained. The Three Elements align to our system of governance quite naturally (see Exhibit 3.2).

The Creative Element

The creative element rests with the people. In all systems where individuals are governed, the creative element emanates from its people, for isn't a nation and/or any governed group the assemblage and coming together of

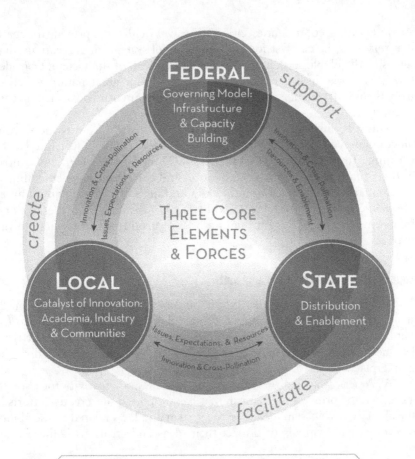

EXHIBIT 3.2 The Three Elements and Government

disparate and individual elements? A nation is only as good as the sum of its parts. It is a network of individuals, groups, and communities that comprise the whole.

In this context, ideas, resources, and issues flow from local communities to both the federal and state governments. Local communities—and more important, individuals—are the source of innovation and creativity in the marketplace. This is why it's vital that our local communities receive necessary resources and support to ensure that they thrive.

Individuals, communities, cities, and towns of all types provide the spark that serves as the catalyst for growth. As in all systems, it is creativity that serves as the lifeblood that spawns activities for all of the system. Consider how this works in our country. Commerce in our great nation is driven from the minds, talents, and creative efforts of many Americans from coast to coast.

Think about four of our most active "hotbeds" of innovation, from Silicon Valley to Austin, Texas; from Research Triangle in Raleigh, North Carolina, to the Massachusetts corridor. Think of the enormous contributions that these centers of innovation and commerce have contributed to the marketplace, both domestically and globally. These communities are made up of a number of individuals who, through their creative and innovative energies, have brought a host of products and services to the market.

Support and the Federal Government

The federal government's role is to support and provide the necessary infrastructure for the system, just as our muscular and skeletal systems do for our bodies, as well as other bodily functions that control and dictate activity. Let me provide you with an example you can relate to as applied to the marketplace.

As America has led the world in innovation and creativity for close to a century, the primary mechanism that has supported our creative efforts is the ability to protect an idea. Yes, the system and laws related to the ability of everyday individuals to protect their ideas and creations is the pivotal player.

Our copyright, patent, and trademark laws provide the environment necessary to make our ideas commercially viable. These laws allow us to retain ownership of the output of our ideas and creations. This commercialization of our ideas allows us, then, to provide products and services to the marketplace. This sophisticated yet pragmatic system has provided us with a strong platform on which to be an economic giant throughout the world.

Another example associated with the supportive role of government is the use of our roads and highways and waterways as public means of commerce. What if governments did not designate these critical aspects of commerce as a critical part of the public domain? Not only would there be anarchy, but we would have a patchwork of roads, highways, and waterways that would be controlled by private individuals. While this would make those individuals quite wealthy, it would stifle domestic commerce.

Opening up these critical conduits of commerce enables greater volumes of commerce to flow through them. Moreover, maintaining this critical infrastructure of commerce is vital to ensure that commerce flows unencumbered and free. There are other activities the federal government engages in to support our system which include its support of education, health, and the social welfare. These functions are critical infrastructure for any country.

Facilitation and the State

The facilitative component is the state, as very often in the flow of commerce and resources in the system, it is the state whose primary role is to serve as the conduit between the local communities and the federal. Each state within our country plays a critical role as a facilitator and conduit. It ensures that resources, issues, and other critical items flow from both the federal government and local communities.

This could entail new ideas and programs that are being administered in other parts of the country to important federal dollars that are targeted to stimulate specific activity, for example, the process of the federal government disseminating funds to local communities to maintain highways, bridges, and local roads. While to many individuals this activity may seem meaningless, it goes a long way to maintain this critical vehicle of commerce.

THE FEDERAL GOVERNMENT SUPPORTS, FACILITATES, AND CREATES: A FRACTAL VIEW

The federal government carries out its supportive role through support of specific activities, including the provision of infrastructure such as roads, highways, and waterways; tax systems; and the legal system, to name a few. The federal government as the primary support function in our system of government has the three elements embedded in it. Again, this reality is no different from any other system and is replicated in any environment.

The federal government also has many tools at its disposal to carry out its duties as a support function. These include its ability to enable or facilitate growth and support through levying and collecting taxes, its ability to spawn new economic activity through the legislative branch, and its support of commerce through the building of infrastructure.

The tool of taxation is a facilitative function. Through its ability to levy taxes, the federal government facilitates a myriad of economic and social programs. Taxes support many critical federal agencies such as the Department of Education, Health and Human Services, and the Department of Commerce, to name a few.

The tax system of our government—as well as any other government—is one of the most important facilitative mechanisms. It has to provide the necessary infrastructure for a nation. It is critical to nation building and fosters vibrancy and a resilient platform in which to launch a national agenda. This is the primary problem facing the debt crisis in Europe, as countries such as Greece, Spain, Italy, and Portugal are significantly challenged in their ability to collect taxes.

The government also facilitates growth and sustains performance through the institution of the Federal Reserve Board, which is our nation's central banking system. Its primary role, according to the Federal Reserve Act, is to conduct the nation's monetary policy and to maintain the stability of our financial systems. Although most federal oversight functions are supportive in nature, I categorize the Fed's role as primarily facilitative due to its responsibility to regulate commerce through the use of tools such as interest rates and the supply of money in the system. It also has responsibility to oversee depository institutions. And, as we know, banks play a pivotal role in the flow of commerce, as they act as a conduit in our marketplace.

The federal government also has creative activities. An example that comes to mind is its ability to enact laws and policy that "create," if you will. These creative activities include policies and laws that serve to spawn new commercial and business activities. For example, in the 1930s, under the leadership of President Franklin D. Roosevelt, the federal government enacted a series of acts that established certain agencies, which was known as the New Deal. Because we were on the brink of economic collapse in the Great Depression, the New Deal's objective was to enact policies and laws that would provide immediate, much needed recovery, relief, and reform to the system. The sole focus of these activities was to serve as the catalyst to spawn and create new commerce and economic activity.

THE FEDERAL GOVERNMENT AND OVERSIGHT

A critical supportive role of the federal government is to regulate and provide oversight of new products, services, and activities that flow through the stream of commerce. This fundamental function is key to ensuring the protection and overall well-being of all citizens. As new products are introduced into the stream of commerce, one of the many federal agencies acts as a filter to assess and determine whether it is fit for public consumption and use.

Agencies that come to mind include the Food and Drug Administration (FDA), the Office of the Comptroller of the Currency, and others. The FDA, for example, is very proactive and responsive in monitoring and addressing the introduction of new products into the system. Through the years it has demonstrated a robust and effective system to protect the public's overall well-being. However you put it, this role boils down to managing risk, for there is no other component in our system of governance that is as uniquely positioned and situated to manage systemic risk.

Through a network of various agencies, the oversight and regulatory function of government should effectively and at times proactively monitor or recognize and respond to issues or risks that threaten individuals and the overall system. However, an example where government oversight and its response were too slow was with the financial services industry and the most recent credit collapse in 2008.

History also shows that over time the government has struggled to keep pace and monitor this highly dynamic and volatile industry. This pattern of uncertainty can be traced from the credit collapse to the 1990s savings and loans collapse, even dating back to the stock market crash of 1928. And because of the proliferation and advances in technology, this industry will become even more dynamic. Although Dodd-Frank will go a long way to address these missteps and issues, there are still components of the 2008 fallout and others that are important to highlight regarding the government's ability to monitor and respond to risk in the system.

A HOLISTIC APPROACH

Organizations are highly dependent on operating activities in a system that promotes their growth and sustainment over time. This is especially relevant in an increasingly dynamic, interdependent and complex world. While the U.S. system of governance has it flaws, it does provide companies with an environment that fosters continuous and vibrant growth.

The Three Elements and forces work in tandem to provide a holistic system to govern systems (see Exhibit 3.3). These realities ensure that all living systems either grow or are sustained. Naturally, this new framework applies to organizations as systems. By incorporating these elements and forces into a single framework, we can leverage a new model in which to govern daily corporate activities. This framework is essential to mastering strategic risk.

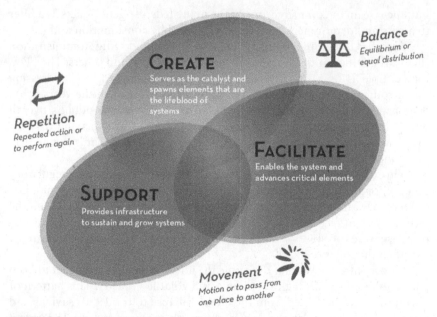

EXHIBIT 3.3   The Three Elements and Forces

SUMMARY

Applying the Three Elements to organizational activities takes on enhanced significance when we think of them in the context of the Three Forces that dictate performance in systems. As a company's success is dependent on its ability to keep pace with consumers, stay abreast of competitive forces, and monitor activity in the marketplace, incorporating mechanisms to manage these forces is vital for success. Further, due to the realities of organizational systems, accounting for these forces is also relevant when we consider how determinative employee behavior and performance is on overall performance.

As our commercial and social lives continue to be impacted by the pace and intensity of change due to technological innovation, applying the forces and elements holistically provides a strong response to these challenges.

QUESTIONS

1. How do you account for changes in the marketplace and customer behavior in your daily and strategic processes?

2. Is your management of these changes integrated into the introduction of new products and services?
3. Do you have a systematic process that continuously evaluates the volume and intensity of activities?
4. If you do, what groups and organizations are a part of the process?
5. Is the review of the volume and intensity of activities managed in the business units?
6. Is there a sense of organizational discipline in your company or group you manage, and how are you ensuring that you are consistently improving it?

REFERENCES

Baker, Dean. 2008. "The Housing Bubble and the Financial Crisis," *Real-World Economics Review*, 46.

Cheng, Ing-Haw, Sahil Raina, and Wei Xiong. 2012. "Wall Street and the Housing Bubble: Bad Incentives, Bad Models, or Bad Luck?" Princeton University Working Paper.

Farah, Samar. 2006. "Latino Marketing Goes Mainstream," *Boston Globe*, July 9.

Medina, Hildy. 2007. "Hispanics Grabbing the Keys," *Hispanic Business*, November. www.hispanicbusiness.com/2007/10/31/hispanics_grabbing_the_keys.htm

O'Dell, John. 2004. "Latinos in U.S. Embrace Toyota, *Los Angeles Times*, May 6.

Stein, Jason. 2004. "More Hispanics Buyers Pick Toyota," Orlando Sentinel. May 27.

Valdez-Dapena, Peter. 2013. "Asian Automakers Trouncing Detroit in Key U.S. Market: Hispanics," May 7. www.hispanictrending.net/hispanic_business

Transforming the Corporate Agenda: Applying the New Learning to Master Strategic Risk

The requirements of our new age demand a unique approach in the way companies account for the risks and complexities of the twenty-first century. To rise to these challenges, organizations as systems must be governed holistically, incorporating mechanisms that keep pace with an increasingly dynamic marketplace. Through a keen focus on the critical elements and forces that serve as fundamental pillars in systems leaders can build robust capabilities, enabling them to unleash the true power often lying dormant in organizations. These elements will serve as a compelling catalyst for operational excellence, ensuring optimal performance even in the most challenging of times.

ALIGNING THE THREE ELEMENTS AND FORCES FOR IMPACTFUL RESULTS

Organizations in the context of systems provide a unique lens to evaluate the effectiveness of critical activities and functions. While this differs from the traditional way in which we think of corporate activities, it does not conflict with the internal structures in place today that support the sale of products and services. The focus on organizations as systems also supports traditional approaches to operational excellence. While the first few chapters introduced these new concepts, this chapter will demonstrate how the elements and forces, when combined, can provide a compelling operational framework.

Operational excellence is focused on two important influencers of performance: (1) how organizations are internally structured, which focuses on a company's underlying operating model; and (2) how effectively organizations execute day-to-day activities. To ensure alignment with these influencers, companies pay careful attention to how important activities and internal capabilities are aligned to attain strategic objectives. These objectives are rightfully focused on the customer.

To meet these objectives companies focus on furthering capabilities such as continuous process improvement, improving execution, measuring and monitoring key activities, and enhanced delivery of products and services to customers. Organizations also leverage processes that ensure integrated strategic planning and focus on ensuring that the right leadership is in place to further its daily and strategic objectives. While it is important to bring these essential activities together to optimize performance, this is not enough, as they alone fail to account for the internal and external forces that influence performance.

This approach to operational excellence must be expanded in order to account for the forces and influences present in today's marketplace. The forces and influences center on the pace and intensity of change in our world, whether it is in the form of shifting consumer trends and behaviors, emerging technology, and the pace at which transactions and activities are conducted, to name a few.

When we consider how companies account for these influences today, it is often from a knee-jerk and reactive posture. Think of the a myriad of corporate failures over the past few years, and those of the not-so-recent past; they all revolve around similar themes and patterns. This chapter is not focused on organizational design and structure, but is dedicated to expanding the traditional understanding of operational excellence. Through monitoring and developing enhanced capabilities focused on the fundamental elements that serve as the foundation of organizations as systems, companies can effectively account for the risks that undermine strategic objectives.

The Three Elements and Forces provide a holistic governance model to drive key objectives and manage strategic risk (see Exhibit 4.1). I have

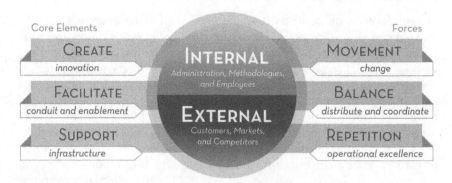

EXHIBIT 4.1 The Universal Guide of Governance

termed this model the *universal guide of governance* for two reasons: (1) it can be universally applied across industries, and (2) it is a concept that applies in both organizational and natural systems.

Ultimately, it's about evaluating the adequacy and overall health of the pillars of growth and sustainment. This approach gets to the heart of the key drivers of performance in organizational systems. Only with a more holistic yet focused approach that considers these fundamental pillars can leaders anticipate the demands of an unrelenting corporate agenda.

THE THREE ELEMENTS AS KEY DRIVERS OF ORGANIZATIONAL PERFORMANCE

The Three Elements and Forces holistically account for the internal and external realities organizations face. While it is important to identify the elements and forces and how they apply to organizations, it's essential to demonstrate how companies leverage them to drive performance. Due to the importance of the creative element as the initiator and catalyst in organizational systems, a special emphasis will be placed on the role of creativity and innovation. Through examples of how companies are addressing this important capability, you will be provided with specific examples to unleash this vital lever.

Driving Growth through Continuous Creativity and Innovation

In a world of continuous change, creativity and innovation must be a fundamental pillar of an organization's strategy and operating platform. This should be a strategic priority for any company desiring to remain relevant and competitive in today's competitive marketplace. While technology companies such as Apple, Facebook, and Google today lead in innovation, more "old-line" companies should follow their lead in driving continuous creativity. There are many lessons or models these companies have built that ensure a steady flow of products and services to the marketplace, ensuring continuous growth.

One approach is to create an innovation center of excellence (COE). Creating a COE that focuses on innovation is not new to industry. Several top companies have established this critical function and made it a strategic imperative. The innovation COE often is a corporate function, governing and coordinating the process of innovation throughout the enterprise. This function drives the creative activities in an organization and instills creativity into the culture.

Where these COEs should reside in an organization can be a rather exhaustive debate. However, I believe that there could be horizontal COEs that focus on enterprise types of issues and vertical COEs that are line-of-business–centric. For example, for major lines of business there should be a COE for innovation focused on the particular products and services of the particular line of business. While I am a proponent of ensuring that critical capabilities sit at the top of an enterprise, I've always been an advocate of ensuring that functions that support or drive business unit activity should reside in and be in the flow of those specific activities. There is tremendous value to be gained through this alignment. Quite often, however, those functions that have responsibilities for a particular business unit are far removed from the flow of daily and operational activities and therefore not as effective and tend to lose an important perspective.

Consider the role of the technology organization in driving innovation in companies. The office of the chief information officer (CIO) have become critical catalysts of growth as technology has become such a pivotal player in shaping and changing our lives. While there may exist a COE of innovation in technology, this function would not only focus on driving value within the operations of technology, but work in tandem with line-of-business innovation COEs in creating new products and services. Consider this in the context of developing critical business unit applications or leveraging the Internet to drive the sale of products that were once relegated only to the brick-and-mortar stores.

The Talent Factor and Innovation

Driving innovation through the office of the CIO also means recruiting and retaining top talent. With a sharp focus on building a strong cadre of exceptional talent, innovation in companies of all types can enhance growth significantly. In Chapter 3, I referenced the significant impact made by centers of innovation in America. When we consider how these centers have added trillions of dollars in value to the economy, serving as essential engines of growth on the national, state, and local levels, it is obvious that this model of creating growth can be replicated in organizations.

The key centers of innovation I reference again are in the Silicon Valley; Research Triangle; Austin, Texas; and the Boston corridor. As we all know and as the data reflect, many of the high-flying start-ups and successful technology companies were started by former students who were educated at nearby universities. These companies continue to thrive and draw top talent not only from the nearby academic institutions but now attract talent from across the globe. Organizations outside of these hotbeds of innovation should also adapt this model and build strong innovation centers though this approach. However, recruiting and retaining the right type of talent to build and drive technology innovation requires an approach far different than what is done today.

During my banking days, we recruited top talent across the enterprise. Often, recruitment efforts that engaged in recruiting the best and brightest focused on placing these coveted resources in a form of management training program or specific business unit type of training program. For talent that would focus on a shared service organization like the finance department, these resources would, for example, rotate through departments in the division such as Internal Audit, Treasury, the Office of the Controller, and business unit finance groups, to name a few.

The second type of program saw top talent matriculating through a program in a business unit such as Capital Markets. While the other programs were prestigious, by far, the most coveted and competitive of programs was this training program. Of course, it was related to the future income potential in this division, but my point here is to highlight the fact that this group attracted the most talented individuals from top schools throughout the nation.

This should also be the approach in building a center of innovation in technology. What must also change is our thinking on how to incent resources in technology that focus on innovation. By incentives I'm referring not only to being more creative in structuring compensation, but also to how we reward risk in traditional functions such as technology.

CREATIVITY AND INNOVATION THROUGH THE LENS OF INDUSTRY LEADERS

Establishing a formal function that focuses on championing and furthering innovation will initially assist to ensure that this fundamental catalyst of growth remains visible and is eventually integrated into routine corporate activities. However, there are other alternatives to further innovation and creativity. Let's take a look at Google Inc.

Google—Building a Culture of Innovation

Founded in 1998, Google Inc. quickly became a pioneer in innovation. While its success is tied to the tremendous growth of the Internet, creativity through innovation serves as the catalyst for its meteoric rise. Consider that in 2011, Google earned approximately $87,000 in profits per employee. This figure exceeded those of Wall Street top performers such as Goldman Sachs, IBM, and even Apple.

Consider Google's system of innovation. Through several key principles, Google fosters and drives innovation.

Open Sharing Through a philosophy of open sharing, Google ensures that employees understand almost everything that is going on in the company. This assists employees in understanding why decisions are made, enabling them to connect this information to the company's mission and their individual jobs. The company even shares actual slides taken from presentations to its board of directors and presents them to employees in company-wide meetings.

Google has also found that sharing information openly and broadly leads to robust discussions and the exchange of ideas among teammates, which may eventually lead to new outcomes and innovation. This approach differs from what traditionally occurs in old-line companies as, generally, information shared in board sessions, save the typical earnings data, is kept close to the vest.

This notion of open sharing also corresponds to the reality of change and access to information in our new age. As information is available to employees and people everywhere at the touch of a button, we have come to expect access to information instantaneously. Promoting a culture that ensures that information is shared openly creates an alignment to the behaviors and expectations of employees.

Risk Taking and Failure Within Google, risk taking is integrated into the fabric of the company as strong messages are conveyed to employees that it is okay to fail. This guiding principle is conditioned only if teammates learn from their mistakes and incorporate these learnings as they move forward.

Google's culture allows for extensive experimentation and risk taking. Through its "launch and iterate" process, it reinforces this important concept. This approach differs from a company like Apple, whose approach is to "perfect it before you sell it." As part of its product development life cycle, almost all products released to the market are tested first. Throughout this testing process, critical user feedback is incorporated into the product, allowing adjustments along the way. In the process, Google tests new products with actual customers, thus requiring less investment and in the end allowing more innovation.

The approach differs from traditional manufacturing concepts, which require a high-quality, low-defect approach, and are generally viewed as fostering excellence. In encouraging risk and experimentation, Google believes this aligns with how the world really works. Hence, embedded in its DNA is the notion that continuous innovation means that you may not always get it right the first time.

Ideas Taken from Everywhere Ideas are taken from everywhere, such as from employees, external partners, and others. Google even wants insight into the informal conversations taking place in hallways, as it believe its teammates are critical to driving creativity. It has even implemented a 70/20/10 system to harness the creativity from its employee base.

In this model, during any given 40-hour workweek, 70 percent of an employee's time is spent on their core job, 20 percent working as a part of another team, and 10 percent on what they view as "blue sky" ideas. The company believes that allowing teammates to see other projects across the organization will further enable innovation. Providing teammates with 10 percent of their time to work on anything they like also furthers innovation.

Google also pushes for original ideas rather than for ideas that are copied from others. It incorporates this approach by not only investing in creating new ideas but also enhancing existing products and services.

Also reinforcing Google's approach of taking ideas from everywhere is how it is building its workforce. Employees are taken from everywhere across the planet. Google aggressively pursues recruits from countries around the world. This allows it to leverage perspectives and ideas from individuals possessing tremendously different backgrounds and experiences. Combined with a common set of company principles, this allows the process ideation to flow effortlessly through the company's "ecosystem" of innovation.

By incorporating an approach that incorporates the components a company like Google has leveraged, companies can begin to build a strong foundation in which to foster a culture of innovation and creativity. These components also provide a rich flow of ideas, which not only embeds this practice into the corporate culture but ensures that innovation and creativity are constant.

The IKEA Way

Another highly successful company that has integrated innovation into its core operations is IKEA. For over 50 years this trailblazer in innovation has taken the approach that its business is more than selling furniture—it sells lifestyles. Today, IKEA operates an extensive chain of furniture showrooms across the planet, owning and operating over 200 stores in countries throughout Europe, Asia, Australia, and the United States, to name a few. In these countries, it has cornered 5 to 10 percent of the furniture market. To demonstrate the power of its innovation machine, every year IKEA changes approximately one third of its products.

The way IKEA approaches innovation is to ensure that creativity is leveraged and integrated throughout its core operations. For example, understanding its customer base, IKEA provides a play area for children, which also serves special meals. The play areas are typically staffed and allow parents who shop at IKEA to take their time shopping. These areas are strategically placed and are generally in the middle of each store.

Other examples of IKEA's innovation include its "Product Recovery" program, which cuts down on waste by reusing materials whenever possible. This program allows customers to download or look through their catalog in 3D as well as watch product demonstrations on video and play with the look of some products. IKEA has recently launched newly co-branded hotels with Marriot. Through this collaboration, IKEA hopes to attract the new Millennial traveler, who also fits the same profile as the type of customer that purchases IKEA's home furniture. The features in these hotels attract customers interested in a combination of contemporary design, low prices, simple service, and a touch of self-sufficiency.

Bell Labs—A Trailblazer of American Corporate Innovation

Any discussion of creativity and innovation would not be complete without mentioning Bell Labs. While much has been documented of the legendary innovator's enormous contributions to modern civilization, there are several things the company did that could be leveraged by companies today. The legacy of Bell Labs as an innovator transcends the current creativity we now observe, as what it brought to the world has shaped several industries.

During the last half of the twentieth century, Bell Labs introduced and launched what are now the building blocks of innovation for many of the consumer products we now use. Examples include the transistor, which today resides inside the chips that fuel our mobile devices and computers. Bell Labs built the first fiber-optic cable system as well as developed the first communications satellites and cell phone systems. It created a mind-blowing number of innovations—too many to mention—which served as the foundation of our new technology products today.

There are several key drivers that served as the impetus of Bell Labs' success, including:

- *Idea ecosystem.* Bell Labs created an ecosystem that cultivated and allowed an easy transfer of ideas. As part of its system of labs, Bell Labs established several satellite facilities. These facilities fostered a robust two-way transfer of ideas between the researchers/scientists and the factory workers. It enabled the "thinkers" (researchers/scientists) to immediately apply their ideas to practical things.
- *Critical mass of thinkers.* Not only did Bell Labs assemble the best and the brightest, but it forced this critical mass of thinkers to work side by side, requiring them to interact with one another. Its facilities were architected in a manner that created this atmosphere.

- *Autonomy and freedom.* Freedom at Bell Labs gave its researchers the ability to work autonomously and independently without pressure. This meant that quite often they were given significant time to work through ideas, as researchers were not held to aggressive schedules.
- *Risk taking.* Researchers were permitted to fail and were not held accountable for failing.

The key components of the way in which Bell Labs was designed can be leveraged today in companies. Yes, the Bell Labs approach required a significant investment and a mind-set that was committed to the long-term benefits of its activities, which yielded groundbreaking results. And while the Bell Labs model is one that is not focused on speed to market, there is much to be gained by focusing on innovation as a part of one's core operations in order that it can flourish.

IDENTIFYING ADDITIONAL CENTERS OF CREATIVITY AND GROWTH IN THE MOST UNLIKELY OF PLACES

Another approach to uncovering additional growth opportunities in organizations is to build this capability in facilitative and supportive functions. A critical exercise for all organizations is to identify the centers or areas that are "hot spots" that can be leveraged to drive innovation and creativity. While today this is done by default, through a deliberate focus, organizations build additional generators of growth, exploiting their creative potential.

To unleash additional opportunities companies should think of the fundamental elements in the context of natural systems. This is in the context of how natural systems are fractal in design. As in natural systems, there are creative elements within organizations' facilitative and supportive functions. While it is easy to identify those areas in creative and even facilitative functions where revenue can be generated, quite often organizations miss opportunities to identify areas in supportive functions where this value can also be driven.

McDonald's and Its DNA of New Product Development

Let's consider an example that is close to home—McDonald's. While much has been written about this industry darling, I'd like to focus specifically on how McDonald's leverages its owner operating model to drive creativity. Through its extensive network of retail outlets, which serve to facilitate and support sales, it has been a pioneer of innovation. One of the primary reasons McDonald's Inc. has maintained a long track record of sustainment and growth is due to its ability to "mine" new products and services from its creative, facilitative, and supportive functions.

McDonald's is the star of the fast-food industry. It has survived through challenging economic times and steadily delivers value to its shareholders. It is an organization that has over a long period of time delivered growth and has sustained its operations. When we examine the McDonald's operating model and organizational structure, it can be aligned quite naturally with the Three Elements. McDonald's drives creativity and innovation in three primary areas:

1. *Products.* Products include the food and beverage items that are a part of its ever-changing menu.
2. *Franchises.* Through a global network of franchises, McDonald's sells and distributes its products to customers. This critical network also provides the global operation with a robust pipeline of innovation.
3. *Core operations.* Through the design and structure of its locations, McDonald's drives value. It has led the industry in leveraging its operation to drive growth.

The primary way in which McDonald's drives revenue growth is through the continuous introduction of new products. This is a hallmark of McDonald's, as through the years it is a keen observer of customer trends and behaviors. McDonalds has developed quite a track record in responding to these changes and shifts by offering products that meet these trends. Its ability to respond and deliver products that meet these new dynamics has been a formidable engine for its growth through the years. Think about the impact of the Big Mac, the Happy Meal, its new product line in McCafé, and, for that matter, how it became the first fast-food restaurant to offer a breakfast menu. Let's consider McCafé, the most recent innovation of McDonald's, and a not so recent innovation, the Happy Meal.

McCafé   Picking up on the resounding success of Starbucks, in 2005 McDonald's introduced its McCafé menu of products. It offers a blend of features from Starbucks and from the tried-and-true McDonald's brand we've come to know. The coffee is less expensive than at Starbucks, and McDonald's now attracts people who wouldn't normally come to its locations.

Since its introduction in 2005, McCafé continues to drive profitability and growth to McDonald's sales. In 2009, sales from McCafé products topped $1.5 billion, and as of 2011, McDonald's took market share from Starbucks. The overwhelming success of McCafé has prompted Starbucks to sell and distribute its coffee through McDonald's rival, Burger King. To continue to leverage its success with McCafé, in 2010 McDonald's continued to add beverages to its products in the space by offering a whole line of smoothies.

The Happy Meal In 1977, McDonald's launched the first Happy Meal in the United States. Since then, the Happy Meal has created a frenzy and massive following with children the world over. Through the years, McDonald's has also improved the Happy Meal as a product, altering its contents to meet new trends and shifts in consumer behavior. For example, the company changes Happy Meal toys almost every week, tying toys to popular children's movies and characters. The Happy Meal has helped to build a loyal following and customer base as children are drawn to the franchise primarily to discover what toy comes with the Happy Meal from week to week.

Core Operations (Support): Driving Growth through the Drive-Thru The first fast-food operation to introduce the drive-thru window, McDonald's introduced this game-changing concept to the burgeoning restaurant industry. Today, McDonald's drive-thru business accounts for over 60 percent of its sales.

In 1975, the first drive-thru was created at a McDonald's location in Sierra Vista, Arizona. As with most great innovations, the drive-thru window was born out of sheer necessity. Located near a military base, the McDonald's location had a high-volume customer base of soldiers who frequented the store. However, because the soldiers would come in fatigues, they were unable to leave their cars. To accommodate this significant part of its customer base, the location began to serve the soldiers through a drive-thru.

Now some 30-plus years later, the drive-thru window accounts for 50 to 70 percent of revenue in a food industry, with annual sales exceeding $200 billion. The creation of the drive-thru window, now a key aspect of fast-food restaurants, is an example of how a supportive activity in any retail operation can be a difference maker. Drive-thrus have become such an important aspect of the fast-food companies that the industry has dedicated many resources to understand its most critical drivers.

With the goal of enhancing efficiency and effectiveness in order to enhance revenue, comprehensive studies now focus on many key factors. These factors include measuring performance along order accuracy, average wait time, exterior appearance, suggestive sell incidence, service time, cleanliness, and the ability to manage capacity, to name a few.

Even technology giant Apple Inc. has separated itself from its competitors through creation of its network of retail Apple stores. The emergence of its retail store, combined with Apple's powerful innovative engine, has served as the key catalyst for its growth during the past few years. The

Apple Store is effective because it creates a unique community, serving as a place where customers and curious shoppers can enjoy stimulating customer experiences and training and development. Apple even sells a tremendous amount of its accessories out its retail stores.

There is also a strong correlation between Apple's most recent store expansion and its growth in market share. For example, from 2003 to 2009 it opened approximately 123 U.S. stores. During that period, it also saw its U.S. market share jump from 3 percent to 9 percent. This strong correlation between the expansion of its retail stores and growth of market share has also been observed in its European markets.

The emergence of technology and the Internet has enabled organizations to drive the creation of new products and services out of core technology and operations functions. As we continue to gain new ground and experience advancement, the possibility to exploit opportunities in these areas will only proliferate. Nevertheless, to harness these exciting green fields of opportunities, the way organizations think of technology must be elevated and leveraged as a true enabler and creator of new products and services.

GROWTH THROUGH FACILITATIVE FUNCTIONS AND CAPABILITIES

Facilitative elements in organizations run the gamut and play a similar role as found in natural systems. As Exhibit 4.1 indicates, facilitative elements in companies enable and serve as critical conduits of growth and sustainment. As discussed in Chapter 2, they include functions such as sales, marketing, and even leveraging important technologies such as the Internet.

However, rather than focusing on traditional facilitative activities, I'd like to reference a not-so-obvious and little-covered aspect of this element, and that is the art of the cross-sell. There is no better example of mastering cross-selling than looking to banking industry giant Wells Fargo.

Wells Fargo

Long before the day when Wells Fargo purchased failing Wachovia Corp. in a historic fire sale, it had developed its industry-leading cross-selling capabilities. It is no secret that Wells Fargo's ability to cross-sell has enabled it to sustain long periods of growth over time. Further, there is strong evidence that this industry giant is not as operationally sound or efficient as it could be. There is also a strong case that can be made to demonstrate that prior to being purchased by Wells Fargo, Wachovia was years ahead in managing a leaner and more efficient operating platform. However, this is not the focus of my point but does underscore the sheer power and enormity of Wells Fargo's cross-selling capabilities.

The facts are clear. Wells Fargo's cross-selling makes other banks envious! While the majority of banks sell a consumer products, Wells Fargo averages six products per customer. And although this is an industry-leading figure, Wells Fargo's top brass would like to push that farther to a total of eight per customer. This number is in the context that the average American household has approximately 16 products tied to financial institutions. For example, in 2006, Wells Fargo generated approximately $1.3 billion of after-tax revenue from cross-selling alone in its mortgage services portfolio customer base.

There are many factors that have helped to build this capability and embed it into the Wells Fargo culture. One of these is its focus on rigor and discipline. Rigor and discipline are important parts of the sales process as the average customer is taken through a detailed profiling system. Rigor is also reinforced through a very hands-on approach by managers through coaching and inspecting employee work. This practice enables managers to provide much-needed feedback and tips on how work can be more effective.

Wells Fargo's compensation structure is also a strength, as it supports cross-selling and ensures that teammates cross silos to collaborate and further the best interests of each customer. By breaking down traditional silos and divisions it has been able to enhance efficiencies and increase transparency.

For example, at the beginning of the last decade, Wells Fargo decided to combine two of its most critical banking platforms, the consumer and corporate Web banking platforms. It wanted to leverage the opportunities that existed between these two customer groups but realized it had to remove critical barriers in order to first empower its customers and further enable its bankers. Wells Fargo's bet paid off, as this strategy led to substantial growth in the number of corporate clients. From the combined platform launch in the year 2000 when it only had some 2,000 clients, the number of corporate clients rose substantially to well over 25,000. What Wells Fargo realized that was over 100,000 users also worked for those corporate clients, which provided it a unique opportunity to cross onto the consumer platform.

In 1995, as one of the first banks to launch online consumer banking, Wells Fargo also enabled single sign-on for its wholesale customers. This step created tools that spanned product lines, which eventually provided customers an integrated and consolidated view. It also allowed employees to have transparency that transcended traditional boundaries into other product lines.

The bank's unique approach to teaming and furthering a unified selling approach has assisted in removing remaining fiefdoms. Wells Fargo is uniquely organized to support these tools structurally. Richard Kovacevich, its CEO at the time, took all retail, commercial, and consumer business units and placed them under one leader and business unit. This helped place an emphasis on the strategy that emphasized the total size of the customer relationship. As bankers were not seeing much growth in their traditional sources of income, Wells Fargo understood the power of cross-selling. Other financial services organizations that early on understood the power of the cross-sell prior to Wells Fargo were American Express and Citigroup in the 1990s under the leadership of Sanford Weill.

GROWTH THROUGH SUPPORTIVE FUNCTIONS AND CAPABILITIES

Exploring and exploiting additional areas of growth in supportive functions can provide a competitive advantage, especially due to the power of technology.

There isn't a more critical issue to manage today than an organization's ability to extract, leverage, and harness the value of data to enhance performance. The issue of a company's data management efforts is focused on a number of key issues and areas, including understanding:

- Internal customer data
- External customer data and consumer trends and behaviors
- Competitor activities and behaviors

Understanding customer activity is critical. This entails tracking and capturing their internal transactions to understand not only their needs but also behaviors. It provides organizations with the ability to proactively market and sell products to their customer base. However, this alone is not enough as it pertains to the issue of leveraging customer data to enhance sales and marketing efforts.

It is also critical to understand prevailing trends and behaviors as they pertain to general behaviors and trends in the marketplace. For example, consider the emergence and importance of mobile banking and its critical connection to the adoption and popularity of handheld and mobile devices. This phenomenon is a clear example of how this connectivity works. Again at the front and center of a dynamic consumer is technology.

Mobile Banking

There are few examples that highlight the importance of monitoring and tracking consumer trends and behaviors as the example we find in the adoption and usage of mobile devices and their impact on banking and financial services. This example also highlights how critical technology has become to us and its impact on how we interact and conduct daily activities.

Mobile banking would not be possible without the comfort we all have with the Internet. The Internet enabled many of us across the globe to be comfortable with interacting and transacting critical activities outside of the confines of the brick-and-mortar store. We have yet to fully comprehend the impact the Internet has and will have on us regarding how we are evolving as a civilization. The adoption of Internet use, of course, paved the wave for mobile and smartphone usage.

Further, an online banking report in 2003 reported that it took about 10 years, that is from 1996 to 2006 for Internet or online banking to reach 40 million users, and will take about the same amount of time for mobile banking to reach the 40 million users. Even Americans between the ages of 55 and 64 are adopting smartphones at an amazing rate. It is at a rate faster than of any age group. However, in the United States, the largest group of adoption is between the 25- to 34-year-old population.

Transactions in mobile banking include the ability to conduct balance checks, account transactions, initiate payments, and a host of other types of transactions. In 2008, a Berg Insight Study forecasted that worldwide American mobile banking customers would grow from 20 million in 2009 to 913 million by 2014. By 2015 mobile banking will top over 1 billion. As of 2011, smartphone adoption was surging not only in the United States but worldwide. Globally, its usage is at 27 percent, and in places such as Europe its penetration is at 51 percent, according to a recent Nielsen study. For low-income economies, smartphone usage is popular and on the rise. Further, in many emerging countries such as China, India, the Philippines, and countries in Africa, where the mobile infrastructure is stronger and more stable than the fixed-line infrastructure, mobile banking carries with it much more promise.

Understanding and tracking the behaviors and trends of consumers using mobile technology is critical in applying this technology in other areas and facets of our lives. Financial institutions that understand this and incorporate all of the critical data about mobile and smartphone usage, trends and behaviors can leverage this data to propel and support its efforts in this emerging space. The data that is captured in the use of mobile and other handheld devices can also be leveraged to understand customers that go beyond the data needed for banking services. Tracking the competition can also provide organizations with valuable information and insight. This data can provide valuable insights into product and service offerings, beyond traditional offerings and help it exploit opportunities in non traditional areas.

These non traditional areas include other retail products such as insurance, mortgage, credit card, auto lending, and others.

REPETITION AND OPERATIONAL EXCELLENCE

Repetition in organizations both private and public is in its purest sense about establishing organizational discipline. Repetition supports operational excellence by instilling rigor and discipline within an organization's culture. Fostering an environment that reinforces these important capabilities ensures consistent execution.

Traditionally, organizations have focused on areas such as risk management, technology, and finance. This applies, for example, to functions such as internal audit and compliance in their need to monitor and measure the adequacy of internal controls. This notion of organizational discipline also applies to critical process improvement capabilities such as lean, Six Sigma, and others.

Whether it is organizations like GE that excel in fostering a culture focused on efficiency and quality through methodologies such as Six Sigma, or in organizations that promote discipline in managing risk as Wachovia did in its heyday through its merger and integration methodology; establishing a strong organizational culture is paramount to an organization's ability to create an identity.

Having a strong organizational identity and culture is linked to employee satisfaction and pride. Think about how the power of strong organizational culture and identity is the hallmark of many industry darlings, from GE and its focus on quality, to Nordstrom's with its legendary customer service brand. Or think of innovative organizations such as Apple, Microsoft, and Google. Whether an organization focuses on customer service, quality, risk management, or other areas, what ultimately propels its focus forward is the practice of repetition.

WACHOVIA AND MERGER INTEGRATION

During my time at Wachovia, we successfully developed a strong process to integrate those companies that merged with us. This was no easy task as we learned from the mistakes of the past.

In the 1990s, Wachovia, through its predecessor organization, First Union, acquired a number of banking franchises on the East Coast. These transactions, although successful, did not come without a cost, as we did a poor job in integrating the companies. During this period, we paid dearly, as customer attrition was significant losing many of these important assets during the integration process. However, this was the primary purpose of entering these merger transactions, as acquiring these relationships was a critical part of this valuable prize.

Customer attrition was due to the many issues that arose during the transition. At that time, First Union did a poor job of planning and accounting for the critical processes and impacts to customers as they migrated onto the bank's platform. These issues quite naturally impacted customers and their ability to transact routine banking transactions.

Eventually, these challenges came to a head. In one instance, First Union's 1998 purchase of CoreStates, the fallout was devastating. The poor execution of the integration caused a significant erosion of the CoreStates' customer base, and First Union's poor execution of the merger impacted already soured retail customers. The attrition rate of the First Union/CoreStates transaction was greater than 20 percent, well above what would be considered normal at that time. However, if First Union was serious about growing through merger, it had to do something about its merger and integration methodology and processes.

The announced merger of First Union and Wachovia in the spring of 2001 ushered in a new era regarding the company's management of merger and integration risk. Both sides appreciated the importance of executing the merger with the utmost care. First Union, from prior experience, learned how important it was to implement an integration with little customer fallout, and the legacy Wachovia organization, possessing a strong customer service culture, wanted to ensure the safe migration of its customers to the new platform. In order to mitigate the risk and ensure a successful integration, both management teams came together and created what was considered during the early to mid-2000s one of the most effective models for integrating two companies. And, yes, the entire process is centered on the power of repetition.

The merger and integration methodology created by Wachovia worked as follows: After the announcement of a merger or acquisition, both companies agree on an individual/leader from either company who will serve as the chair and leader of merger and integration activities. This individual was normally a leader who was from the acquiring organization, unless it was a merger of equals, in which case leaders from both companies would serve as co-chairs.

The leader generally was someone who was respected enterprise-wide and had a strong background and understanding of how the bank worked. The leader chosen was also taken from his/her full-time responsibilities to take on this assignment full time. This merger leadership function was also supported with a small project/program office to help coordinate activities.

In addition to this leader, all critical areas of the bank assign critical resources to the merger and integration enterprise team. These individuals are assigned to the effort full time and represent critical areas such as retail and commercial banking, wealth management, technology, operations, customer service, and risk management, to name a few. As the merger and integration calendar and timeline is established, this enterprise-wide process kicks into full effect.

For most integrations, instead of converting all accounts at one time, the conversion was broken up into mini integration and merger events. Often, these mini mergers are segmented by state and/or region. Wachovia often did this to manage the scale of these conversions and also to learn along the way about potential hiccups in the process. However, the power in the merger and integration methodology was that prior to each state or regional integration, the enterprise-wide merger and integration team would meet in what is commonly known as a merger readiness reviews.

During this process, all key stakeholders from various groups would walk through a very structured and disciplined process. During a readiness review, stakeholders who are a part of the upcoming integration are required to walk through their preparedness for the upcoming event. As the event approaches, the seriousness and rigor of each review escalates. However, one of the benefits of repeating this "readiness" exercise prior to the event is that it enabled critical gaps and issues to be identified and mitigated. The process also allowed all of the critical players to interact in one forum, thus enabling varying points of view in analyzing the problems.

By 2008, Wachovia had completed over five major mergers and integrations. These mergers included the acquisition of national banks, brokerage companies, and auto finance lenders. They included:

July 1, 2003 Prudential Securities

November 1, 2004 Metropolitan West Securities

November 1, 2004 South Trust Bank of Birmingham, Alabama

September 5, 2005 WestCorp

May 7, 2006 Golden West/World Savings Bank

At Wachovia, over time we built a strong culture whose identity was built on our ability to integrate and execute mergers flawlessly. The secret to developing such an effective process was repetition. As Wachovia snapped up financial service companies along the way, a key differentiator was this capability, as organizations valued the significant impact a smooth merger would have on their customer base. Yes, Wachovia developed high ratings for customer service; however, we became known throughout the industry for our attention to detail and precision in integrating and bringing together organizations.

MANAGING MOVEMENT AND CHANGE

Of all the forces that influence organizational systems, there is none more compelling than the force of movement. Movement and change are the primary wielders and conductors in the flow of life. For example, the force of balance is held captive to its weight.

In the context of what activities should be measured and how often they should be measured, the forces of change and movement come to mind because in a dynamic, volatile, and complex marketplace an organization's ability to anticipate, respond, and manage "change" is of paramount importance. In today's marketplace, the most impactful reality that is driving and will continue to affect the rate, pace, and intensity of change is technology. And there is not a more compelling and impactful force on us today than the use of the Internet and its role in our lives.

A critical exercise in this process is to identify those areas in an organization that are most impacted by change and movement. Some clear examples that come to mind include product development, customer data, and technology. There are other areas, but these three are most impactful when it comes to maintaining a competitive edge.

THE VALUE OF A TRANSFORMATION AND CHANGE COE

Building internal capabilities that account for transformation and change is critical to a company's sustaining itself over time and remaining relevant. I've been a part of an internal organization that informally played this role. But there are also significant benefits to establishing transformation and change COEs. Organizations must build and foster an environment that is accustomed to executing on daily activities while undergoing transformation and change. This is essential in order to keep pace with the competition and ensure that the organization stays abreast of best practices.

Continuously inserting change and transformational initiatives in an organization also reinforces operational excellence. It assists in embedding continuous transformation into the company's DNA and reinforces individual employees' need to embrace change. This can be impactful when we consider the role of employees as leaders and individual contributors.

A transformation and change COE can also provide a valuable lens into the pace and intensity of change occurring in an organization. This function could account for monitoring and measuring balance in the system, as the COE has a unique window into the portfolio of enterprise activities. It can serve as a type of air traffic controller. A traditional COE or Project Management Office (PMO) should be a centrally located function, having an enterprise view. A typical COE today is engaged with the following:

- A portfolio or enterprise view of all change occurring in an organization.
- A clear understanding of the organization's strategic initiatives and the individual projects linked to them.
- A collection of cross-enterprise tools and processes that will enable it to drive strategic objectives.
- Provides robust reporting to senior and executive management, enabling it to base decisions on this flow of critical information. Focus on driving efficiency and enhancing revenue.
- Providing risk management through independence and escalation, allowing for greater organization transparency and accountability.

A portfolio COE should also have a primary focus and mandate of not only monitoring change but introducing change into the organization. Currently, the COE function takes on this role by default, meaning that through its many activities in managing and tracking efforts that drive efficiency and growth, it often introduces new capabilities.

Take, for example, an organization that desires to reduce expenses. It might leverage offshoring as a capability to further this goal. This may be the company's formal foray into leveraging offshoring as a continuous process to not only assist with its efficiency efforts but to also leverage strategic suppliers to introduce state-of-the-art capabilities. Regardless of the reason, these types of efforts one by one introduce transformation into an organization, providing a formidable foundation to change culture.

However, by focusing on introducing change into the organization continuously, PMO COE ensures that an organization not only keeps abreast of new tools and capabilities but brings along employees in learning to operate in an environment of healthy change. Instilling a culture of continuous change is a catalyst to driving operational excellence. It forces the continuous evaluation of core operations and creates a healthy tension in the organization. Through this dynamic, associates take on a mind-set of pushing old boundaries and seeking new ways of adding value.

This notion of fostering an environment of continuous change again is a part of natural systems. In natural systems, while many things remain the same, all environments remain under a constant state of flux. This reality ensures that natural systems maintain themselves and experience growth. This also applies to organizational systems.

While organizations do evaluate where they need to make investment and keep abreast of change, this exercise is spotty at best. This new lens or understanding is about creating a model and reinforcing organizational discipline to ensure a consistent and repetitive evaluation of the fundamental pillars that fuel organizational success. Ultimately, enhancing operational excellence is about understanding these critical connections and ensuring that a continuous process and sense of discipline are well established in the corporate culture.

THE IMPORTANCE OF MEASURING KEY CONTROLS AND ACTIVITIES

Often, corporations struggle to determine which activities to focus on, what to measure, and why certain activities should be measured. Today, there is a considerable amount of activity centered on measuring and monitoring critical activities and internal controls. Functions such as internal audit, risk management, corporate compliance, and the office of the chief financial officer (CFO) are pivotal to this important exercise. However, these efforts are often too narrowly focused and reactive in nature. Many times they do not go far enough in measuring and anticipating risk. These areas today focus on important activities as individual and institutional trading activities, the adequacy and resilience of systems, key financial controls, and core operations.

Further, these efforts are mainly focused on monitoring and measuring risk-related activities. There is an expanded role of these functions along with senior management to monitor and measure those activities that are at the heart of organizational systems.

Evaluating What Matters Most: The Human Body Example

Consider how we evaluate the overall "effectiveness" and health of organizations in the context of the approach taken by modern medicine to evaluate the overall health of our bodies. We all know the process, as we have, in one way or another, been through an annual physical or some form of medical evaluation. This process focuses on measuring the "vital signs" in the body that point to good health. This approach or methodology evaluates a patient's blood pressure, breathing, pulse, and temperature.

Gathering information on these key indicators provides a physician with a solid snapshot of how healthy an individual is. These cursory tests points to the effectiveness of the heart, respiratory and circulatory systems, and blood. Further tests also assess how healthy certain critical organs may be. These tests or measures focus on the critical systems and organs of the human body, providing a clear picture of how effectively they all work in tandem to sustain life.

If this approach is taken to measure the effectiveness of the most vital elements and activities in the human body, why wouldn't we apply it to the manner in which we evaluate organizations? The human body is more complex than organizations, and for years this approach in measuring one's overall health has been effective. This approach applies to how scientists measure the vitality and overall health in ecosystems and even how we measure the health of the economy. Ensuring that the key elements and forces in all systems work effectively is key to long-term sustainment.

Evaluating Organizational Performance Today

Today, there are various ways that organizations measure performance. These systems of measurement focus on evaluating the effectiveness of internal controls and monitor how processes and activities intersect to drive profitability and growth and control expenses. While this approach to monitoring and mitigating "risk" to customers and earnings is appropriate, it must be expanded to provide a deeper and expanded assessment of the overall health of an organization.

Take, for example, the role of Internal Audit or Risk Management. Both of these internal functions measure risk by evaluating key control points and the processes tied to important operational activities that support the delivery of services and products to customers. They also involve assessing the adequacy of key financial controls to ensure that a company has a strong financial footing. Again, this focus provides only part of the picture in understanding the overall health of a company.

When we consider the various ways in which companies fail over time, the failure can often be traced to the breakdown or impending failure of fundamental elements that are at the heart of corporate performance. Consider the colossal collapse of Enron. Its ultimate demise was due to many factors such as greed, arrogance, and flawed trading practices, to name a few. There was also a fundamental breakdown in governance, as Enron's auditor failed in its role and the board failed to monitor and address the significant issues the company faced.

To deal with tremendous losses it engaged in accounting practices that would hide these losses. Mired in fraud and misrepresentation, the former industry darling became the Peoria of the marketplace, with several of its top brass being convicted and sent to prison.

We can thank Enron for Sarbanes–Oxley, as Washington was swift to enact legislation to prevent this manipulation of accounting practices from ever happening again. However, Enron's cover-up and ensuing misrepresentation was only the symptom a much larger theme lurking—the failure of its underlying strategy to generate revenue and growth. While there was a breakdown in internal controls, this was a direct result of management's desperate need to "manufacture" growth and revenue.

Evaluating the core elements in organizational systems responsible for growth and sustainment would provide an effective approach to ensure operational excellence. This could entail implementing new tools that measure the effectiveness of these elements. For example, one tool could be in the form of a dashboard where senior executives could provide a snapshot of the overall performance or health of these elements. This dashboard would measure specific factors associated with ensuring consistent activity in the areas of innovation and creativity. They could even evaluate how effective key functions are in keeping pace with change, whether they are creative, facilitative, or supportive in nature. Management could then determine, based on what the data reflects, what it must do in specific areas in order to increase productivity. This type of focus would benefit strategic planning activities.

This type of effort also enables management to be proactive in managing change, enabling it to keep pace with customers and the competition. Consider how this may impact sales or trading as a facilitative function, for example. Or take it a step further and look how change impacts underlying systems from both operations and technology perspective. How relevant and current are these systems or practices? Staying abreast of new developments and capabilities in the marketplace and with competitors providing management with an opportunity to make various trade offs, which may lead to stronger performance. Alternatively, it may also enable management to make more effective strategic decisions by helping it to determine where to best allocate capital.

ASSESSING KEY DRIVERS THROUGH THE UNIVERSAL GUIDE

As you are well aware, a useful tool to leverage in evaluating the adequacy of key risks, controls, and activities is a standard assessment. Typically applied to assess the risks and controls in the context of compliance, financial, and operational issues, the assessment methodology ensures consistent and repetitive monitoring of activities. Whether conducted by internal or external resources, through the years conducting periodic assessments has proven to be a formidable tool in an organization's tool kit to manage risk. This tool also offers unique benefits in a company's desire to manage strategic risk.

Assessing key drivers of risk and growth through the universal guide's lens offers a unique approach. It provides companies with not only a framework in which to account for the formidable risk companies face but can unearth new opportunities for growth. Through a strategic risk assessment (see Exhibit 4.2) and a growth and opportunity assessment (see Exhibit 4.3), companies carefully parse through these opportunities and risks in a more comprehensive exercise.

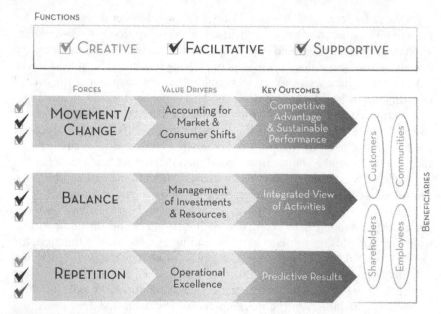

EXHIBIT 4.2   Strategic Risk Assessment

EXHIBIT 4.3   Growth Opportunity Assessment

Strategic Risk Assessment

Let's consider the strategic risk assessment. The assessment is centered on accounting for the three most formidable forces that dictate and influence organizational systems: balance, repetition, and change (see Exhibit 4.2). Creative, facilitative, and supportive functions should all be evaluated in the context of how they address or account for these forces. A simple example that most can relate to is in the application of a part of the assessment on a risk management activity or practice such as disaster recovery/business continuity to the force/influence of repetition. Risk is a support function.

What events such as 9/11 and other catastrophic natural disasters have taught us is the importance of ensuring that, after or during a major disruption of services, we quickly resume business processes or activities. That we ensure there is a contingency plan in place to handle the fallout relating to the disruption. As we know, these interruptions have the potential to cause the marketplace, a company, and its brand tremendous financial and reputational loss.

However, the best-laid disaster recovery and business continuity plans are not brought to life unless they are continually and periodically tested. This vital control must be tested repeatedly. There are many benefits to "repeating" your disaster recovery and business continuity tests: (1) through continuous and repeated testing, employees become more proficient and adept at what to do during a disruption or major disaster; (2) the process is naturally refined and is tweaked, as the test will uncover flaws in the plan; and (3) as new processes, products, and services are deployed, they should be integrated into current practices and therefore ensure that new risks are mitigated.

If you were to continue this process, the risk management function would be evaluated across the additional forces. Again, the assessment considers only the critical functions under each element and applies them to the forces.

The approach to the assessment also ensures alignment to the most critical organizational drivers, outcomes, and stakeholders (see Exhibit 4.3). By focusing on enhancing operational excellence, management of critical resources and assets, and the organization's competitive advantage, companies begin to thrive.

Strategic Suppliers Driving Value

An important aspect of this evaluation should be to incorporate the organization's strategic suppliers. Too often, organizations leave significant value on the table by underleveraging the enormous capabilities strategic partners possess. While many of these organizations are willing to partner with the organizations they support, companies must put forth a more conscious and deliberate effort to explore opportunities.

Whether it is in the form of leveraging strategic partner technology and capabilities or keeping abreast of industry trends and the competitive forces, partnering with your strategic suppliers across enterprise functions will drive value.

Growth Opportunity Assessment

Another approach is to apply the assessment to need to exploit additional opportunities of growth and value creation (see Exhibit 4.3). This approach assesses the three types of broad corporate activities and functions (creative, facilitative, and supportive) and evaluates their subfunctions and activities. The exercise is one that could be included as a precursor to an organization's periodic strategic planning efforts, as it may reveal additional areas of opportunities in which to direct resources. Again, this process should evaluate these opportunities in the context of the Three Forces, especially the forces of change and repetition.

SUMMARY

Through an approach that views organizations through a system's lens, companies can leverage the universal guide to enhance the management of strategic risk. This lens applies a more holistic discipline in addressing the dynamic and complex challenges companies face while ensuring the integration of key learnings and capabilities.

While fully addressing the challenges and opportunities the three elements provide, focusing on creativity and innovation as part of the systematic engine will ensure continuous growth over time. As some old-guard organizations have mastered this capability, we see in "New Age" companies a trend, driven by the enormous change in the marketplace, wherein creativity and innovation is more interwoven into the fabric of their organizational culture.

Ultimately, to sustain growth over time and to manage risk integrating the critical components of the Three Elements and Three Forces is necessary. This is especially true when we think of the impact of change and how it holds sway over so many of the key activities of an organization. Whether, it be in how a company addresses change from a new product and services or consumer trend perspective, or as it relates to new and emerging technologies or even the discipline of risk management. The reality of integration is also vital as we consider the forces of repetition and balance.

However, it is only through the discipline of continuous assessment and evaluation that an organization can yield value from the approach.

Through a systemic and repeated application of these principles, companies build the culture necessary to succeed in an ultra-competitive marketplace.

QUESTIONS

1. Identify areas in your organization that serve as "centers of creation." Where do these centers reside?
2. How are innovation and creativity cultivated and fostered in these areas?
3. Do you have an active innovation function, and if so, how effective is it?
4. What processes and practices are in place to ensure innovative employees operate in a dynamic and challenging environment?
5. How do you integrate and account for managing external change in your business? Is the process institutionalized?
6. How does your organization account for the impact of change internally as it applies to people, process, and technology?
7. Is the manner in which you account and manage change and risk an integrated and dynamic process?
8. What strategic exercises and assessments do you conduct regularly, and are there gaps in these activities?
9. Do you have a systemic process in place to capture and exploit innovation and capability derived from your core technology and operational functions?
10. When evaluating daily activity in high risk areas, is there a process in place that continuously measures and monitors this activity? How are you alerted when there are gaps in the monitoring of these activities?
11. Are the processes that manage and measure risk in your organization integrated? And are they summarized holistically to adequately communicate risk levels and their interdependencies?

REFERENCES

Capell, Kerry, with Arianne Sainsin, Cristina Lindbald, Therese Ann Palmer, Jason Bush, Dexter Roberts, and Kenji Hall. 2005. "IKEA." *Time*, November 13.

Gertner, Jon. 2012. "True Innovation." *New York Times*, February 25.

———. 2012. "How Do You Manufacture Innovation?" *Time*, March 23.

Hardy, Quentin. 2011. "Google's Innovation—and Everyone's?." *Forbes*, July 16.

Oches, Sam. 2012. QSR Drive-Thru Study, "How the Best Drive Thru Operations in the Industry Make the Wheels Go Round." QSR Special Report, October.

Popelka, Larry. 2013. "Google Is Winning the Innovation War against Apple." *Bloomberg BusinessWeek*, May 20.

Riordan, Michael. 2005. "No Monopoly on Innovation." *Harvard Business Review*, December.

Rothacker, Rick. 2012. "Wells Fargo's Carroll Eyes Cross-Selling by Brokers." Reuters, February 8.

Touryalai, Halah. 2012. "The Art of the Cross-Sale." *Forbes*, February 13.

Tuttle, Brad. 2013. "Marriott & IKEA Launch a Hotel Brand for Millennials: What Does That Even Mean?" *Time*, March 8.

Webley, Kayla. 2010. "A Brief History of the Happy Meal." *Time U.S.*, April 30.

Wells-Fargo's Package Deal, Bank Investment Consultant, October 2010, pp. 31–34.

Wojcicki, Susan. 2011. "The Eight Pillars of Innovation." *Think Quarterly: The Innovation Issue*, July.

CHAPTER 5

Risky Business: Why the Environment Should Matter to You

Mastering strategic risk requires that companies develop robust environmental sustainability agendas. The Three Elements provide insight into the formidable challenges we face as they help us understand how the critical players in our high-stakes environmental drama are inextricably bound. Through this new lens individuals, the Earth, and industry form a compelling and highly symbiotic web of relationships—a set of interactions that must be held in balance in order to sustain life not only today but for generations to come.

OUR SELF-CENTERED INTERESTS

As I hovered over my desk anxiously awaiting the call I had been expecting for several hours, the caller ID on my cell phone identified a private number coming through. Quite naturally, my first thought was, "This must be a telemarketer." Frustrated, I took a deep breath and continued with the conversation on my office phone. I was testy, to tell the truth, as the call I was waiting for should have been from Hollywood, California.

At the time of the call, I was deeply engrossed in a productive conversation with a consultant who was providing much-needed guidance on my new project. I wasn't willing to interrupt her, especially to answer a call from some random telemarketer, so we continued the conversation. After ending the call, I reluctantly checked my voicemail; the supposed telemarketer had left a message. As I listened to the message, I stood in silence, startled by what I was hearing. The message stated, "Mr. McPhee, this is Sherri from Mr. Poitier's office. Please return the call when you can."

Believing that the next step in the process was for Sherri to schedule a phone meeting with Mr. Poitier, I immediately dialed his office. I had talked to Sherri the day before, and she assured me that she would tell Mr. Poitier of the letter I had written to him some four months ago.

"Good afternoon, this is Sherri."

"Sherri, this is Joel McPhee returning your call."

"Mr. McPhee, Mr. Poitier read your letter and wants to speak to you immediately. I'm going to connect you—do you have a minute?"

"Of course, I do, Sherri." What else was I supposed to say?

There I stood in my office and began to think and move at a harried pace! Attempting to gather my thoughts, was I dreaming? This was finally the day I would have the long-anticipated phone call with Mr. Poitier. After a few rings, his clear and distinguished voice greeted me, "Mr. McPhee, Joel, how are you today, this is Sidney Poitier." Trying to collect my thoughts, I could hardly believe I was on the phone with the legendary actor and Hollywood icon. Yes, Sidney Poitier is a beloved actor the world over; however, for me he has always meant something more. He was my childhood hero!

Sir Sidney Poitier not only shares my Bahamian roots but grew up almost on the same street as my mother. My mother's family and other families who lived on or near Deveaux and Young Streets in Nassau at the time all knew each other very well. And as young children, Mr. Poitier and my mother knew each other. To this day, they remember each other very well.

Growing up in the Bahamas, as a child I would see Sir Sidney Poitier as we would spot him from time to time in downtown Nassau or in the International Airport. And almost always, I would walk up to him, remind him of our connection, and tell him how much I admired and appreciated his work. He was always gracious, ending each conversation by inquiring about my mother.

However, the context for my call was far different from those childhood encounters. In early September of that year, I reached out to Mr. Poitier to solicit his assistance in moving forward my fledgling book project and documentary. At that time, during the fall of 2009, my project was far different from the book you are now reading. In addition to beginning to write a book, I had created a short "teaser" documentary. However, getting Mr. Poitier's attention proved to be a daunting challenge.

What I learned from Sherri during those months of correspondence was that Mr. Poitier was working tirelessly to deliver a manuscript to his publisher. He was up against an aggressive deadline and had little time. For three long months I exchanged e-mails and telephone calls with Sherri, who always assured me that she would make things happen. And she did!

"So I have read your letter, Joel, and I believe you are on to something, yet I sense there is still something more powerful lurking within your passionate and well-written letter that needs to be brought forward. Now since I have read your letter, I would like for you, in your own words, to describe this project, your concepts, and why they are of such importance at this time."

I was stunned and caught completely off-guard. My mind raced with a number of thoughts: "Really?" "What do I say?" "How should I say it?" I was ill-prepared. For close to four minutes I stumbled hopelessly along, desperately trying to find my conversational cadence in articulating the key points of the project. I was failing miserably, and it was painful! So much was going on in my head. To be honest, I was still attempting to wrap my head around the fact that I was talking to Poitier, while at the same time realizing I was squandering what I considered to be a once-in-a-lifetime opportunity. How do I shift my focus in order to interact with him as a simple human being, sharing information? I finally found my footing and stated my case.

After what seemed to be a lengthy pause, Mr. Poitier stated, "Joel, it is clear that you have put much thought into this work, but let me share my perspective on a project of this type. As you know, I've seen a lot, and as I have experienced life, one thing remains clear the world over. Every person who picks up a book, movie, or product of this type wants to know one thing and one thing only, and that is, what's in it for me? Yes, Mr. McPhee, my conclusion is, at the end of the day, we are all selfish!"

Momentarily I had to take a step back. I needed to really contemplate what he had articulated. His advice was not only insightful but timely, considering the early stages of the project. We then continued to exchange ideas. The conversation ended up far better than it had begun, and we parted ways. However, his words remained firmly planted in my head. For weeks I wrestled with his simple yet illuminating thought. We can't all be selfish. Am I selfish? This couldn't be, as I know many individuals who are far from being selfish. Could this be true? Ultimately, after several weeks of reflection and internal debate, I reluctantly yielded. Yes, we are selfish, each and every one of us!

Looking back at that conversation made me realize how often I've operated out of my own self-interest, and how we all often operate from self-centered interests. This advice coming from him proved to be pivotal in developing my book idea.

Our self-centered attitudes and behaviors come clearly into view when we consider our crises concerning the environment and sustainability. His words ring true when we consider the critical players of our modern world. For if the critical players act solely out of self-interest, we will pay a heavy price, impacting the lives of generations to come. The critical players include individuals, industry, and the environment.

THE TRUTH ABOUT SYSTEMS

We live in an interconnected world—a world, though seemingly composed of disparate components and parts, that is netted together by an intricate web of dependent relationships. Over time, we somehow have come to view our world through a compartmentalized and detached lens. However, if there's one thing our new era has illuminated, it's how dependent we are on one another. As technology and the Internet have fueled this integration, it has served as a powerful force, linking systems, forms of technology, and processes that straddle our personal and commercial lives. It has also played a formidable role in altering our understanding of the world by forcing us to think more holistically, enabling us to recognize how truly connected we are.

This reality, coupled with how the speed of commercial and social activities has intensified, is forcing us to view and align activities in our world in a more integrated manner. Recently, this was evident with the 2008 credit meltdown and the ensuing global recession, as the impact of seemingly separate activities was felt in every corner of the planet. Today, we are also highly interdependent when we consider our environmental, economic, and social issues. When one part of the world experiences change, the reverberations are felt everywhere.

While we are adapting to understanding these interdependencies, we still struggle to fully understand our interconnectedness with and dependency on the environment. Another possible reason for our complacency is that we believe there is a choice. However, as more data are showing us on issues of sustainability and the environment, we have little time to lose in ensuring a vibrant future.

OUR COMMERCIAL ECOSYSTEM

Individuals, the Earth, and industry are tightly linked as they relate to the flow and realities of commerce. This connection or web of relationships is highly symbiotic, interdependent, and interconnected, just like the relationships that exist in ecosystems. I refer to our system of commerce and how it works in this manner due to its uncanny similarity to ecosystems in our natural environment. An ecosystem is defined as "a system of complex interactions of populations between themselves and with their environment" or as "the joint functioning and interaction of these two compartments (populations and environment) in a functional unit of variable size."

As described in Chapter 2, in ecosystems there are three primary players. There are producers, consumers, and decomposers. Producers create and serve as the catalyst for the entire system, while consumers act as the conduit or facilitate the process. Finally, decomposers play a critical support function for the entire system.

Other characteristics of ecosystems include but are not limited to:

- Ecosystems contain complex interactions and relationships between members in the ecosystem. These interactions and relations between the participants are at the heart of how the system functions.
- Activities in ecosystems involve the activities of animals. Animals play a pivotal role in their sustainment.
- They are large, dynamic entities with large amounts of energy and matter.

Our commercial ecosystem possesses similar characteristics as those found in ecosystems in nature. These similarities include:

- In environmental ecosystems, there are two primary features that are responsible for sustainment of the system. There is first the physical and second the biological/chemical environment that members/participants live in. In commercial ecosystems, there are also two primary features that are responsible for sustainment of the entire system. There is first the physical, which is composed of natural resources, and second the commercial environment, in which commerce and marketplace activities transpire in order to meet the needs and desires of individuals or human beings.
- As in environmental ecosystems, in commercial ecosystems the viability of the system is tied to how healthy the interactions are between the participants/members. Interactions between all participants/members are tightly linked; therefore, impacts to a set of members inevitably affect any one aspect of life of the system.

We operate in a commercial ecosystem consisting of three players—individuals, industry, and the Earth (see Exhibit 5.1). Linked through their common interests, these three players demonstrate how dependent we are on one another for growth and sustainment. This new insight not only explains how symbiotic the stakeholders are but presents a compelling case on why we must transcend our collective self-interests in furtherance of a more vibrant tomorrow.

In the commercial ecosystem, individuals or human beings are the catalyst and spawn the activity that serves as the lifeblood of commercial activity. The basis of this activity is our fundamental needs and desires. This includes fundamental needs such as food, shelter, health, physical needs, and safety. As human beings, we consume, and it is the role of consumption in our commercial ecosystem that ensures activity and propels the system forward.

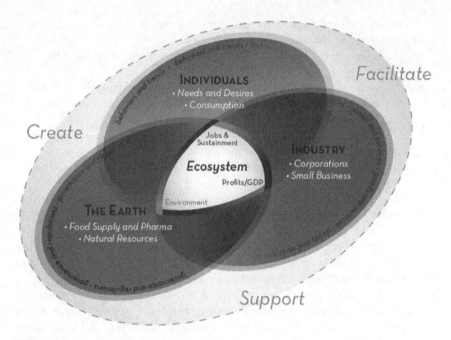

EXHIBIT 5.1   Our Commercial Ecosystem

There are also desires that span the gamut and include social, entertainment, and other areas. These fundamental needs and desires serve to create or produce critical elements for the system.

The consumption of goods and services is fundamental to ensuring the optimum performance of many marketplace activities. Without human consumption the wheels of commerce would come to a grinding halt. Not only would commerce falter, but life on Earth would not exist, for to be alive on this planet means that we must also sustain ourselves.

Corporations, both private and public; small businesses; and enterprises of all types facilitate these needs by providing products and services for our consumption and use. I refer to this category as industry. These products and services span many industries. A critical connection here is the important linkage to marketing and advertising. Marketing and advertising is a very important tool in the overall system of commerce, for it enables entities to initiate, cultivate, and further agitate in all of us new desires or a reinforcement of some fundamental need. It is a powerful force in the flow of our commercial ecosystem.

Finally, there is the supportive component. The flow of products and services are supported by both the earth and human beings, from the oil and gas that comes out of the earth to provide us fuel for our automobiles and energy for our homes, to the pharmaceutical products we use to help us with daily ailments and disease. For example, it is estimated that approximately 25 percent of Western pharmaceutical products originated in the planet's rainforests. More astonishing than that is the fact that approximately 70 percent of all new drugs in the United States originate and are derived from or originate from the land.

Consider the impact and importance of agriculture and of timber or the criticality of precious and industrial metals. Metals such as aluminum, stainless steel, nickel, titanium, and copper are vital to the development of emerging countries such as China and India. They provide the critical infrastructure necessary to support these economic giants.

Government also provides the necessary components to support these activities. Government provides the laws, regulations, and policies to ensure that goods and services not only meet the needs of individuals but also are appropriate for sale and usage by consumers/individuals. Government plays a critical role as it relates to the governance of our precious and limited natural resources in our commercial ecosystem. This function is paramount, and ensures objectivity and balance in the system.

Understanding these players in the system also underscores why industry and business must be separate from the role of government and governance in the system. Because industry is primarily focused on production for profit and gain, this primary objective of industry in the stream of commerce runs contrary to the role of governance, which in itself is an objective notion.

Embedded in this model is the core of the system, which provides insight into the connectivity between jobs, production, and profit, and the environment. While consumption through needs and desires spawns what becomes the lifeblood of the commercial ecosystem (goods and services), this dynamic in turn is the catalyst to job creation. Job creation not only provides us with the means to purchase goods and services, thereby sustaining ourselves, but enables to pursue work that provides us with meaning. And the final cog in this important wheel is always the environment because it supports it all through the natural resources and the food we consume.

Because of this interdependence, the self-interests of individuals and industry, if not held in check, would overwhelm our already strained environment. This new perspective not only explains how symbiotic the stakeholders are but presents a compelling case for why we must transcend our collective self-interests in furtherance of a more aggressive plan to address the sustainability and the environment. Bringing forward how dependent these three stakeholders are provides a formidable business case regarding the environmental sustainability. It demonstrates how the overall health and long-term profitability of commercial activities are directly tied to environmental concerns. Industry, as a key stakeholder in this web of relationships, must take a more active role in addressing and mitigating issues tied to the environment. Consider the work that the multinational corporation Unilever is doing in the area of sustainability and the environment.

DRIVING GROWTH AND SHAREHOLDER VALUE THROUGH SUSTAINABILITY

Possessing a rich history of pioneering social responsibility, it's no wonder Unilever is a global leader in corporate sociability. The company produces products that represent the highest standards of quality, are socially and environmentally responsible, and reflect strong input from the communities it serves. Unilever quite simply produces products for a global customer base that enhance and improve the quality of life for individuals throughout its massive global footprint. It serves a customer base of over 2 billion worldwide that stretches from South America to Southeast Asia and from Africa to western Europe. It is a consumer branding behemoth, serving customers in over 100 countries.

Corporate responsibility is deeply embedded in Unilever's DNA, as it has been a strategic imperative throughout its 100-year history. The company views the issue of sustainability and sales growth not as being mutually exclusive goals but as inextricably tied to achieving profitability over the long term. Corporate responsibility is a strategic imperative.

In 2010, Unilever launched a new business model that placed the issue of sustainability at the center of its worldwide operations. As a result of this new business model, it has committed to a number of aggressive sustainability goals by 2020. These goals are to:

- Reduce the impact its products have on the environment by 50 percent. This applies to lowering greenhouse emissions and waste.
- Obtain all of its agricultural supplies from sources that are sustainable.
- Directly impact the health of a billion individuals across the planet through these efforts.

Some three years after the launch of its new sustainability business model, Unilever has produced strong financial results and outperformed the competition. In addition to Unilever's strong belief that its approach to sustainability will fuel its growth, it is also convinced that this approach will significantly reduce the company's expenses. However, ultimately, the company believes that its sustainability strategy will deliver long-term value to its shareholder base.

Unilever is confident that this approach to the long-term view will only enhance its ability to sustain itself and remain competitive.

Brand Imprinting

Preceding its 2010 sustainability efforts, in 2004 Unilever embarked on a unique branding mission. It desired to ensure that its core values became more visible in all of its product lines. What was the impetus of this new focus and refueled mission, you may ask. Unilever read the tea leaves! It understood how much customer demands were changing and how conscientious customers were becoming. Its consumer base across the globe was becoming more interested in health and environmental issues, and to meet these new customer requirements, Unilever believed it needed to strengthen its approach to how it managed corporate environment and sociability issues.

To unleash the power inherent in its unique market position, Unilever embarked on incorporating environmental and social, considerations into the development of its brands. This meant that eventually it would skillfully weave environmental and sociability components into the core of its brand strategy. Hence, sustainability and the environment would become a key part of all business decisions. Unilever was clear: Sustainability and the environment were a competitive advantage. They were not separate and distinct, as it wanted all decision makers to integrate these components into all products.

Known as its Brand Imprint initiative, Unilever required all key decision makers in a product's value chain to come together. The purpose of bringing such a broad group of stakeholders together was to understand the environmental, social, and economic issues critical to each brand. This group represented a wide array of interests, and came from areas such as research and development (R&D), production, sourcing, operations, and the marketing group.

The Brand Imprint initiative was also supported by a structured process that ensured that each functional leader would inspect and monitor his or her individual performance. The performance was then measured against the impact each brand would have from an environmental, social, and economic perspective. What made this approach effective was that the functional leader or owners of each brand, and not the sustainability experts, owned this process.

The six areas of importance to Unilever were measurements on market forces, key opinion formers, social, the economy, the environment, and consumer concerns. Through this process, the sustainability team and managers of the six areas would examine the data for each individual segment. They examined each segment, looking for a number of factors, which included benchmarking, stakeholder engagement, customer surveys, and market research, to name a few. This due diligence and intense analysis would then be reported and leveraged as a baseline to develop a plan for each brand. This process led Unilever to establish a formidable management reporting framework that focused on key performance indicators and metrics that incorporated sustainability measures.

Unilever's unique approach provides a compelling example of how issues of sustainability and the environment can be leveraged to assist in driving performance. Its rich legacy and culture in pioneering this effort has resulted in a powerful strategy that has given it a competitive advantage in a highly competitive global marketplace. Whether through its Brand Imprinting efforts or the launch of its 2010 sustainability model, Unilever's approach to business accounts for the symbiotic relationships that exist between industry, individuals, and the Earth. By skillfully weaving the themes of sociability and the environment into the core of its operations, it has provided a powerful business case.

DEMYSTIFYING THE MYTH . . . WHAT REALLY IS A CORPORATION?

Corporations exist because of individuals. Companies spanning all industry types, both public and private, whether large or small, derive their purpose and power from people. Their ultimate survival is grounded in their ability to provide goods and services to individuals and communities. Hence, at the center of commercial activities are the needs and desires of the individual. Governments provide organizations with the authority and privilege to provide critical and necessary products and services to citizens. This point is of paramount importance, for often because of commercial success and issues of scale and its sheer power, corporations lose sight of who they are and why they exist.

Yes, a corporation's primary responsibility is to provide value to shareholders. However, it is equally important to acknowledge that the lifeblood of companies is human beings and communities. They cannot exist without these pivotal players. Throughout the years, there have been many arguments to further the case for corporate social responsibility. These arguments center on linking social/humanitarian needs and efforts to corporate profit and loss (P&L) performance. Other justifications for corporations to be socially responsible are tied to other strong points, including:

- Enhancing employee relations and strengthening relations with communities and other critical stakeholders
- Increasing market share and attracting new customers
- Gaining a competitive advantage by increasing profits

Although there is strong empirical evidence that links corporate social responsibility activities to the shareholder agenda, there is a more fundamental reason for corporations to contribute to the environmental sociability agenda.

Government, through the power derived by and given to it by the governed (its people), enables corporations to operate. The governed, also through government, give industry and corporations access to critical natural resources that are fundamental and necessary to the production of goods and products that flow through the stream of commerce. While ownership of resources and land is granted due to commercial structures, ultimately, these rights emanate from the collective. We therefore must, even in the pursuit of profit and gain, ensure that we operate organizations with the best interests of communities and individuals in mind as well.

We live on a planet of limited natural resources. We have come to realize that natural resources are fundamental to our ability to survive and thrive in this world. These needs are essential for the existence of the human species. Industry, through corporations, plays a critical role in how these resources are consumed and utilized. Again, we must remember that it is government, on behalf of the governed, that gives authority to industry to provide goods and services, through federal, state, and local legal entities.

Yes, it is the role of governments to govern and police how resources are expended, utilized, and consumed; however, it *cannot* do it alone. Industry and companies must be at the front and center of managing our limited natural resources because they can provide pivotal leadership. Corporations of all types and across various industries can serve as stewards of what is utilized.

Because of the highly symbiotic and interconnected relationship that exists between individuals, industry, and the Earth, the debate transcends altruistic and ethical considerations to one that is centered on sheer necessity and the future survival of the planet. From global corporate titans, such as pharmaceutical giants Pfizer and Novartis, to global retailers such as Walmart and McDonald's; from G.E. to oil and gas conglomerates, such as Exxon and Royal Dutch Shell; to clothing retailers such as the Gap and Spanish retailer Zara Inc.—these and many more are dependent on natural resources to facilitate and supply what is needed in the marketplace.

A LESSON ON THE ENVIRONMENT AND SUSTAINABILITY

You'd be surprised to learn that one of the global leaders in environmental sustainability is a company whose products and services are in the financial services industry. However, this company, over the past 20 years, has embarked on a transformative journey to integrate sustainability and the environment into the fabric of what it does. For five consecutive years it has been listed on the Dow sustainability index as well as garnering top awards, such as being named in 2010 one of the top 15 green companies.

With over $22 trillion in assets under custody and administration, State Street Corporation is a global leader in financial services. Its client list is made up of any company's wish list of enviable enterprises to serve. They span multiple disciplines, including central banks, monetary authorities, top hedge funds, governments, and various mutual funds, to name a few. Environmental sustainability is a serious matter at State Street, as it is deeply embedded into its governance processes, products, and services, and integrated into its corporate culture.

Despite a slowly rebounding global economy, State Street has also remained steadfast in its commitment to environmental sustainability. From the boardroom to its top brass, its vision is to become a global leader in environmental social governance. Its vision and strategy, like Unilever, is tied to its strong belief that it will create incremental shareholder value and sustained performance only if its efforts in this area are fully realized.

To achieve its vision, State Street has set several key activities in motion. Specifically, it has:

- Developed a transparent governance framework and structure.
- Established sustainability goals focused on improving performance in waste, greenhouse emissions, water consumption, and recycling.
- Instituted a long-term process that enables it to connect with different areas of the company, tracking and keeping abreast of global trends. This process also leverages employees' and clients' knowledge and interests.

State Street has also integrated environmental sustainability into its culture through a series of initiatives and actions. A few examples include:

- Holding an employee awareness Sustainability Week
- Offering online environmental sustainability training module, created to inform and educate employees
- Conducting surveys to gather employee opinions and to identify opportunities to engage employees differently on the issues of sustainability

Often, corporate leaders view these issues as being mutually exclusive from the important goal of driving profitability and growth. However, as consumers the world over continue to become more educated and gain access to information, this dynamic will force businesses to produce more environmentally sound and sustainable products. This, coupled with a highly visible drama being played out concerning the deleterious impacts of our individual and collective impacts on the planet, will further drive these issues.

TD Bank and Its Green Initiatives

With a goal of being as green as its logo, TD Bank is also leading the way in championing the environment. TD is serious in its commitment and has set in motion a series of green initiatives aimed at responding to our global crisis. An example of its strong commitment to the environment occurred in 2007, when at the beginning of our period of financial uncertainty, it announced its first ever chief environmental officer. These examples and many more underscore its passion and vision for the environment.

In May 2011, TD Bank opened what was the first Net Zero commercial bank branch in the United States. Located in Ft. Lauderdale Florida, at that time the branch was only one of eight buildings in the United States to be registered as Net Zero. And it was also the only bank out of the eight. Net Zero is a designation given by the Department of Energy. The designation indicates that a commercial or residential building in a given year produces as much renewable power as the total energy it uses.

To execute on its commitment, TD Bank has created a three-pronged strategy centered on energy, employee engagement, and paper. The company carries out its activities in these areas through:

- Energy:
  - Since 2011, every new TD Bank branch or store is designed and built to achieve Leadership in Energy & Environmental Design (LEED) certification. It is also installing solar panels at more than 50 of its stores across the United States. By incorporating solar panels, its goal is to generate approximately 12 to 18 percent of the stores' energy needs.
  - To recognize its efforts, in 2012 the Environmental Protection Agency (EPA) awarded TD Bank the Green Power Partner Leadership Award.
- Employee engagement: TD bank realizes how critical employees are to its efforts and has created a series of initiatives that will institutionalize environmental sustainability into its culture:
  - Through forums, such as senior committees that bring together executives from across the enterprise, it allows leaders to collaborate on environmental issues. These efforts also focus on how to drive effective change in daily business operations.

- Online systems allow employees to pledge and conduct green acts. These systems also allow employees to track and measure performance.
- Through a community day entitled TD Tree Day, the bank demonstrates to each community in which it operates how serious it is about the environment. This day is a volunteer day in which employees from Florida to Maine plant hundreds of trees in their communities.
- Paper: TD Bank is committed to reducing the use and waste of paper. Through a program entitled TD Forests, the bank has committed to two goals:
  1. Reduce paper usage by 20 percent by 2015.
  2. Directly impact the area of forest habitat in North America (United States and Canada) by two football fields of forest each day.

Realizing that State Street and TD Bank are not alone in implementing environmental sustainability efforts, their active commitment provides strong examples in an industry not known for championing this cause. Quite often, companies whose products and services are not directly from nature fail to realize how interconnected their businesses are to the environment. However, highlighting and telling these stories will assist in making the connection for other companies, enabling them to view pragmatic and simple solutions to implementing their environmental sustainability efforts.

OTHER FACTORS DRIVING COMMERCE

The consumption of goods and services also highlights another reality regarding the individual and how we create what eventually becomes the lifeblood of our commercial system. As individuals, we consume for two reasons: (1) out of necessity and (2) because of desire. However, there is an additional critical connection to make between our desires, human behavior, and innovation/creativity. This connection demonstrates how powerful innovation can be when coupled with emerging technology, human behavior, and new trends. This linkage also demonstrates how transformative these drivers are when we anticipate how cutting-edge innovations can both influence and drive behavior.

An example is the significant impact Apple and Steve Jobs have had on our world through technology. Not only has Apple experienced tremendous growth since its introduction of the iPod, iPhone, and iPad, but it has altered behavior. Of the many ways in which these devices have had a major impact on our lives, none is greater than how they have pushed us from keyboard to touch screen, thereby enhancing accessibility and capabilities.

The iPad alone has captured widespread and broad acceptance of touch-screen technology and has influenced and changed the way we work. This example demonstrates a number of powerful lessons and observations:

- How industry can drive and alter human behavior and activity by understanding emerging technology and how it can be used to enhance our lives
- How, by making these important linkages and connections, industry through innovation can introduce products and services that serve to initiate human consumption
- How by anticipating the impact and providing products and services that further drive consumption, companies experience tremendous economic success

Apple engineers have recently published a report it claims supports the impact of its innovative products on employment and the job market. In addition to the 57,000-plus employees who work for Apple, it has conducted a study that as a result of the iPad and other products, it has added some 517,000 jobs to the American economy. Consider how truly impactful this is.

Consider how important food and agriculture are to the food industry globally and to other industries such as energy. Or consider natural resources and the critical role they play in clothing manufacturing, real estate, and the building of critical technology devices such as laptops and home computers. Fossil fuels, water, and essential chemicals are necessary in order to build them.

IMPROVING OUR INTERACTION WITH THE PLANET

The forces of change, balance, and repetition are relevant when considering issues of environmental sustainability. When we think of the enormous change we experienced in the nineteenth and twentieth centuries and how tremendous shifts have altered the needs of a growing planet, we see clearly that a more balanced approach is needed. And while repetition often ensures optimal performance, it does have its drawbacks—we need not repeat behaviors that carry negative consequences, especially ones that carry lingering impacts.

Though we face a future of wonderful opportunity, we must shift the manner in which we manage our world. This new approach should account for the history of human activity. It should ensure that we incorporate the lessons of the past as we prepare the path for a brighter tomorrow. As we move forward, two critical factors must heavily influence our approach: our relationship to the Earth, and the relations among fellow men. These two critical considerations must be addressed in order to usher in this new era.

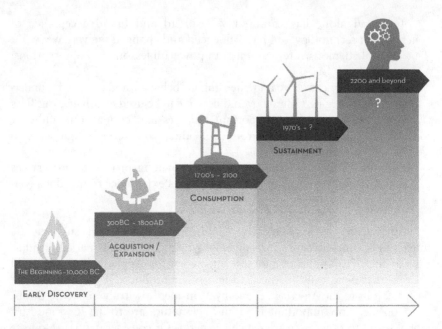

EXHIBIT 5.2 Timeline of Human Activity

Examining our history of interacting with our planet's natural resources and with one another, what emerges are four phases of human activity that I would categorize as early discovery, acquisition/expansion, consumption, and sustainment. I also categorize these phases into the timeline of Human Activity (see Exhibit 5.2). Some of the phases overlap with others; however, they are distinguished from each other based on the volume and pace of a particular activity during a distinct measure of time.

Early Discovery

During this time, man knew very little about himself, his world, and the universe beyond him. This was a time of a different form of exploration. One marked by a focus on learning more about immediate surroundings and what could be leveraged to survive in a very primitive world.

Acquisition and Expansion

Humans slowly moved into a period of acquisition and expansion. As the timeline depicts, this took place over thousands of years, from 3000 B.C. to 1800 A.D. This time period was marked by advances in military tactics, weaponry, transportation, forms of communication, language, and other enhancements to the life of premodern man. The earliest evidence of the creation of the wheel took place somewhere between 3500 and 3350 B.C. Soon after, in the second millennium, wheeled vehicles began to appear throughout the ancient world from the Indus Valley to Central Europe, even onto Mesopotamia. Wheeled vehicles made mankind more mobile, thereby enabling them to transport supplies, food, and armies over greater distances.

This is also the time of Alexander the Great. He is considered by many historians as the first world conqueror, as he expanded his empire far beyond Greece. He created one of the largest empires in ancient history and spread the Greek culture beyond Persia down into the Indian subcontinent.

Along with Alexander the Great, many other world leaders emerged during this time frame: Attila the Hun, Genghis Khan, and Napoleon. This period also marked the rise and fall of the Roman, British, and Spanish empires. It captured a time when these empires acquired and expanded their territories through force, manipulation, and military might. When we think of what occurred in the short history of our nation, the same can be said regarding our activities both in North America and abroad. They began with the Pilgrims and continued for several hundred years to the west, beyond the original 13 colonies. These conquests also left lasting effects on the indigenous people of those lands, which, over time, have transcended their cultural, educational, political, and social structure.

It is interesting to point out that the indigenous people of many of these conquered lands understood the importance of balance and caring for the land. Through the history and knowledge passed down in their traditions, they had developed a reverence for the land and her natural resources. They were appropriate stewards of their resources, consuming the resources they needed while maintaining the balance of nature.

As the world became more complex, it became difficult to acquire and expand through force and manipulation. We no longer have vast territories to expand into, and our global community—through entities such the United Nations—has established a code of conduct between nations. Thus, the time of expansion has passed as it relates to governments and the will of its leaders. However, commercial expansion continues through the private sector. Corporations continue to grow commercially through the purchase of resources and assets to further their economic interests.

Consumption

As we moved from the expansion phase, we began to consume more natural resources during the consumption phase, which I consider to be from the mid-1700s through today. This period also corresponds with the Industrial Revolution, which took place from approximately the mid 1700s to the mid 1800s. The Industrial Revolution was the key catalyst to a more consuming world, as there were major changes in agriculture, mining, transportation, manufacturing, and technology. The Industrial Revolution was a critical time in Earth's history, as we also experienced an explosion of growth in the world's population. Since the birth of the Industrial Revolution, the pace and intensity of human consumption has been staggering. This has converged with the explosion in population growth to create our crisis.

If we were to track the population growth since thousands of years B.C., we would see a somewhat slow growth in the population until the twentieth century. From 1900 until today, the planet has exploded in its population. It grew from 1.6 billion in 1900 to approximately 7.6 billion in 2009. This is astonishing when compared to the fact that from 10,000 B.C. until 1900, the planet grew to only 1 billion-plus inhabitants.

When we compare the growth in the population to our use of natural resources and the damage it has inflicted, we see a corresponding destructive impact on our planet. The realities of an explosive growth in population with the corresponding strain on natural resources require us to pause to think about our impact on these resources. The past three decades marked a time when our consumption is at its height. Although this is reflective of modern man's failure to appropriately balance the pace and intensity of consumption, it also is a direct result of the explosion in population.

We live on a planet with limited physical resources, while over several centuries we've applied a model that is depleting her lifeblood: the natural resources that sustain and nourish our planet. Examine the impact we've had on a critical part of life on Earth: the rainforest.

When we look at a map of landmasses that were rich in vegetation some 50 years ago, we see there are very few left. Only one large land mass remains: the Amazon rainforest of Brazil. Rainforests once covered approximately 15 percent of the Earth's land surface, while today they only cover 6 percent. Conservationists estimate that in only 40 years our remaining rainforests will be destroyed. Why the focus on rainforests? Because the depletion of rainforests serves as a critical illustration of the challenges we face not only today but also in the future.

The Amazon rainforest is massive, encompassing more than 7 million square miles. Its total area would make it the ninth-largest country in the world—larger than Saudi Arabia or Mexico. More important, more than 20 percent of the world's oxygen is produced in the Amazon. Because of the Amazon's significant impact in recycling carbon dioxide into oxygen, it is described as the "lungs of our planet." Additionally, it is estimated that approximately 80 percent of the world's diet—cocoa, avocados, various fruits, coconuts, nuts of all types, and spices—originated from tropical rainforests, as well as significant cures for deadly diseases, viruses, and infections. Even products such as rubber, gum, and resins originate from it. Our rainforests are threatened by climate change, greenhouse gas emissions, and deforestation by humans. If we do not change the way we live, our behavior will eventually destroy this critical component of our planet's comprehensive ecosystem.

Sustainment

Overlapping the end of the consumption phase is the beginning of the sustainment phase, beginning in the early 1970s. Some might say the sustainment phase began in the early 1900s, when Theodore Roosevelt developed a national agenda that focused on preserving the environment. His efforts and those of others around the globe at that time recognized the importance of conservation and being better stewards of our world. However, I selected the early 1970s as the beginning of the period of sustainment because it marks the United Nations' first formal conference on the environment.

Held in Stockholm, Sweden, in 1972, the conference for the first time brought together representatives from multiple governments to discuss the global environment. Governments began creating departments to address environmental issues as well as passing legislation such as clean air and water acts. This time period also ushered in an awareness of the environment as people around the globe were recognizing the risks of nuclear energy. The period of Sustainment will continue throughout the twenty-first century and beyond.

There is a critical need to hasten our efforts to find more effective ways to sustain the environment. We continue to strain our natural resources, inflicting further damage on the planet. Think of the strain that India and China alone will place on natural resources. The emergence of these economies takes considerable resources when we think of the nearly 3 billion Chinese and Indian people whose lives are being transformed by the global economy.

Due to these factors our efforts to more effectively manage our current resources and to transform our attitudes toward the environment take on enhanced significance. The consumption and sustainment phases overlap due to our behavior and the pattern of growth in emerging economies. In a few decades, we will be well on our way in migrating from the consumption phase and will see more of our efforts of sustainment and conservation pay off. Think about the various initiatives that are under way, such as the upgrading of the old electrical grid to a "smarter grid" and our efforts to harness sun, wind, and water as viable sources of alternative energy.

Today, we are experiencing a concerted effort by governments around the world to take on this global crisis. These efforts will only intensify as we work to stop—and in some cases reverse—the damage we've inflicted on our natural environment.

An approach that embraces a spirit of sustainment is the only logical approach and direction. As we've experienced the steady depletion of natural resources such as oil, water, and our rainforests, we see that excessive consumption is not the answer. Further, when we examine the strain our activities have on the environment, we see that are moving to a time when will have no other choice.

MAKING THE CASE FOR THE ENVIRONMENT

Acknowledging how our commercial ecosystem function enables us to manage natural resources more effectively. It will ensure that we sustain commercial activities far beyond our time in this existence. This new perspective also demonstrates how vital our natural resources are to sustaining and initiating commercial activities. Managing natural resources for not only present-day but future usage and consumption ensures that life on our planet will not only be preserved but thrive well into the future. It is essential to our survival.

Industrialists look to environmentalists as a major obstacle in furthering the free market agenda; however, when examined in the context of this commercial ecosystem, their seemingly disparate agendas are one and the same. The only difference between the two is one of time. And in this context, in order for us to ensure a vibrant future for future generations, the only way is through managing the delicate balance of excessive consumption and utilization of the natural resources we have at our disposal.

This divisive and highly charged debate could be resolved by hastening our efforts to capture the benefits derived from alternative energy sources. By focusing on further developing these alternative sources of energy, we would not only preserve our much-needed traditional sources of natural energy but infuse additional inputs into the stream of commerce. As we are aware, these efforts to further develop and create new industries would spawn enormous commerce globally.

THE CORPORATION AND THE COMMUNITY

Corporations are visible in communities. Their presence can be felt through involvement in a host of social and humanitarian activities. They also provide tremendous support in other areas that cover issues in health, human services, education, and the environment. Without this commitment from corporations, many critical local and national concerns would suffer greatly, for they play a pivotal role in fulfilling many needs.

Though corporations provide talent and resources to address various issues in the community, there is one area in particular where it can enhance its presence. This is in the role it plays in assigning leadership and talent to community activities in the form of membership on committees, task forces, and other forums. Providing top talent and capable resources to these efforts enables corporations to be visible and active in communities. However, often decisions to place internal talent on these committees are based on the visibility and influence of these committees and task forces. Alternatively, top talent in organizations should be placed on committees and task forces that need them most. These efforts often are focused on some of the more challenging and less glamorous issues that often plague communities.

THE REALITIES OF LIFE DOWNSTREAM

We exist too far downstream to appreciate the impact of our behavior and actions on the environment. Our attitudes, both individually and collectively, toward environmental sustainability are influenced by how far removed we are from our natural environment and its linkage to food, shelter, and clothing. Through ingenuity and progress, we are several steps removed from the process of how goods, products, and daily comforts arrive on our doorsteps and dinner tables. Today, our homes are heated in the frigid winter and cooled in the withering heat with just a simple push of a button. These comforts shield us from the realities and challenges directly tied to the sources of our many conveniences.

Consider life in the late nineteenth century as compared to life today. As an agrarian society, we were closer to the growth and harvesting of the food we ate. During that time the world over, most individuals either grew or harvested their own food products. This also holds true if we step back farther in time as it relates to how clothing is manufactured. Consider this too in the context of the fundamental need of building a home.

This disconnection, though providing us with amazing modern-day comforts, has equally desensitized us to impacts our individual efforts have on the sources we are critically dependent on for growth and sustainment. How would our attitudes and behaviors differ if we witnessed firsthand how the products and materials that provide us with food, clothing, and shelter are grown and harvested? What if we gained deeper insight into these processes or lived in those areas most impacted by this reality? Would this impact our concerns? Would this create a sense of urgency toward our efforts to sustain the environment?

The fact that we care little to learn and of how the critical flow in the "natural resources chain" of food, energy, and materials affect us does not mean we have no impact or do not pose a threat to these resources. The environment has become a victim of mankind's progress and new lifestyle. Life downstream, though temporarily providing many with comfort and ease, will ultimately topple, creating a great imbalance.

IN THE END, IT'S ABOUT THE INDIVIDUAL

The modern corporation is a force like none other. Its impact and reach touches every aspect of our lives, influencing political, social, and economic agendas as well as other global challenges. As the primary facilitator of commerce, companies are uniquely positioned to leverage their power and influence to champion the importance of environmental sustainability. As a benefactor of the handsome rewards taken from the earth, it has considerable work to do to fulfill its true role—a role centered on stewardship and one anchored in accountability.

However, no matter how powerful and dominating a global player industry has become, it will continue to remain responsible and accountable to individuals. We should also focus on individuals for two reasons. First, no matter how formidable the corporation and industry may be, it will not and cannot exist without individuals. Individuals consume, and our behavior stokes the fires that ensure a vibrant marketplace.

Second, companies rely on individuals in the production and delivery of goods and services. It is the individual who serves on the critical front lines. We sell, trade, service, and provide critical support in the process of delivering products and services to the ultimate end user or consumer. This also highlights the importance of local communities to companies. Without them the corporation would not be, for what are our communities but collection of disparate yet highly interdependent groups of individuals?

Understanding the critical linkage between corporations, individuals, and local communities places the issue of the role and responsibility of companies squarely on the table. It illuminates the important role corporations must play in leading the way to solving many of our challenges.

There cannot be a discussion about the environment and sustainability without mention of the impacts of global warning and climate change. These two realities will continue to cause irreversible impacts to ecological systems the world over, damaging forests, coastal swamps, and marshes. Global warning and climate change also impact our delicate water management system through early snow melt and runoff.

We've all experienced other impacts firsthand as we observe how extreme and unpredictable the weather in our individual regions has become. Or consider that over the past 20 years oceans have become warmer, sea levels are rising, and extreme droughts have impacted precious crops.

We live in an integrated world. We've evolved and learned over time to compartmentalize things as we often have the proclivity to think of various activities as separate and distinct. But the truth is that, as we move forward in time, we must learn to integrate activities and think holistically about the challenges we now face.

The reality of systems, especially when understood in the context of the universal guide, dictate that seemingly disparate and distinct elements are highly connected and work harmoniously in furtherance of the whole. It is a reality that calls on these functions to perform holistically and in a highly integrated manner.

For example, in the case of the human body, each element, function, and system works in concert and harmoniously with the others on behalf of a unified whole. These separate components come together and work to ensure that the human body either grows or is sustained. Corporations must also understand and operate in a manner that accounts for these dynamics and realities.

When we consider these challenges and what can be done to stem the momentum of these formidable circumstances, we are left with only one conclusion. As individuals, we must all act! Though corporations and organizations of all types play a significant role in this drama, the answers and solutions come back full circle to us. This chapter opened with the spotlight on our self-interest, and so must it end. Eventually, it will be our individual attitudes, behaviors, and actions that will make a difference.

SUMMARY

We live at a critical juncture as it relates to the many issues concerning the environment and sustainability. And at the center of these issues sits the corporation, a ubiquitous and critical stakeholder whose actions will affect life on our planet for generations come.

To further the sustainability agenda, it will be useful for organizations to integrate within their culture programs that promote and foster this important agenda among employees and the communities they serve. Though the corporations must lead in this effort, they alone cannot be accountable, for ultimately as individuals we must step forward and do our part.

QUESTIONS

1. How developed is your social and environmental responsibility program?
2. Do you measure these activities and set annual targets?
3. Do your employees understand the organization's commitment to social and environmental responsibility, and are they an active part of these efforts?
4. Do your customers and communities understand what your position is on environmental and sustainability issues?
5. Can you demonstrate a strong linkage between creating shareholder value and your corporate social responsibility efforts?

REFERENCES

Adam, David. 2009. "Amazon Could Shrink by 85% Due to Climate Change Scientist Say." *The Guardian*, March 11.

Anderson, Richard. 2010. "Unilever Says Sustainability Key to New Business Model." *BBC News Business*, November 15.

Betts, Richard A., Yadvinder Malhi, and J. Timmons Roberts. "The Future of the Amazon: New Perspectives from Climate, Ecosystem and Social Sciences. Philosophical Transactions of the Royal Society Biological Sciences. 363, no. 1498: 1729–1735.

Brandel, Mary. 2010. "State Street: A Green Dashboard Monitors Data Center Efficiencies." *Computer World*, October 25.

Brumfield, Ben. 2013. "Global Warning Is Epic, Long-Term Study." *CNN World*, March 8.

Bunker, Stephen G. 1980. "Forces of Destruction in Amazonia." *Environment* 22 (September): 84–86.

Flynn, Margie, and Marissa Beechuk. 2013. "How TD Bank Measures Employee Engagement on Sustainability." July 22.

Halpert, Julie. 2012. "iChildren: How Apple Is Changing Kids Brains." *Fiscal Times*, March 21.

Healy, Beth. 2013. "State Street to Lay Off 630." *Boston Globe*, January 9.

King, Bart. 2011. "TD Bank Opens Nation's First Net Zero Branch." *Sustainable Brands News and Views*, May 16.

Unilever Brand Imprint, engaging brand strategy.

Uren, Sally. 2012. "6 Ways Unilever Has Achieved Success through Sustainability and How Your Business Can, Too." EcoBusiness.com, January 24.

Walsh, Bryon. 2011. "Hot Planet, Cold Planet." *Time*, December 12.

Webber, Alan. 2011. "The Apple Effect: How Steve Jobs & Co. Won Over the World." *Christian Science Monitor*, September 17.

CHAPTER 6

Governance, the Cornerstone of Risk: The True Role of Accountability in Organizational Systems

At the end of the day, mastering risk also hinges on ensuring that organizations maintain effective governance processes and structures. Fostering strong governance serves as the lifeblood of an organization's success. At the core of governance is the important role of accountability. From the boardroom to the mail room, accountability depends on the actions and inactions of the key leaders, managers, and employees. The ultimate success of organizations of all types depend on the proper functioning of governance and accountability. Conversely, a company's inability to leverage these pivotal players can lead to its demise.

GOVERNANCE IN NATURAL SYSTEMS: THE HUMAN BRAIN AS AN EXAMPLE

Governance has been and will continue to be a much-debated topic because it is a vital aspect of our world. Unfailingly, we experience and expect it in our daily lives, whether it is through the laws and regulations that order activity on the local, state, or federal level or through organizations and political bodies that enforce and monitor national and internal affairs. Or even consider the notion of governance in nature, as there is an innate structuring and systematic cadence of the systems that operate our world. Governance sits at the epicenter of all of life!

When considering how we would define governance, we would agree that it encompasses a set of processes, mechanisms, systems, and even institutions that are established to manage and monitor activities. Governance is also associated with rules and the expectation that the activities that have been established will be ordered and coordinated effectively and with great efficiency. It ensures the proper functioning of all important components. To explore this further, let's look at an example taken directly from nature.

The amazing and mysterious human brain is the greatest wonder known to man. Of all the organs in the human body, none is more determinant of human behavior and important for its basic functioning. The brain oversees an elaborate network of systems that control the most sophisticated activities in our bodies. By far, it is the most complex organ!

The natural question you may ask is: why there is a discussion about the brain in a chapter that focuses on corporate governance? Its because the role of the human brain and its importance to the human body is akin to the role and proper functioning of governance in corporations. Similar to the human brain, there is a network of functions and systems that ensure organizations operate effectively. While there are other examples found in natural systems, few can rival the similarities found in the example of the brain. The brain provides a thorough example of how governance should operate.

This holds true especially when we consider how the role of governance in companies has evolved over time. Due to the reality of a complex and highly intense marketplace, the importance of internal and external activities has catapulted governance to the top of the corporate agenda. In this context, the human brain, which directs both involuntary and voluntary activities, is similar to how the role of governance in organizations has evolved to oversee a myriad of internal activities.

The importance of observing the brain from this perspective provides further direction into how we can order corporate systems of governance, enabling us to more effectively link and structure internal functions and activities in a manner that assures a strong control environment. Let's take a deeper look at the human brain.

The brain is the primary control center of the human body. It governs almost all activities critical to sustain life. As with the many functions and processes in organizations that provide a patchwork of governance controls, the brain's varying but connected components and parts also come together to direct and regulate activities.

Structured into three interconnected sections, the brain is composed of three layers: the central core, the cerebral cortex, and the limbic system. The central core regulates movement and balance, processing sensory information, pulse, sleep, and arousal. The cerebral cortex controls the brain's most sophisticated emotional and cognitive functions. It oversees thought, planning, perception, and emotion. Finally, the limbic system governs blood sugar levels and blood pressure, controls emotional states and memory processes, and regulates body temperature.

This elaborate network works in tandem to regulate and process a host of information, emotions, and core bodily movements and functions. Collectively, they serve as key control points to ensure that our bodies function as they should. If any of these critical components failed to operate as designed, the functions they support in our body would be rendered ineffective. As human beings, we are highly dependent not only on each of these functions operating effectively but also their coming together to "govern" activity.

Whether it is a company's board of directors, its external/outside auditors, policies and procedures, or officers who possess a fiduciary responsibility to shareholders, these essential control functions can similarly render an organization as ineffective. The brain, as the primary governance function in the human body, plays a similar role as the different governance activities in an organization.

The competitive requirements of a highly intense marketplace and the complexities of our new age have placed the importance of corporate governance at the forefront of every corporate agenda. While the highly publicized governance failures of the past few years have ushered in a new era of government intervention through the enactment of a host of new legislation, we remain far from solving our governance challenges. As we continue to evolve, the criticality of corporate governance in ensuring effective oversight will only be enhanced. Due to these forces, there has never been a more opportune time to require enhanced objective oversight of vital corporate activities.

Critical governance mechanisms and pillars include establishing:

- Internal policies and procedures, as well as clearly defining critical roles and responsibilities.
- Creating an independent board of directors. The board must also be supported by a complementary network of subcommittees.
- A strategic planning process, ensuring not only a long-term sustainable plan but also have mechanisms in place to adjust planning along the way.
- Selecting an independent auditor to provide objective oversight of internal control activities.
- A policy framework that ensures that customers, suppliers, and employees are treated in a fair and equitable manner.
- A culture that fosters accountability, supporting its system of policies and procedures.

WORLDCOM AND THE BERNIE EBBERS STORY

It was Wednesday, July 13, 2005, on a cloudy summer day in Lower Manhattan. Though the skies were overcast, rays of sunlight pierced sharply through the scattered cloud cover overhead. Like any given day in New York, the city was bursting with life as the traffic, noise, and congestion dominated the city scene.

It was the typical hustle and bustle of city life. You could hear a distant drill hammer pounding away on a nearby construction site, and horns honking as legions of cars navigated their way frenetically through the congested streets.

At a nearby location, WorldCom CEO Bernie Ebbers anxiously awaited his fate in the U.S. District Court, Southern District. With piercing blue eyes, steely white hair, and accompanying beard, Ebbers's appearance resembled that of the mythical character Gandalf in the *Lord of The Rings* trilogy. An imposing figure, the former college basketball player towered over many, just as his intimidating personality loomed over high-flying WorldCom, the company he launched onto the global corporate stage. However, today, and at that very moment, Ebbers sat ever so patiently to learn his fate.

But this day would be far different from those freewheeling days at WorldCom. It was a day when the proverbial chickens would come home to roost. As Judge Barbara Jones explained his 25-year sentence, Ebbers wept, because the 63-year-old CEO would most likely spend the rest of his life in prison. The 25-year sentence handed down was one of the harshest punishments ever given to a corporate executive in the U.S. court system.

Ebbers's conviction and WorldCom's unprecedented fall signaled one of the largest corporate governance failures in corporate history. It was also one of the largest accounting scandals in U.S. history. In all, Ebbers and his fellow executive officers at WorldCom were a part of a staggering $11 billion accounting fraud.

The Back Story: How It Began

A native of Edmonton, Alberta, Canada, Bernie Ebbers found his way to rural Mississippi through a scholarship at Mississippi College. After college, he became manager of a garment manufacturing plant. This move allowed Ebbers to hone his management skills, as he was highly successful, receiving several promotions through the years. After leaving the garment plant, Ebbers purchased a motel; this purchase would be the first of several other motel acquisitions. He would eventually amass a small bundle of motel properties. Ebbers would go on to manage a chain of hotels, which criss-crossed the state of Mississippi.

In 1983, Ebbers and three partners devised a highly ambitious plan to enter the long-distance business. Though new to the telecom space, Ebbers would eventually find himself riding a cresting wave of growth and opportunity in the industry. It was the 1980s, and his timing was impeccable as a recently enacted law removed barriers to media ownership.

The deregulation of telecommunications left the industry in a state of limbo. This, combined with the breakup of AT&T, created an opportunity for smaller companies to enter the market. The emergence of the Internet also coincided, and the convergence of these two factors provided a unique opportunity for those who acted quickly.

Ebbers was brilliant in the early days as he handpicked CFO Scott Sullivan, and the two created an aggressive and timely acquisition strategy. It was a strategy that turned the newly formed start-up into a telecommunications powerhouse. His acquisition spree in the telecom space began in 1983 when he purchased long-distance reseller LDDS in 1983. At first, the company experienced slow growth, but then in 1989, when it went public, it skyrocketed! In 1994, LDDS became one of the top five long-distance companies in the United States.

In the mid-1990s Ebbers created WorldCom as he combined LDDS with two smaller telecom companies.The companies were MFS Communications and UVnet. At its height in 2002, WorldCom boasted over 20 million customers and owned a third of all U.S. data cables. Over the course of this exponential growth, Ebbers would snap up close to 70 companies.

Ebbers was notorious for having a penchant for the details, as he carefully managed the affairs of WorldCom. The stories of his obsession and painstaking attention to details became WorldCom folklore; there would be numerous accounts of his personally poring over individual employee expense reports. He would even carefully monitor individual employee actions in exercising stock options, often calling them directly and aggressively challenging their activities.

As the company's primary strategist, Ebbers was focused on two activities: (1) growth by acquisition and (2) maintaining a strong stock price. He wanted to ensure that WorldCom's stock remained high and realized that by continuing an aggressive acquisition strategy. Ebbers realized this tactic would fuel incremental growth. He understood what mattered most to the Street; therefore, in the midst of anemic growth and earnings pressure, his focus was on bolstering its shares.

However, after a few years, this strategy became particularly troubling considering the state of the telecom industry. Over time, conditions became speculative at best as the underlying economic fundamentals of the industry indicated it was standing on an unhealthy foundation.

Conditions at WorldCom began to deteriorate rapidly when in 2000 its proposed $100 billion merger with Sprint fell through. Due to this one monumental event, WorldCom's shares were dealt a heavy blow. This event was also coupled with the fact that the telecom bubble was losing steam and would soon grind to a screeching halt. As the pressures began to mount, Ebbers and his CFO, Sullivan, went to work. As the facts would later reveal, they decided to "cook the books."

Ebbers and Sullivan intentionally shifted expenses wrongfully from one column of the balance sheet to the other, just to inflate earnings. These actions also inflated the company's value, as losses were turned into huge profits. Though this appeared to be a simple task, it was highly impactful and wrongful as an accounting practice. This uncomplicated yet effective move resulted in approximately $3.8 billion in operating expenses being listed as long-term capital.

As the telecom industry was experiencing slow growth, the Securities and Exchange Commission (SEC) began to launch a series of investigations. It was particularly perplexed as industry giant AT&T was struggling to deliver earnings while WorldCom was flourishing. As the SEC launched its initial investigations, WorldCom's Internal Audit division also began to dig deeper into the situation. The Audit division would eventually discover the fraud. However, both of WorldCom's audit functions, its internal audit group and external auditor should have discovered the fraud long before.

It was also discovered that not only was Sullivan making false and misleading statements, but he directed internal staff to make false accounting entries and misrepresentations.

The rise and fall of WorldCom points to many challenges in corporate governance. However, a critical factor in the demise of the promising telecom company was its failure to lay out an effective strategy. Often, when discussing the topic of governance, the importance of effective strategic planning is left out of the discussion. As the telecom industry was changing, Ebbers and his leadership team at WorldCom failed to respond with a viable plan. Even though Ebbers and his top lieutenant succumbed to fraudulent behavior, the catalyst for their desperate and ill-advised acts was the lack of a formidable strategy.

STRATEGY AND GOVERNANCE

WorldCom's demise was ultimately a result of a rampant culture of greed. It was a tone that was set at the very top of the organizational chart. Throughout its system of governance, there were flaws in important control points. These problems included the failure of key executive officers in adhering to their fiduciary duties, a company board of directors that failed to provide oversight of key organizational activities, as well as a host of other issues, and the failure of its accounting and audit functions, both internal and external, failed to address such blatant misrepresentation.

In addition to these challenges, Ebbers's reign over WorldCom mirrored that of a king ruling his empire with unfettered power. He did what he pleased with very little resistance from those who had the authority to question his decisions and strategy.

There has been much written of the many missteps along the way and how critical checks and balances in WorldCom's governance failed. However, one of the primary factors that served as the catalyst of the entire fiasco was the lack of a compelling and robust business strategy. A company's strategy is the key pillar in the governance of critical activities. It is the cornerstone of its ability to master strategic risk.

When we consider corporate failure throughout our most recent past, a consistent theme woven through these devastating narratives is an inadequate strategy. While much can be attributed to an organization's failure to execute, the ability of any organization to chart and maintain a viable long-term strategy rules the day and is the primary determinant of its ability to thrive. From Blockbuster to WorldCom, Wachovia to Kodak, many corporate failures can be attributed to strategy.

As we have observed time and time again, the failure to craft a formidable strategic plan creates a domino effect, often leading to a host of challenges along the way. It can serve as a major distraction, as a company can squander valuable time and resources in an effort to address its strategic position through misguided actions that add very little value over the long term.

An organization's strategy should be in sync with a host of external and internal forces that are connected to the formidable challenges in managing movement and change. These forces include shifts in industry trends and dynamics, seismic and significant movement in customer behavior, and the timing of executing new products and services. Too often, companies miss the mark by reverting to tactics that fall far short of addressing their overall strategy. These tactics include attempting to fuel growth through acquisition, intense expense reductions, and even reverting to fraud by "rigging" financial results.

When we think about this in the context of the overreliance on growth through acquisition, we see that through the years many companies have employed this strategy to fuel growth; however, this approach can be flawed due to the lack of certain fundamentals in growth and earnings not being present. Quite often, increasing profits through acquisition masks a company's internal weakness. These weaknesses run the gamut and is tied to its ability to drive and sustain profitability and growth through core products and services.

Additionally, a common theme among many acquisition sprees is that they are more opportunistic rather than aligning to a clear strategic plan. This approach also presents formidable challenges, as acquiring companies often find it challenging to fully integrate new processes, services, and systems into internal operations. We see this reality currently being played out as the second-largest bank in the United States, Bank of America, struggles internally to effectively align and optimize its internal operations. Too often, these activities also fail to address systemic challenges.

The pivotal role of strategy is also connected to the force of movement and change. As we experience shifts in the marketplace and with customer trends, an organization's strategy must, in turn, respond to these changes. Responding and adapting to changing market dynamics ensures that a company remains relevant and keeps pace. We've seen many companies that have failed because of their inability to recognize these shifts, often responding a little too late.

While companies should still engage in long-term strategic planning (five to ten years), as we continue to experience such dynamic change, aggressively planning in shorter time frames (two to five years) will be necessary. And as we continue to experience uncertainty in the marketplace, the strategic planning process should become even more robust. As we move further into this time of dynamic change and continue to experience technological advances, there will be a corresponding need to strengthen this planning process.

Boards of directors and senior executives should continually probe and force management to answer the tough questions. These questions transcend clever tactics and approaches to engineer earnings and should be centered on ones that are laser focused on the fundamentals. Have we addressed flaws in internal operations? Are the pivotal drivers of growth operating effectively? How competitive are our products and services? How well are we positioned in the marketplace, and what can we do address any gaps?

This line of inquiry should also include important questions concerning talent. Do we have the right talent in our most key governance roles? This includes the functions of CEO, CFO, CIO, controller, legal, risk, and internal auditor. When considering whether the right talent is in place, any evaluation of these critical functions should include questions that assess whether these leaders possess the right attitude to ensure objectivity and integrity. Can they "toe the line" when it comes to making tough decisions and uphold their fiduciary responsibilities?

The leaders who hold these vital governance functions serve as the last line of defense when there is an internal breakdown of a company's governance controls. Unfortunately, these leaders often serve as protagonists, as they initiate and set in motion the actions that eventually lead to an organization's failure. They are vital defenders of the governance framework and hold the keys to the long-term viability of the organizations they lead. Yet due to selecting the wrong talent to lead in these critical areas, a series of corporate pillaging occurs.

Senior management and the board of directors should always ensure that a company's strategic plan and the path ahead is viable and is supported by foundational elements. These foundational elements should be based on considerations that assess the competitiveness of the company products and services, industry trends, the competition, and marketplace dynamics, as well as core earning realities.

COMPLACENCY AND GOVERNANCE

An inadequate strategy can also lead to organizational complacency and a lack of direction. This holds true when we consider the most recent demise of legendary Eastman Kodak. The once–darling of the marketplace and Americans everywhere was forced to declare bankruptcy. However, many point to the symptom of the problem, rather than dig a little deeper to its core. Yes, Kodak was slow to move into the digital market, but was there more to this story? While this observation is true, are we to believe that there were leaders, managers, and employees in the organization who did not see this coming? And if they did, why didn't anyone listen?

We've seen and experienced through the years how companies like Kodak, after experiencing a lengthy run at success, are quick to vanish into obscurity. When companies become successful, there is a natural tendency to become complacent. And why wouldn't they? There is no difference in the manner in which organizations as systems respond to success and how an individual does. At the helm of a company is a group of individuals leading and guiding it along the way. And as human beings, these individuals as a collective of leaders fall prey to the same pitfalls individuals do.

Though this may be true, it is important to consistently capture and incorporate insights from employees and managers throughout the organization. As each and every individual plays a critical role in the delivery of products and services, staying abreast of new developments, market trends and strategies is critical in the governance process.

THE ROLE OF ACCOUNTABILITY IN SYSTEMS

Typically, corporate governance dialogues focus on important players such as the board of directors, external auditors, key senior executives, and others that possess fiduciary responsibilities. While these functions play important parts in a company's system of governance, there are factors or an additional lens with which to examine and understand the criticality of governance and accountability in systems. This lens entails understanding the role of accountability in systems. Accountability in companies drives at the heart of organizational culture.

Accountability is also a part of mastering strategic risk. Accountability in systems of nature shows up in the form of rules, laws, and the roles particular elements play. In natural systems, there are built-in processes that automatically trigger when a certain anomaly or breakdown occurs. These triggers or controls quite often mitigate risk by effectively accounting for the disruption that occurs, allowing the particular process or system to eventually function normally. However, unlike natural systems, organizational systems are highly dependent on the behaviors and actions of individuals.

Elements and functions are interdependent and work in harmony. If a particular element or subsystem fails, it hurts the performance of the entire system. This is the manner in which systems of nature are ordered as they are void of the human element. In organizational systems, because of the human element or our behavior, employees and leaders alike who serve in critical functions must also be held accountable. And as with the components of the universal guide, as discussed in Chapter 4, the process of accountability is a continuous, repetitive process.

Accountability in organizational systems ensures that we humans, no matter the part we play, are held responsible for doing our part. If we come up short, our shortcomings are addressed, or, if necessary, we are replaced. Hence, holding leaders accountable impacts corporate culture and performance. Ultimately, in an intense marketplace, mastering strategic risk requires that all players be held accountable. Competitive forces and shareholders demand it.

ACCOUNTABILITY AT ADULANT TECHNOLOGIES

To amplify the impact of accountability in systems, let's consider high-flying Adulant Technologies. Adulant is a company that has been on a tear due to the explosion of growth in its industry. For the past four years it has experienced double-digit growth year after year. Supported by a well-fortified balance sheet, Adulant is poised to experience sustained growth for the foreseeable future. Although the company has been in existence for over 50 years, its newly found growth and success is helping to fuel a resurgence in company pride firm-wide. However, all is not well at Adulant.

Despite a surging stock price and a favorable position on the street, Adulant suffers from what beleaguers most large complex organizations. It is mired in unneeded political bickering and back-biting. Across the enterprise, from its Technology division to Human Resources, leaders skirmish daily in attempts to garner more turf. Its corporate battlefield leaves no room for the faint of heart as the corporate climbers leave a bloody trail of bodies on their climb up the corporate ladder.

Helen, a 16-year industry veteran, recently was recruited to Adulant to bring in new leadership. She was recruited from Adulant's main rival to play a pivotal role in its new strategy. However, Helen's hands are painfully tied as at every point of launching her new efforts she is met with stiff resistance. Now at the company for 18 months, Helen is fed up and ready to move on!

The problem at Adulant has become systemic and is deeply embedded into the fabric of the organization. To make matters worse, even the most egregious violators of company core values are not held accountable for their behavior. These groups include HR, Legal, Marketing and others. Though most of this activity is relegated to more of its support groups, the behavior and culture is slowly making its way to line-of-business units.

There's little accountability in the system as those functions that are traditionally thought of as the protectors of corporate stewardship are, unfortunately, mired in the mess. And as the drama continues, those who wield the type of power required to make a difference turn a blind eye. Fearing confrontation and making the tough call, they bury themselves in their pleasurable pastimes and cashing in on the company's success.

Does this story sound familiar to you? Do the players and cast of characters remind you of something close and dear to you? Your current place of employment? Too often, this sad little saga is played out without there being little accountability.

Unfortunately, this scenario at Adulant is quite commonplace among successful companies the world over. And while the sheer momentum of an organization's success often is able to overcome the fallout from these debilitating circumstances, a significant amount of unrealized potential and performance is left on the table. There are a host of losers in the stifling saga as employees, corporate culture, shareholders, and communities all lose greatly. Governance in systems also requires that there be accountability and checks and balances.

THE IMPORTANCE OF ROLES AND RESPONSIBILITIES

The role of governance in systems also brings to the forefront the importance of roles and responsibilities. This entails ensuring that all of the components and parts are clearly defined and understood. In natural systems, when all functions and players do not play their part, the survival or sustainment of the entire system or process is at risk. In nature, as in organizational systems, there can be grave consequences that impact, destroy, or throw the entire system out of balance.

Organizations are no different, as it is important that all stakeholders play their part in the sustainment and advancement of the organization's system objectives and goals. Without clearly delineated roles and responsibilities, processes and functions within organizations become ineffective and are suboptimized. Clearly defining roles and responsibilities sets a strong foundation on which to drive performance. This reality also drives home the importance of conducting an RACI model (Responsible, Accountable, Consulted, Informed) exercise.

Redundant and overlapping functions and roles lead to the underutilization and unnecessary expenditure of organizational resources. These suboptimized resources can be redeployed and placed in areas or functions where they are needed or can be reduced to lessen expenses. Overlapping and redundant roles and responsibilities often occur in shared services organizations such as Technology, Risk Management, and even Finance.

Mangroves

An example in nature that demonstrates how different roles and responsibilities work in tandem to ensure the proper functioning of systems is in the ecologically important mangrove. We've all known of and experienced mangroves, as they are found in most coastal regions. They also are found on islands, at the mouths of rivers, and near lagoons. In the United States, mangroves are most common in Florida.

Mangroves are critical to our lives because they play a vital role in the preservation of important food sources and our water management system. Mangroves have a hand in the following critical aspects of life:

- They serve as an important feeding ground for many saltwater fish and also as a nesting sanctuary for a host of birds.
- They assist us with water runoff—as they help to prevent soil loss.
- They act as a barrier or buffer for natural forces such as waves, hurricanes, and other types of storms.
- They play a major role in the fishing industry, as a majority of game and commercial sea life are dependent on mangroves, especially in South Florida.
- They produce a significant number of nutrients for sea life, as they continuously shed leaves, which produce tons of nutrients on an annual basis. The leaves, which are broken down, are eventually released back into the sea and provide food for sea life.

The players in mangroves include plants, shellfish, crabs, birds, and raptors. These players represent the core of the mangrove ecosystem. They enable critical processes by transferring critical energy and by supporting its vital food chain. Without these players and the processes they drive, these systems would be out of balance.

Not only are these components and parts interdependent and rely on one another, but they also are clearly defined. A reality that is consistently found in natural systems that often also is commonplace in organizational systems is how clearly distinct and well defined roles are.

The Outside Auditor

Whether an enterprise is large or small, the criticality of the External Auditor function cannot be overemphasized. The external auditor plays a critical role in governance systems in organizations, serving as a key mechanism to ensure the key governance controls are intact. They wield considerable influence over the process. The auditor ensures accountability of management to shareholders.

Because of its critical role, the outside director must be truly independent. Independence can be reflected in a number of ways, which include ensuring that there are no strong ties between the auditing firm and the company and rotating auditors periodically.

The external auditor should possess the following characteristics:

- The requisite industry knowledge and experience.
- The ability to communicate challenging information and to ask difficult questions. This includes understanding and examining investment holdings, family relationships, and other business relationships. The company's audit committee should also evaluate external audit firm engagement and have an understanding of the firm's practice in the company.
- Champion full financial disclosure.

The board of directors' audit committee must take painful steps to evaluate the adequacy and reasonableness of the external auditor's audit plan. This entails examining the scope and coverage of external auditor activities. To do a good job of this, the audit committee must be composed of qualified individuals who have a deep knowledge and understanding of finance and accounting.

The importance of a company's outside external auditor comes into full view when we consider the high-profile missteps of the most recent past. The accounting firm Arthur Andersen served as the external auditor for Enron, Tyco, Global Crossing, and Adelphia. This placed this firm at the center of these high profile accounting scandals.

A CRISIS OF CORPORATE CULTURE: THE STORY OF NEWS CORP.

Bribing police officers and officials, conspiring to intercept communications, wiretapping, and illegally listening to individual cell phone voice messages were all done as part of a carefully calculated scheme. They were activities targeted at a global list of who's who, which included celebrities, politicians, actors, and professional athletes. You'd think by this description we'd be setting the stage for a heart-pumping international espionage thriller, set in the same vein as the *Bourne Identity* series or a James Bond movie, but you'd be surprised to realize this was the backdrop behind Rupert Murdoch's News Corp. scandal.

It was a phone-hacking scandal that first broke in 2006. The illegal activities eventually impacted close to 4,000 victims. However, at the center of the News Corp. scandal is a crisis of corporate culture. It is a crisis in which the 53,000-employee media conglomerate reflects an environment that is a mirror image of its brilliant yet highly controversial leader, Rupert Murdoch.

At the high-flying media company, the culture is one that tolerates pushing the boundaries, and where breaking the rules is accepted and doing "whatever it takes" is the motto of the day. The global media empire amplifies the voice and attitude of Murdoch, who is known as a leader who consistently displays a disdain and contempt for the rules. Within its walls, many insiders described it as a lawless culture, which was reflected on every rung of the corporate ladder.

The subsidiary where the scandal occurred was at *News of the World*, which in 2006 was the largest English-language Sunday newspaper in the world. It was one of several newspapers under the Murdoch News structure and media empire. News Corp. possesses a formidable network of complementary brands in the sports and news information services that stretches from the United States to as far away as Australia.

Under its umbrella are such noted and popular global brands as the *New York Post*, Dow Jones, the *Sunday Times of London*, *The Australian*, and the *Wall Street Journal*. At one time News Corp. owned the Fox Entertainment Group and had a significant interest in the Direct TV Group and Twentieth Century Fox. In all, Murdoch has to date assembled the world's second-largest media empire.

The event that triggered investigations into the activities of *News of the World* was a story it printed in 2005 about Britain's Prince William's knee. The story prompted the royal family to complain to authorities, sensing the potential of voicemail hacking on behalf of the paper. After a full-scale investigation and legal proceedings, the paper's royal editor and a private investigator were convicted of conspiracy to hack into voicemails. Little did Murdoch and top officials realize that this conviction would unravel a pattern of fraud and abuse.

Eventually, it was discovered that from 2005 to 2012 *News of the World* and its various officials were a part of a string of phone and e-mail hacking scandals. One of the ways in which the news outlet hacked into a target's voicemail entailed accessing voicemail messages by using a default factory-set personal identification number (PIN) that could be used by another phone. This was possible if a customer, upon purchasing their phone, did not change the PIN that was initially assigned. By obtaining the factory preset PIN, any target's voicemail box became vulnerable to being hacked. The hacking scandal included private investigators, newspaper editors, and executives, who all played a role in retrieving private information from individuals' personal messages.

The discoveries of the phone hacking scandal led to the arrest and conviction of a number of the paper's management and individuals acting on its behalf. In addition to years of investigation and subsequent lawsuits, the scandal prompted the British prime minister to launch a full-scale public inquiry into the activities of the British media. In 2011, after close to 170 years in print, *News of the World* was forced to close its doors.

The scandal exposed the many governance challenges at News Corp., including the lack of an independent board of directors, instances of conflicts of interest, such as Murdoch's having roles as CEO and chairman, and a blatant system of nepotism, among others. Within News Corp., Murdoch's children not only were appointed to coveted board of directors seats but were also given senior roles. This was even in the face of there being better qualified internal and external candidates.

In August 2013, News Corp. shareholders from the United States to the United Kingdom filed a resolution demanding that the News Corp. CEO and chairman step down. In a separate filing, an additional resolution was brought forth calling for News Corp. to end its highly controversial structure, which enables the Murdoch family, who hold only a minority of shares, to control News Corp. This arrangement enabled Murdoch to take the company public while still retaining control of the company.

The 2013 resolutions were preceded by resolutions filed in 2012 that called for News Corp. to enhance management oversight. They were aimed at ensuring that News Corp. was better organized to more effectively reduce and manage business risks. A separate Committee of Inquiry and the British Parliament in their individual findings also concluded that Murdoch, who single-handedly built the newspaper empire, was ill-prepared to lead NewsCorp. It also concluded that the company lacked effective governance, as there was evidence that Murdoch did not take the time to become aware of the hacking scandal. It even suggested that he turned a blind eye to the brewing scandal.

Since the phone-hacking scandal, many changes have been put in motion at News Corp., which were the result of a $139 million cash settlement between News Corp. and its shareholders. Among the sweeping changes are mandates that News Corp.:

1. Establish a more independent and active board of directors
2. Maintain an anonymous whistleblower hotline

3. Create a compliance steering committee to report several times a year to an audit committee
4. Address how it nominates and compensates its board
5. Develop policies and procedures on political activities

The News Corp. hacking scandal underscores how critical it is to set the right tone at the top of an organization. It provides an important lesson on how leaders and the messages they send through behavior can permeate even the far reaches of organizational systems. As reflected in the settlement, the company was lacking several important governance mechanisms—deficiencies that normally point to the tone by leaders at a company's helm, who care very little for checks and balances in the day-to-day management of their organizations.

THE INDEPENDENT BOARD OF DIRECTORS

The discussion of governance is not complete unless we further explore the issue of the role of an organization's board of directors. While many of the failures of companies in the recent past have been tied to a number of strategic and operational missteps, the ultimate arbiter of a company's strategy and direction is its board of directors. The board also has oversight of critical operational activities, ensuring that a company's control environment is effective.

Whether it is in the implosion of Enron, WorldCom, Global Crossing, or other high-profile corporate failures, in each case the company's board of directors played a critical role in its ultimate demise. Take, for example, the collapse of Adelphia Communications.

Adelphia Communications

Adelphia Communications, once the sixth-largest cable company in America, came crashing down as the high-flying cable giant was rocked by internal fraud and mismanagement. In the federal case brought against Adelphia, company founder John Rigas and his son, Timothy Rigas, the firm's CFO, along with three others were charged with securities violations. As the trial revealed, the Rigases used an elaborate system to distribute monies to its various family-owned entities and, under this scheme, pocketed a bounty of cash for themselves—close to $100 million.

After being found guilty, the 82-year-old senior, John Rigas, would be sentenced to 15 years in prison, and his son Timothy sentenced to 20 years for their hand in the implosion of one of America's most promising cable companies. The company, which began as a small family business and rode a wave of success, ended up filing for Chapter 11 bankruptcy after amassing a staggering $9 billion in debt. It was a bittersweet story, of how the senior Rigas took a $300 license in 1952 and parlayed it into a billion-dollar business.

The dynamics surrounding the operating environment and management of Adelphia presents a recurring theme when we consider our corporate landscape. It is a reality where a closely held and successfully run family business is catapulted onto a more visible and demanding public corporate platform. It is the type of growth that presents once-in-a-lifetime benefits to those who have shepherded the organization from its inception.

These new demands require a management philosophy that embraces objectivity and enhanced transparency. However, the new requirements that are thrust onto the old family guard take them out of their comfort zone. Accustomed to operating with a tight rein, these leaders naturally resort to those operating principles that bore them their success.

However, while these companies transition into public entities, many of these leaders attempt to insulate themselves from outside influences, as they desire to tighten their control of the company's activities even more. Including family members and/or board members who are connected to these leaders and the company's history enables these leaders to hold tremendous influence over company matters. But this dynamic does little to ensure the long-term viability of the new entity.

Whether it is in the form of a family taking its business public or any other corporate scenario, the lack of board member independence undermines a critical mechanism of checks and balances. An independent board ensures that decisions are transparent and undergo intense scrutiny. It ensures that the best interests of shareholders and the enterprise transcend those of any one person and require that critical decisions are taken through an objective vetting process.

At Adelphia, the board was not only stacked with family members but also included long-term family friends, who were viewed as nothing more than cronies of the elder Rigas. Nine of the company's board members were family members, with a number of them also holding coveted senior executive roles in the company. Family members such as Timothy Rigas served in dual yet conflicting capacities as he was Adelphia's CFO while serving as the chairman of the board's audit committee. This was, of course, a clear violation of the fundamental corporate governance conflict-of-interest tenet. And the conflicts extended deeper into the operations of Adelphia as family members and board member friends helped to create an illusion of success as the company in reality was buckling under the significant weight of enormous debt.

Board members at Adelphia amassed a staggering $3.1 billion in loans as well as used company resources to fund real estate holdings. They even used the company's deep pockets to purchase an interest in a professional hockey team, the Buffalo Sabres. Family members on the board also commingled the accounts of the company with their own personal businesses. Adelphia Communications was being used as a virtual cash machine by the family.

In addition to these egregious actions, under oversight of the board, Adelphia "cooked the books" and overstated the company's earnings. Eventually, the board sued its external auditor, Deloitte, for failing to inform it of the unscrupulous activity that was occurring at the company.

SUMMARY

The demands of today's marketplace have placed an even greater emphasis on the need for strong governance systems in organizations. These demands include the speed and pace of commercial activities and how this dynamic has intensified market competition, the interconnectivity of activities and of commercial relationships, and the pace of change and innovation.

Unlike natural systems, where functions, processes, and subsystems run on autopilot, organizational systems are highly dependent on our human efforts to ensure their viability. Similarly, in natural systems, when there is a breakdown in function or process, the entire system is at risk. Ironically, in both natural and organizational systems, these failures produce a similar result.

In organizational systems, the success of processes and structures are dependent on human behavior. Human behavior is the primary determinant of how effective governance will be in organizations; all other mechanisms are solely dependent on this key factor. Too often, fundamental human tendencies such as selfishness, greed, pride, and fear render leaders ineffective. Therefore, a pivotal factor in shaping an organization's culture is selecting leaders who possess the mettle to lead. In addition to these leadership attributes, a formidable system of governance should include:

- An independent and active board of directors
- Key executives who can be relied on to shepherd the organization, even in the face of the most challenging circumstances
- Qualified and objective outside external auditors
- Clearly defined roles and responsibilities as well as a robust set of policies and procedures
- A culture that demands accountability
- A robust and dynamic strategic-planning process

However, these standards alone are not enough, as they will only come to life and gain traction with effective leaders in place. They require leaders who operate as effective stewards, and who often have the temerity to make the tough call, even in the most challenging of circumstance.

QUESTIONS

1. Describe your current corporate culture. What do you like about it, and what needs to change?
2. Is there consistency? Are your stated core values consistent with how the organization operates?
3. Are the company's stated core values and objectives integrated into how all employees are evaluated?
4. Are leaders and associates held accountable for acting in a way that does not reinforce company values and leader expectations?
5. Is your board of directors independent?
6. Do you reward inappropriate behavior, and do you make certain actions that reinforce your organization's core values visible?
7. How robust is your strategic planning process?
8. How dynamic is your strategic planning process?
9. Does it account for significant shifts in your industry that consider consumer trends, the competition and integrates new and emerging capabilities?

NOTES

1. Ackman, Dan. 2005. "Bernie Ebbers Guilty." *Forbes,* March, 15.
2. ——— 2005. "The WorldCom We Hardly Knew." *Forbes,* June 26.
3. "Adelphia Founder Sentenced to 15 Years." 2005. *CNN Money,* June 20.
4. Bassets, Danielle and Michael S. Gazzaniga. 2011. "Understanding Complexity in the Human Brain." National Institute of Health Public Access (NIHPA), April 14.
5. Chu, Henry. 2011. "Rupert Murdoch's News Corp. Drops Bid for BSky" *Los Angeles Times,* July 14.
6. Chumley, Cheryl K. 2012. "Rupert Murdoch's News Corp. Settles Suits over Phone Hacking Scandal for $139 Million." April 23.
7. "Ebbers Out at WorldCom." 2002. *CNN Money,* April 30.
8. Engleman, David. 2007. "10 Unsolved Mysteries of the Brain: What We Know—and Don't Know—About How We Think." *Discover,* July 31.
9. Fisher, Daniel. 2013. "News Corp. Pays Itself $139 Million for Phone Hacking Scandal—Minus Legal Fees." *Forbes,* April 22.

10. Hancock, David. 2009. "World-Class Scandal at WorldCom." CBS News, February 11.
11. Kay, Joseph. 2005. "The Rise and Fall of Bernie Ebbers." World Socialist. www.wsws.org/en/articles/2005/07/ebb-j16.html, July 16.
12. Lowenstein, Roger. 2004. "The Company They Kept." *New York Times*, February 1.
13. McCafferty, Joseph. 2003. "Adelphia Comes Clean." *CFO Magazine*, December 1.
14. McCarthy, Michael. 2004. "Next Up on Scandal Parade, Adelphia." *USA Today*, February 23.
15. Markon, Jerry and Robert Frank. 2002. "Adelphia Officials Are Arrested, Charged with Massive Fraud." *Wall Street Journal*, July 22.
16. Phillips, Helen, 2006. "Introduction: The Human Brain." *New Scientist Life*, September 4.
17. Phillips, Matt. 2013. "Phone Hacking Scandal Still Pinching Rupert Murdoch's News Corp." Yahoo Finance, May 8.
18. Stecker, Tiffany. 2002. "Restoring Mangroves May Prove Cheap Way to Cool Climate." *Scientific American*, July 31.
19. Tan, Mark. 2002. "WorldCom Accounting Scandal." *The Guardian*, August 9.
20. Warne, Kennedy. 2007. "Forest of the Tide." *National Geographic*, February.
21. Wrage, Alexandra. 2013. "5 Compliance Lessons from the News Corp. Scandal." *Forbes*, April 3.

CHAPTER 7

The Game Changer: Stewardship— Taming the Land Grabbers, Passive Aggressors, and the Mighty Ogre

A true leader has the confidence to stand alone, the courage to make tough decisions, and the compassion to listen to the needs of others. He does not set out to be a leader, but becomes one by the equality of his actions and the integrity of his intent.
—Douglas MacArthur

The twenty-first century has raised the bar on leadership standards. These new requirements transcend the old paradigm, as it has become a strategic imperative for leaders to guide their organizations as true stewards. As the speed and complexity of commercial activities continue to intensify, organizations are required to muster a strong cadre of capable leaders—the type of leaders who will serve as formidable anchors that will enable organizations to withstand the sea of change we will continue to face in this new era.

THE COUP D'ÉTAT

It was a hot and humid Texas summer morning, the type of morning in which the temperature was already unbearable at 10 A.M. As Sam and his teammates made their way to a nearby hotel through the sweltering heat, they wondered why they had been summoned to this private meeting. It felt like a clandestine operation. A few minutes after gathering in a small banquet hall, they were provided an overview of the purpose of our meeting.

Justin Davies, the executive who pulled this small group together, wanted to talk strategy and pave a path forward regarding the company's critical priorities—or so they thought! However, at the crux of the meeting was Davies' personal agenda to further his own career to become a part of the company's most senior executive operating committee. And to achieve this, he believed he needed to ruthlessly unseat an already established committee member. It was a coup d'état!

Sam and his colleagues were senior leaders in the Finance division at Polaris, Inc., a rapidly growing diversified finance company that specialized in consumer products. However, with all its recent success, Polaris was plagued with significant organizational culture issues. Through the years, it had developed a culture of passive-aggressive behavior, one that allowed leaders and employees to shy away from the hard conversations and avoid confronting the brutal facts.

This culture at Polaris stifled decision making and often impacted customers as critical decisions were delayed, mired in a morass of corporate bureaucracy and politics. And this culture of passive-aggressiveness permeated the organization, all the way from the boardroom to specially created task forces. Davies understood the problem and, over time, learned how to skillfully leverage this dysfunctional system to navigate his way up the corporate ladder. He quickly amassed new responsibilities and in a short time had become a key leader within Corporate Finance.

At this meeting, along with the small group of finance leaders, Davies invited a top-ranking executive of one of the nation's Big Four consulting firms. He invited the consultant because of his specific knowledge about the division's activities and the Operating Committee member who was the target of the coup. The division was Technology and Operation. And Davies wanted to find the proverbial buried bodies.

As he carefully made his motives clear, he warned Sam and his colleagues that knowledge of this discussion must not ever reach his target's ears. To Sam's surprise, in front of the group Davies pointedly asked the consultant what he knew about the weaknesses in the target division. He believed that his only way to becoming a member of Polaris's operating committee was by undermining the senior executive. Everyone knew this because he was very open about his aspirations to run the division. Davies also took cheap shots at this leader whenever he could. And his timing was right!

At the time of that meeting, the target executive was under siege as potentially debilitating regulatory issues swirled around Technology and Operations, and Davies knew it. After a long and robust dialogue, the group identified several significant issues within the target division. Eventually, the Operating Committee Member Davies targeted did resign from the organization under his own terms. And Davies? He was not selected to replace the retiring executive, as the outgoing leader was allowed to recommend his successor for his job and his seat on Polaris's operating committee. Ironically, Davies's actions were not confined to this target; no, Davies was consumed with undermining other executives throughout the organization.

IT'S TIME FOR CHANGE

Unfortunately, this is and has been the way of corporate systems for years, as often leaders are rewarded for the type of behavior Davies displayed. However, organizations can no longer afford to allow this type of leadership to flourish. The realities of our new era require a more centered form of leadership—the type of leadership that ensures leaders view themselves as stewards of organizational resources, are held accountable for exhibiting the wrong behaviors. These leaders should stand as shining examples to the entire enterprise.

Think about it: How much time did Davies spend clawing his way up the corporate ranks? Or consider the precious corporate resources other executives expended in trying to fend him off. Realizing that these political antics transpire all the time in organizations prompted me to explore what true leadership is. What are some of the more salient aspects of leadership that are missing in the corporation of today? Why is leadership such a critical issue? More important, how does leadership in corporations relate to mastering strategic risk?

Mastering strategic risk requires that all systems possess effective supportive elements. Just as the supportive elements in systems of nature must be effective and consistent in order to ensure optimum performance, so, too, must the supportive elements be effective and consistent in our man-made world. In organizational systems and in our broader marketplace systems, leadership plays a vital role in supporting critical activities.

Think about the Three Elements model introduced in Chapter 2 and how functions/activities such as administration, governance, and management are essential. These supportive activities ensure that the other two elements—create and facilitate—within an organizational system are ordered appropriately in order to optimize the use and consumption of the resources that become the lifeblood of the system.

At the center of administrative and governance functions within a corporation is the role of leadership, for it is competent leadership that ensures that systems are managed effectively. Consider the highly publicized demise of a number of corporate giants over the past several years. Enron, Tyco, Blockbuster, Washington Mutual—at the heart of these critical corporate missteps is the failure of leadership.

Mastering strategic risk also requires strong leadership when we consider the role corporations must play externally in local, national, and global communities. Their role touches myriad issues that transcend commerce and can significantly affect social, political, and environmental concerns. A point of reference to consider is the role industry plays in our commercial eco-system. As discussed in Chapter 5, corporations are one of three stakehold-ers (individuals, industry, and the Earth) that are essential to our modern reality.

Because corporations play such a vital role in the global wheel of activi-ties, the leadership bar within its hallowed walls must change. A new stan-dard of leadership must be set—one that incorporates and considers the dynamics of our highly complex age and that in the end will consider the realities within systems.

As organizations of all types are besieged with significant challenges, having the right leadership in place is paramount in navigating such choppy waters. As I have observed various dramas played out in the corporate game, what has emerged is a cast of characters or leadership types. Unfortunately, many of these leadership types undermine a robust organizational culture and set a poor example of model leadership. They are:

1. The Passive-Aggressive Leader
2. The Land Grabber
3. The Mighty Ogre
4. The Corporate Steward

The Passive-Aggressive Leader

The Passive-Aggressive Leader is the silent assassin as he moves in a shroud of mystery. He is a highly skilled covert operator. You never see him coming, nor does he leave his fingerprints on anything. This type of leader always seems to land on his feet, regardless of what occurs in the organization. He is the consummate survivor. The Passive-Aggressive Leader manages to say the right thing at the right time and always does Just enough to manage whatever resources or set of issues he is charged to oversee.

He is not bold and courageous, for he views peers and leaders who exhibit these qualities as naïve and shortsighted. The Passive-Aggressive Leader is skilled at carefully observing which way the wind is blowing, and very quickly aligning himself with the prevailing view. He is seldom the first to speak up and is the last to take a stand. He often comes across as unassuming as he skillfully cloaks himself in a contrived sense of aloofness, but he is far from disinterested.

This leader never goes out on a limb, and somehow manages to dance skillfully between political landmines when asked to provide an opinion or position. His way of expressing an opposing view is by being noncommittal.

Behind closed doors he may express opinions, but in open dialogue he hides behind others. At the core, this leader is concerned only with his own ultimate survival. Like other leadership types, he is a corporate climber and works tirelessly to ensure that he gathers all the benefits he can muster.

The Land Grabber

Like General Sherman's infamous march to the sea, this leadership type has a "scorched earth" policy. He takes no prisoners! You usually know this type of leader, for he leaves a path of destruction in his wake. The Land Grabber is often found in a shared services organization. These departments include functions such as Corporate Finance, Technology and Operations, Risk and Regulatory Management, as well as Human Resources and Marketing.

The Land Grabber is bold. He speaks his mind and can appear to hold the organization's interest above his own. However, this is a grave misreading of this type of leader because he is a skilled chess player and his every move is done with an eye to achieving his ultimate prize, which is a lofty position of power high atop the corporate food chain. Winning this game, in his mind, is about achieving more power and an invitation into the inner sanctum of the true corporate power brokers. To this end, everyone is expendable, and he holds allegiance to no one but his own self-centered ambition.

The Land Grabber views his undermining and destructive behavior as his only means to reach the top. The Land Grabber understands how to skillfully align key corporate objectives with his own ambitious scheming. Quite often, it is very difficult to see through his game, as he masks his personal agenda in the guise of corporate interests. Land Grabbers are very politically savvy and know how to align themselves with allies in order to assist them to get where they need to go. They make some very strange alliances and partnerships to achieve this end.

In Front of the Steamroller: A Personal Story   To see what it's like to get in the way of a Land Grabber, you don't need to look any further than me. I stood in the way of a Land Grabber—my very own manager! Although I eventually ended up okay, the road was fraught with many perils.

There we were—12 of us along with two consultants I'll call the ABC consulting firm—discussing the merits of the initiative and whether the company should move forward and begin the project. Every major stakeholder was in attendance, and they were ready to approve the initiative. Prior to the meeting and months leading up to this final decision, I had done all the leg work and we agreed that I would lead the initiative. I was excited to lead such a groundbreaking effort and had tremendous confidence in the consultants who had worked side by side with me in building the business case. We called for a vote and it was unanimous! Everybody wanted to move forward. With a few parting comments, the meeting was quickly adjourned. We were excited!

Then my manager called me over to him in the hallway just outside of the conference room. "Great job, Joel. This is going to be a critical project for the bank. On that note, I wanted to let you know that we will probably not engage ABC consulting and you will most likely not lead the effort." I was speechless! Excuse me? "Yes, Joel, I'm not sure you will lead the effort, and our CEO would prefer to work with XYZ consulting on an engagement of this type." "But didn't we commit to these consultants? And what about all the effort we collectively put into it thus far?" He didn't want to discuss it anymore. Dumbfounded and dejected, I walked away from that meeting in a deep fog.

That conversation took place on a Thursday evening, and I spent Friday trying to figure out what to do. After several hours of thinking through my options, I called Chris, a senior executive I had known for years during my days in corporate finance. He was not only a friend but a supporter of mine during my time at Wachovia. We arranged to meet at Chris's home on Saturday morning. That morning I proceeded to share the story with Chris, who couldn't believe his ears.

I told him that earlier that summer I had met with ABC consulting and they had successfully implemented the program at American Express. My manager gave us 60 days to garner internal support for the program, and if we succeeded, I was assured that I would lead the initiative and ABC consulting would be hired. In response, Chris said, "Joel, we are not going to let this happen. We can't."

Over the next few days, we got support from our corporate treasurer, and our CFO. Later, all four of us met: my manager, the Corporate Treasurer, our CFO, and me. Our CFO laid down the law! He commanded that I lead the effort and that ABC would be the consulting partner on the initiative. They also determined that I would report directly to them, that is the CFO and Corporate Treasurer, during my leadership of the initiative.

After our meeting, my manager called me to his office. "Oh, boy," I said to myself, "he's gonna let me have it!" To my surprise, as we sat down, he turned to me and we began planning for how we would fund the project—ignoring the fact that I had just gotten him rebuked for his attempted power grab. Inside, I laughed—this man was such a politician, a true Land Grabber, but I knew this would not be the end of it.

Soon after our CFO left, the Corporate Treasurer became the new CFO. Although I would be reporting to the CFO, my manager knew he would eventually get what he wanted—more power and a much-coveted promotion. In retrospect, I shouldn't have been surprised. It wasn't personal at all; I was just in his way. He had wanted to replace me with a yes man who would blindly do his bidding and replace ABC with his favorite go-to consulting firm.

I eventually went on to successfully lead the initiative. My manager also got what he wanted—a coveted promotion to executive vice president only three months later. Of course, he would get what he ultimately wanted, for he was indeed a master chess player, and I a mere pawn in his high-stakes game.

The Mighty Ogre

As James waited patiently for his meeting with Don, who led the company's technology group, the voices coming out of Don's office began to rise in heated debate. James felt quite uncomfortable as Don began to shout and berate the recipient of his tirade. Minutes later, the door flung open and Debbie Allen, the audit leader who covered technology, emerged from the office in tears. As James looked to Debbie in disbelief, Don motioned to him with a devious grin that he was ready for their meeting.

After sitting down, James asked Don, "What happened? Is Debbie okay?" Don replied, "Oh, Debbie will be okay. Those damn auditors just don't get it, they're completely useless!"

Ah, the Mighty Ogre! He is an imposing and terrifying leader, and people often shudder at the mention of his name. The Merriam-Webster dictionary defines an ogre as (1) "A hideous giant of fairy tales and folklore that feeds on human beings," and (2) "A dreaded person or object." The Mighty Ogre often sits perched in high places, far above the fray of everyday corporate politics. The rules just don't apply to him, for in the corporate game he is untouchable. The Mighty Ogre is a tyrant, a monster in the corporate world. He strikes fear in employees, corporate partners, and others who find themselves on the wrong side of an issue, challenge, or circumstance with him. He is the ultimate bully.

The Mighty Ogre is often left alone, amassing a long track record of performance. He may be highly knowledgeable in his particular discipline, or he may not be competent at all, as Ogres often use their bullying tactics to mask their mediocrity. He appears to be the consummate expert, leveraging his knowledge to get what he wants. To him, expertise is king in the high-stakes corporate game. Viewing himself as indispensable, he is hard to rein in.

A corporate Ogre also possesses an unrealistic view of his leadership capabilities. This is because the only thing he values is the deep knowledge that people like himself possess. And having this ideology deeply embedded into his psyche has him believing that he is the only one worthy of leading, and not just in his particular discipline, but in other areas of the enterprise.

He may even use his bullying tactics on leaders who manage him, believing that these leaders can be easily disposed of. The Mighty Ogre realizes that his knowledge is valuable and uses it as his number one weapon.

The Mighty Ogre sucks the lifeblood out of organizations. Leading by fear and intimidation is contrary to building and maintaining a high performing organizational culture. This type of environment stifles employee empowerment and makes it hard to get to the right information. The Mighty Ogre sets a poor example of leadership and costs the company.

The Culture in Which These Characters Thrive

Some important factors affect how this drama plays out in organizations. Passive-Aggressors, Land Grabbers, and Mighty Ogres generally thrive in shared services organizations. Although found in some revenue-generating centers, these characters find more of a more fertile environment in the non-revenue-generating centers. A primary reason is that CEOs, operating committee members, and boards of directors will not tolerate any disruption to processes and services that in their mind directly impact the customer and revenue generation.

CEOs and top brass in corporations usually come out of revenue centers. Seldom are leaders within shared services organizations viewed as the future key successors. This is critical due to the fact that leaders and key talent from revenue centers have a few important realities in their favor. First, they generally lead and direct resources that are the lifeblood of revenue. And second, these individuals, because of how they matriculate in the organization, have grown up selling, trading, and brokering products and services to customers.

In many instances, they have strong ties and relationships with large and important customers, depending on the product or group of services.

Also to be considered is the impact of change on an organization. When there is significant or continuous change in a revenue-generating center, the customer feels the brunt of it. This is why it is so important to carefully execute merger-and-acquisition activities, as fatal flaws in the process can result in the loss of many customers. However, the same cannot be said for change in a shared services organization, especially those farthest away from technology and operations. There is often perceived to be little risk to precious customers when change impacts a shared services organization.

It is important to highlight these environmental and cultural realities, for it helps to illuminate how certain behaviors and activities flourish in certain parts of organizations. Make no mistake—higher-level executives often allow these leaders to use their aggressive and selfish ambitions to take on the difficult issues that the leaders themselves do not have the stomach to bear. This is also because those who support these destructive characters do not want to expend their political capital to execute the politically unpopular tasks.

Before moving on to the Corporate Steward, I must share another insight regarding this cast of characters, for in not taming these corporate leaders, there can be formidable fallout. The corporation is an elaborate system that is akin to the harsh realities of life on the rolling plains of the African Serengeti. In this highly vicious environment is a cast of characters just like there are in the wild. There are predators as well as prey.

Land Grabbers, Passive-Aggressors, and Mighty Ogres amass their territory by bringing down their prey, or as I have labeled the prey in corporate systems, the powerless. They prey on the powerless, who are many times left to fend for themselves in a very high-stakes, political, and highly sensitive environment atop the corporate food chain.

As keen students of the corporate game, these destructive leaders intuitively know that the true power brokers in the system will do very little to come to the rescue of the powerless. This is because these power brokers instinctively know that they must be highly judicious in how they expend their political clout in this high-stakes game.

They play their precious political chips only when it matters most—when it is needed to serve their own selfish ambitions. So who are the powerless? The powerless are not identified by race or gender. The powerless are women, people of color, and at times even a member of the majority. It's anyone who isn't part of the corporate inner sanctum. They include corporate leaders who, by a combination of a strong track record, skill, experience, talent, and general likeability, have made it up the corporate ladder.

In the high stakes corporate game, the power brokers are a part of the inner sanctum. They are bound usually by deep connections; in many instances the inner sanctum members are all cut from the same cloth. These wielders of power, because of human nature, often select leaders or confidants who look like them, think like them, and act like them.

Land Grabbers, Passive-Aggressors, and Mighty Ogres almost always covet a seat at the table of the inner sanctum or power broker group. However, quite often they are misguided as they turn a blind eye to the harsh reality that they will never become a part of the core power structure. They themselves may be pawns in the corporate high-stakes game, as quite often the most senior executives in corporations use these individuals to do their dirty work and further their own personal agenda. More importantly, the corporate system has an uncanny way of possessing a very short memory, especially for those doers of bad deeds!

The Corporate Steward

This individual possesses the true qualities that exemplify the profile of the ultimate corporate leader. He is the ultimate team player. As with any leader, he, too, possesses strong personal and professional aspirations. Let's not be naïve, for all individuals who make it to these levels in organizations are motivated in some way by personal ambition. However, they lead in a manner in which personal ambition takes a backseat to doing what is right.

The Corporate Steward is selfless and often says what needs to be said in order to agitate necessary dialogue on leadership teams. He is courageous and truly has the best interest of the organization in mind. The Corporate Steward can at times appear to be naïve in that quite often he risks his own career to see that what is right is achieved. He is held in high regard throughout the organization because his actions speak louder than words. You can generally spot a true Corporate Steward, as he garners a tremendous amount of respect from the rank-and-file.

Take Brenda Stewart, for example, director of corporate strategy for Polytech Technologies Inc. She represents the profile of a true Corporate Steward. Through the years, she has held several key assignments at Polytech, developing a strong track record of performance and exemplary leadership. Stewart is a resolute leader who often comes across as overly confident, as she is opinionated and not afraid to share her candid thoughts with others.

What most of Stewart's peers admire about her is that the things she whispers in private are the same things she expresses in public. They are in strict alignment! Stewart never shies away from a difficult discussion and politely challenges any issue she thinks is not in the best interest of the division. Even when Polytech has its semiannual key enterprise-wide leadership meetings, Stewart exhibits the same behavior.

While these meetings are very formal and have a very rigid format and agenda, during Q&A Stewart often poses tough questions to Polytech's CEO and top brass—the type of questions most people think but are afraid to ask. She is courageous and displays a high level of personal and professional integrity. Stewart also receives high praise for her leadership from employees at all levels when Polytech conducts its biannual employee engagement survey.

A PROFILE IN LEADERSHIP

A leader is best when people barely know he exists, when his work is done, his aim fulfilled, they will say: we did it ourselves.

—Lau Tzu

So what does the ideal corporate leader look like? What attributes should she have? Yes, the Corporate Steward represents a good profile of corporate leadership; however, there are other salient aspects of leadership as well:

- It's all about people.
- Accountability is crucial.
- Change is not a choice.
- We live in an integrated world.

It's All About People

There he was in the midst of a throng of employees. Standing at 5'8", Hugh McColl was a giant of a man. He was saying farewell to the rank-and-file employees of Bank of America (BOA) at an event that was open to the public. The event was held at Founders Hall, BOA's massive multipurpose space that sits at the foot of its main office tower in uptown Charlotte.

There stood McColl at the top of the venue, giving personal farewells to anyone who wanted to say goodbye. Employees were lined up as far as the eye could see. What shocked those of us who attended the event was that almost everyone greeted Mr. McColl with a warm embrace. Here was the CEO and chairman of one of the largest financial services organizations on the planet being warmly embraced by his employees. And these were not the executive types; they were the rank-and-file—those who battle daily on the front line.

To see the joy and excitement on each employee's face saying farewell to their leader, and his reaction to everyone, it was obvious McColl knew each and every one of them. This scene deeply illustrated what true leadership is. At the end of the day, leadership is the ability to inspire, engage and move people. A leader must understand how to resonate with all types of individuals, from the lowly janitor all the way to his most exalted general.

Through the years I had cultivated a strong relationship with Brian Stevens. Brian was a key executive at BOA, and from time to time we would share ideas about various operational, regulatory, and organizational performance issues. We had a wonderful time. What took me back to these conversations with Brian was a story he told me about a meeting he had with McColl that demonstrated his fine attributes as a leader and true steward of his corporation.

There was one conversation in particular when Brian shared a moving story about a meeting he had with McColl. As Brian told his story, I was blown away. He said, "There I was in Hugh's office to pitch the idea I had. After realizing our meeting had gone over an hour, I informed Hugh of the time. To my amazement, he jumped to his feet, buzzed his assistant, and commanded her to cancel all the meetings that remained on his calendar. It was only a little after 2 in the afternoon!

"Needless to say, I was taken aback by his excitement and sincere interest in my idea. However, that day he not only demonstrated a sincere interest in me, as he had done many times before, but he had shown his commitment and care for all people. That afternoon I learned so much about Hugh and the experiences that shaped his perspectives on leadership."

The Value of Being on the Front Lines   One of the stories that came out of the meeting between Brian and McColl was McColl's account of his days in the Army, and how his time in fighting side by side with men from different backgrounds and socioeconomic groups shaped his view of the world. McColl shared with Brian, "that when in a foxhole, it didn't matter what color, shape, or station a man came from; the only thing that mattered was that they were there for each other." True friendship and camaraderie was born out of experiences that highlighted the common bond between men.

Often in organizations, leaders find themselves leading critical organization resources and employees without having prior experience in dealing with people and customers concerning day-to-day challenges. While I believe that you do not need to have sold products or services to be a successful leader, I do believe that having the experience of interacting with customers provides invaluable insights regarding individuals and human behavior.

Being on the front line and interacting with customers provides leaders with firsthand knowledge of how employees and teammates work together and the many challenges they face, first, as individuals and, second, as employees. This type of experience enables those who eventually go on to take on leadership duties at the higher level of organizations to truly understand customers, employees, and the community at large. Nevertheless, legions of people yearn to occupy the loftiest of spaces, yet don't realize that true leadership is forged in the lowliest of places.

In my days in Corporate, the leaders and executives that I admired most were ones who began their days on the front line in some way. Not only did I admire them, but they were often the most revered leaders in the organization. Interacting firsthand with customers provided these leaders with incredible insight into how to handle critical decisions that would ultimately impact customers, employees, and shareholders. Equally important, it equipped them with the ability to truly empathize and connect with those they led.

Accountability is Crucial

"Does anybody have any questions for Austin? If not, let's vote on Brian Steel's recommended promotion," said Susan. Austin and his colleagues were having their regularly scheduled divisional operating committee meeting, and voting on a slate of new officer promotions. Susan Michaels, the leader of the division, desperately desired that her executive team engage in more open and honest dialogue.

The process saw that each leader would present a slate of candidate promotions for their group or division, providing an explanation of why the leader should be promoted. After a while, the process felt like horse trading to Jim, the division's head of customer service, as there was little candid dialogue on each candidate presented. This at times irritated Susan because she eagerly wanted to transform the culture in the division—definitely a passive-aggressive culture.

Just as she opened her mouth to call for the vote on Brian's promotion, Jim did the unthinkable. He decided to challenge the reasoning behind the promotion. Jim asked, "Will we send the right message to our employees if we promote Brian?" The room fell silent as heads began to look down the table at Jim. "Isn't it true that Brian has a terrible reputation, as he often is condescending and curses our vendors and employees of all types?"

Brian was the epitome of a Mighty Ogre! Leaders looked at Jim as if they had seen a ghost. They were shocked that he would challenge this promotion. What confused Jim about this officer promotion was that as a leadership team they talked for hours about how they wanted to change the culture, of how they wanted to raise the bar and hold leaders accountable for poor performance and for exhibiting inappropriate behavior. And what made matters worse was that Brian's behavior struck at the heart of their company's core values; core values that emphasized teamwork, respecting individuals, and integrity, to name a few.

Jim realized they were sending the wrong message to their employee base. He decided to take a stand! After a close vote that ended in Brian not receiving his promotion, Austin agreed to coach Brian over the coming year on his behavior. However, after several months, Jim learned that Brian was awarded that coveted promotion. And, of course, nothing changed as he continued in his belligerent and hostile behavior, serving as an embarrassment to the organization.

This story underscores how critical it is for corporations to hold individuals accountable. From the boardroom to operating committees, from leaders and managers on all levels to rank-and-file employees, holding individuals accountable for their performance and behaviors helps to foster a vibrant organizational culture.

The concept of accountability also plays a vital role in the performance of systems. Accountability in systems of nature shows up in the form of rules, laws, and the roles particular elements play. Elements and functions are interdependent and work in harmony. If a particular element or subsystem fails, it hurts the performance of the entire system. This is the manner in which systems of nature are ordered as they are void of the human element.

In organizational systems, because of the human element or our behavior, employees and leaders alike who serve in critical functions must be held accountable. And as with the force of repetition, as we explored in Chapter 3, the process of accountability is a continuous process. Accountability in organizational systems ensures that we humans, no matter the part we play, are held responsible for doing our part.

If we come up short, our shortcomings are addressed or, if necessary, we are replaced. Hence, holding leaders accountable impacts corporate culture and performance. Ultimately, in an intense marketplace, this reality requires that all players be held accountable. Competitive forces and shareholders demand it.

Change Is Not a Choice

Mastering strategic risk demands that leaders embrace change. This new age requires leaders who know how to navigate through change. As discussed in Chapter 3, the force of movement and its by-product, change, affects organizations internally and externally. And one of the key elements in organizational systems that is critical in managing change is leadership.

Leadership is critical from two perspectives: (1) leaders and key executives must personally and professionally navigate change, and (2) organizations can optimize performance by leveraging change/movement concepts. Let me explain.

The leader in the twenty-first century must keep pace with an ever-changing world, which means staying abreast of the new trends and forces affecting her scope of authority as well as becoming a change agent and champion herself. She must display a willingness to embrace new developments, both internally and externally, that impact her duties, as the people she leads will look to her for critical cues and follow suit. Moreover, poor response to change from a leadership perspective harms not only culture but also performance because leaders too often squander valuable opportunities to enhance business activities.

An important operational practice that organizations should incorporate is to rotate key talent and leaders through various assignments. Companies such as GE, Bank of America, and Mitsubishi have adopted this practice. This model, made popular by the Japanese, has been widely accepted as a powerful developmental tool for corporate leaders.

In addition to developing the leaders' skill set rotating through different assignments has two distinct advantages in the context of change. First, it provides a fresh set of eyes and a new perspective in shepherding resources in a new organization. Second is cross-pollination, as leaders have the opportunity to leverage their capabilities from other functions to their new area of responsibility. This quite often can lead to enhanced performance.

Hiring executives and leaders from competitors and even companies outside of one's industry also provides opportunities to cross-pollinate ideas and new capabilities in the organization. New leaders, whether they are internal or external to the organization, bring a fresh mind-set to the task at hand that can only benefit the organization. They infuse new life as their leadership brings welcome change to a department or organization.

We Live in an Integrated World

Our new era has thrust on us the reality that we live in a highly integrated world. The tremendous turmoil we've experienced over these past few years has underscored this. The Internet and technology have brought us even closer together commercially, socially, and politically. Understanding the integration and interdependence of our world is critical for leaders in organizations, for they are at the epicenter of managing vital resources in a dynamic world.

Consider the role of industry, as outlined in Chapter 5, and how it is one of three critical stakeholders (the others being individuals and the Earth) in our commercial ecosystem. Each stakeholder in this system plays a vital role to ensure that the system operates optimally and in harmony. As a critical stakeholder, industry, through corporations, must not only recognize this interdependency but be at the forefront of fostering healthy interactions among the important players and issues in this system. Whether it is in fostering healthy relationships with customers and communities, or issues such as the environment, the commercial corporation is at the heart of it all. A fundamental part of the corporation's or industry's doing its part is the role of leadership.

Understanding that we live in an integrated world is also tied to the importance of managing risk and change. In a world where transactions take place in a nanosecond and a company's ability to respond to marketplace developments is critical to its survival, it is imperative that leadership is tuned into managing its portfolio of risk. Managing risk is now of paramount importance at the highest levels of corporations globally. The speed of commercial and retail transactions, interdependent relationships, and the Internet have placed it at the forefront of corporate agendas.

The speed with which information now travels has placed even greater emphasis on the need to manage reputational risk. Consider BP's *Deepwater*

Horizon tragedy. This incident reinforces many critical points regarding the importance of managing risk and highlighting how connected and integrated we are; it is one of several recent examples that shows the linkages between the environment, industry, individuals, and shareholders.

It is no secret that BP had a dismal track record of managing safety and risk. In addition to the 11 lives lost during the *Deepwater Horizon* incident, BP took a heavy beating not only in the court of public opinion but also in loss of revenue and market value. From April 20, 2010, the date of the disaster, to June 20, 2010, BP's stock fell a staggering 52 percent. Its share price had dropped from $60.57 per share to 29.20 per share. Further, during its second-quarter earnings announcement on July 27, 2010, BP reported a net loss of $16.97 billion for the second quarter of 2010 and had already spent $32.2 billion up to that point.

Shareholders and residents in the Gulf States (Mississippi, Alabama, Texas, Louisiana, and Florida), as well as special interest groups and governmental officials, were up in arms. But from a purely economic perspective, consider the market share and tremendous impact this had on BP as an organization. No one could have foreseen such a massive loss; however, what if BP had been more aggressive in proactively managing safety issues and cleaning up a reportedly wayward culture of risk? I'm sure in hindsight BP officials would have gladly paid the price to address its issues internally and more effectively manage its risk culture. In retrospect, the benefit and cost to do this proactively clearly outweighed the risk it took in neglecting to manage internal risk.

This issue of the cost and reputational risk transcends corporations, which can cause a natural disaster and extend to organizations in retail, financial services, and a host of other industries. Think of the impact and cost of product recalls due to safety issues in the auto, pharmaceutical, and toy industries. Or, for that matter, a company's failure to provide adequate security for its critical customer data—when information is stolen or lost, it thereby results in a loss not only of customer confidence but the attrition of many of these customers.

Consider how the unavailability and inconsistency of something as simple as a company's web site or the unreliability of technology may cause customers to flee to competitors. And to add fuel to the fire, the power and ubiquity of social media can cause a feeding frenzy as negative information is communicated to millions instantaneously.

Managing in an integrated world takes a special type of leader, one who understands these connections and accounts for them in his day-to-day agenda. Leaders who view their roles as insular and do not account for these dynamics place their organization at a competitive disadvantage. Yes, at the heart of successfully managing critical stakeholders in our modern world is understanding not only how integrated we are but also how to manage change and risk.

Internally, this translates to leaders understanding the interconnectedness of activities. Instead of hoarding resources and building fiefdoms, they must break down internal barriers that perpetuate silo mentalities. If leaders viewed internal resources as truly integrated and governed them accordingly, corporations could gain more efficiencies and opportunities to partner across different groups of activities.

For example, this shows up where instead of concentrating technology resources into a single "shared" organization, various business units have their own technology resources. Termed *Shadow IT,* one can usually find these resources widely dispersed throughout the business unit, often duplicating functions that are being performed in a centralized or shared service technology organization.

Business units and their leaders are big fans of these resources because it allows them perceived flexibility and speed; however, when examined from an enterprise view, they cost companies millions of dollars in additional expense. However, in addition to the extra expense, corporations miss the opportunity to address systemic issues in their Information Technology organization.

SUMMARY

Organizations, whether private or public, have emerged to sit at the forefront of the global stage in the twenty-first century. This is due to the key role organizations play in our external marketplace. Further, the commercial corporation is like none other, as it is one of the critical players in our reality, with its reach extending far and wide and its influence straddling the most important commercial, social, and economic matters of a fragile global agenda. With such a formidable role for the corporation, leadership becomes of paramount importance.

Internally, this translates into ensuring that it has the right leadership in place. The type of leadership required should not only ensure it can return a profit and manage expenses, but should also shepherd vital internal resources in a manner that cultivates a vibrant organizational culture. As the twenty-first century has brought an intensified war for talent and human capital, having leadership that can empower employees and set the right tone at the top can only solidify a corporation's competitive footing.

This is essential, as quite often the system left unchecked can foster an apathetic and cynical culture. Individuals in organizations are not blind: They see what is rewarded, and in many instances order themselves accordingly. They take note of who is being promoted as a key signal from the top.

Too often, limited and precious internal resources are squandered at the expense of selfish political ambitions.

As we hurtle forward in time, corporations can no longer afford to turn a blind eye to the need of developing and promoting the right type of leader. A highly intense marketplace will dictate this; more important, shareholders will demand it. Ultimately, organizations miss the opportunity to engage the hearts and minds of employees, as generally the prevailing behaviors and actions of leadership and key employees carry far more weight than its words.

The challenges we face as a global community require corporations to take on a heightened role. Sitting at the critical intersection of our natural resources, individuals, and government, corporate leadership must rise to the occasion.

QUESTIONS

1. Do your leaders exemplify your organization's core values? How do you formally and informally hold them accountable?
2. Are your top leaders equipped to manage and lead considering the complexities and dynamics of our twenty-first-century marketplace?
3. Are leaders open to change, embracing and leveraging new technology, capabilities, and practices?
4. Have you defined core competencies you desire in leaders, and does your leadership team reflect these competencies?
5. Do the core competencies you've defined support your organization's efforts to compete in a complex, integrated, and dynamic marketplace?
6. How is the culture in your shared services organizations? Is there a separate standard and expectation of leadership from leaders that reside in profit centers?

REFERENCES

Ackman, Dan. 2001. "Forbes Faces: Hugh McColl Jr." *Forbes*, January 24.

Miller, Rick. 2001. "CEO McColl Passing Torch, Mixed Legacy at Bank of America." *Investment News,* January 29.

Milmo, Dan. 2012. "BP's *Deepwater Horizon* Costs Rise $847M." *The Guardian,* July 31.

Williams, Selina. 2013. "BP Expects to Pay More Over *Deepwater*." *Wall Street Journal*, March 10.

Zuckerman, Sam. 2013. "McColl's Mixed Legacy, B of A Chief Won't Retire a Hero in S.F." *San Francisco Chronicle,* September 3.

CHAPTER 8

The Risks of Human Capital: Unleashing the Conceivers, Deal Makers, and Sustainers

The Three Elements point us to a new lens with which to consider how skills align with activities in the marketplace. This new approach benefits both managers and employees as it ensures that individual activities are in sync with what they enjoy, thus serving as a catalyst to drive optimum performance. One of the key outcomes of the most recent recession is that it has served as a major agitator in prompting individuals to evaluate current career paths and future aspirations.

A NEW HUMAN RESOURCES MODEL

The marketplace and the organizations within it are driven by individuals who play critical roles across a broad spectrum of functions. These functions naturally align with the three core elements found in systems and can provide leaders, managers, and employees with a helpful human resources tool to think through career planning and organizational needs. It enables employees to think through their lives and professional aspirations with a fresh lens—one that allows them to explore their talents in the context of what truly motivates them, as well as providing them a new perspective of how it all fits within the broader marketplace. What makes this model compelling is that this human resources guide and the functional personality lens align perfectly with the three critical elements found within systems.

The model is also beneficial to managers and human resources professionals, providing them with an insightful template to think through what is needed and to evaluate talent. It provides them with a tool to truly assess and consider how an individual is wired, enabling managers to better understand how to align talent against important tasks. As a former manager, I know firsthand how challenging it is to select individuals to lead, manage, or perform certain activities.

While candidates may be capable and have excellent experience, it is vital to understand what their true skills, talents, and interests are. It ensures that individuals are in functions that gratify them and are in ones in which they can thrive due to its alignment with how they are in their core. Understanding these dynamics also enables managers to manage employees more effectively. Ultimately, this new approach provides a win-win for the organization and the individual, creating an environment in which individuals thrive.

*   *   *

After several months of revisiting childhood memories with her ailing mother, a spark ignited within Paula. It was time to make a change. Although her career as an analyst at The Hartford, Inc. was somewhat rewarding and challenging, she yearned to explore her creative side. In the midst of the success she was experiencing, Paula took matters into her own hands. In her spare time, she pursued alternative hobbies and even enrolled in various design and creative courses at her local college. Several years later, Paula landed an exciting job in the marketing department of a national candy company. Now, four years later, Paula is a senior brand manager and is having the time of her life.

We all know people like Paula, whether they are our neighbors, family members, friends—or ourselves. After years of working in a particular position, we feel stuck and unhappy, realizing that we need to shift careers to align with what we love to do. A helpful exercise would be to reevaluate what we desire and for managers to reevaluate the talent who work for them. Evaluating and aligning talent to the correct set of activities is of paramount importance in leveraging human resources to drive your competitive advantage. Through a new human resources (HR) model, the three core elements found in systems provide employees, leaders, and management with a powerful HR tool to think through career planning, evaluating talent, and resource planning. This new model is composed of three distinct classifications (see Exhibit 8.1):

1. Conceivers
2. Dealmakers
3. Sustainers

EXHIBIT 8.1   Individual Contributors

Individual Career Planning

I recall a conversation I had during the first quarter of 2008 that gave me insight into how the market aligns to this new model and how it rewards these very distinct skill sets. I had the opportunity to speak with a managing director at a top executive search firm. He was based in New York and had a keen pulse on the economy and executive job market. Soon, it became clear that my timing to find employment, especially considering my experience and skill set, could not have been worse. Although I was excited to have the meeting, I was quickly brought down to earth.

As I painstakingly took the time to outline the highlights of my career, the executive search expert politely took the time to inform me that my skill set and experience were not in demand at that time. He told me that because of the weak economy and grim economic forecasts, corporations needed professionals who could drive revenue. Yes, they were in need of deal-maker skill sets and experiences. And, unfortunately, I had spent most of my career in sustainer roles, providing leadership in various capacities. Coincidentally, this event also prompted me to further explore how skill sets are segmenting, thus eventually leading me to the development of this model.

The model is highly beneficial to individuals in all types of functions and stages of their career. From the new HR model to the functional personality type guide discussed later in the chapter, individuals of all types can assess where they are and chart a new direction. It may apply to your own career if you are unfulfilled in your current job and find that your day-to-day responsibilities do not align with what you love to do and where your true gifts, talents, and skills reside.

Early on in our lives, we may select a career path that appears to suit a particular need or desire. At this juncture, our career path is heavily influenced by a number of factors, including family, friends, or even the powerful influences in our surrounding culture and environment. Over time, as we mature and have different experiences, we discover that we've developed a *career cognitive dissonance;* that is, we come to the realization that our work and career are misaligned with our true talents, passions, and gifts.

This common situation often surfaces when we are well into our careers or are experiencing significant professional challenges. Think about the many people you know—they could be family members, close friends, or even associates—who not only are dissatisfied with their current work but are misaligned career-wise when you take a hard look at their talents and personality type. The concepts in this chapter can be applied to gain a new perspective on how to approach career planning, one that allows them to align their career with who they really are.

Risks, Rewards, and Rule Breakers

There are a few aspects of the model that I must explain up front. First, an individual may possess attributes that place him in one, two, or all three categories—conceivers, deal makers, and sustainers. However, we all possess a dominant set of behaviors that defines us. Second, although creativity is a critical attribute of conceivers, it straddles all three categories. Creative people also can be deal makers or sustainers. Creativity is more about producing an original thought rather than being consumed by thinking through and applying new approaches, which is more aligned with a conceiver mind-set.

Another critical aspect of the model is the risk and reward continuum. People who spawn and execute groundbreaking ideas and products, whether it is in business, sciences, the arts, or other areas, typically are handsomely rewarded for their innovations. Think about songwriters, inventors, innovators, visionaries, and even explorers. Deal makers are next in line as it relates to rewards, as very often their compensation is tied to specific units or sales for selling, brokering, and trading critical goods, services, and assets for their organization. Finally, Sustainers are not rewarded as much as the

Create Market	Facilitate Market	Support Market
Catalysts	**Enables**	**Supports**
Research	Sales/Trading	Regulatory Framework
Development	Import/Export	Legal System
Exploration	Financial Markets	Educational System
Innovation	Technology	Military
Invention	Taxes	Infrastructure
Creative Arts	Venture Capital	Government
high risk		*low risk*
	CREATIVITY	
high reward		*low reward*

EXHIBIT 8.2   Marketplace Activities

other two market participants, although in certain professions they command hefty salaries (see Exhibit 8.2).

As rewards go, the risks follow. Being a conceiver is no easy task, sometimes working thousands of hours creating, innovating, and designing something new with little payback. The result of what has been created can be a huge payoff—or a complete bust. Next on the risk scale would be deal makers, as these professionals are rewarded only on what they deal, trade, broker, or sell. Being a deal maker requires a lot of stomach when it comes to compensation, as individuals in deal-making professions typically receive a small base or guaranteed salary and make most of their earnings from commissions. From a risk perspective, sustainers are often safe when it comes to economic rewards, as often they have stable salaries.

The market rewards these functions differently in times of prosperity and austerity. For example, in recessionary periods, sustainers are more vulnerable, and jobs in this classification are first to go. Conversely, deal makers are in high demand, as they are viewed as key drivers in fueling revenue and growth. The market may handsomely reward conceivers in times of austerity as well as prosperity because they provide the spark that ignites growth, creating the need for deal makers and sustainers.

It's important to note the imbalance in the number of sustainers, deal makers, and conceivers in the marketplace. For example, the sustainers in the marketplace far outnumber the deal makers. It generally takes significant infrastructure to support what is created, from hardware and software to technology and customer services, or support and infrastructure can come from critical technical areas such as Accounting/Finance, Legal, and HR. Likewise, there are more deal makers than conceivers in the marketplace.

This same pattern is evident in natural systems, when we consider the roles and responsibilities in ant and bee colonies to name just two. Typically, there is a similar scaling down of functions, as those elements or insects that are in a supportive role outnumber those that serve in other capacities.

This reality made me pose the question as to why this dynamic is present in the world we've created for ourselves. One answer could be associated with how we are socialized—what we are taught and accept and the ways in which we must act, behave, and think. We are all taught to live within certain boundaries. However, many of us incorporate this way in which we have ordered and structured society as a way of life in all facets of living. Many of us are simply wired this way, as we find it difficult to live and think outside of those boundaries. Others seem to be wired to push and extend those boundaries.

Conceivers are driven by the dream, idea, or vision. They go to great lengths in forming and bringing their idea to life. Whether it is composing a song, creative writing, bringing a invention to market, or furthering a concept or groundbreaking innovation, thousands of hours go into nurturing, development, and execution of the idea. Following through on this takes a formidable amount of patience, perseverance, and will.

Another factor can be the significant influence of art and creativity in our development as human beings. A common theme that runs through many conceivers is that they have some training or background in the creative arts, whether it is through music, the visual arts, or writing. These forms of artistic and creative expression cultivate a fertile environment for creativity. The connection between the role of artistic expression and exploration and developing an individual's willingness to challenge and push boundaries is well known and documented. It's about one's willingness and comfort to take risk.

When I think of my friends and former colleagues who are deal makers, they are innately wired to push and often cross boundaries. They are always prodding and pushing. Conversely, people I know who have characteristics as sustainers almost never break or bend the rules. For example, I used to meet at the gym with a group of friends who exhibited characteristics of all three HR types; some of them are deal makers, and others fit sustainer characteristics. The gym's parking lot had two driveways connecting to the street. The more convenient one was designated as an exit, so each of us would drive past it to the designated entrance.

One day a member of the group, Bob, entered the parking lot through the exit. Another friend, Sue, was taken aback that he would break the rule. Bob, however, didn't think twice about his minor infraction—he surmised that his actions posed very little risk to others so early in the morning. It was fascinating to be a part of such a lively discussion, and, yes, the two friends fit neatly into the classifications. Bob, who broke the rules, is a very successful salesman—a deal maker. Sue is a sustainer who works as a technician, is very process oriented, and follows the rules in every instance.

Conceivers: Creating the Market

Conceivers create market; they are inventors, artists, and explorers and are visionaries. They spawn the critical elements that serve as the lifeblood for the entire system. Characteristics include:

- They tinker, play, and explore different ideas, concepts, and theories.
- They push the boundaries of conventional thinking and test new ground.
- They are not afraid to make mistakes.

Conceivers are always tinkering with conventional approaches and norms; they do not rest, for they are consumed by making critical connections and exploring infinite possibilities. Conceivers see a world of limitless possibilities; they see only opportunity and look toward the future with great expectation. Creativity alone does not make one a conceiver, for the human mind is full of imagination. Let's further explore a popular type of conceiver, the visionary. Visionaries have become visible in today's marketplace due to the impact of technology and the Internet on the world. They dominate the headlines and include popular businessmen such as Bill Gates, Steve Jobs, Mark Zuckerberg, and a host of others.

Visionaries   Visionaries are bold and see opportunities where others see barriers. Creativity alone does not make one a visionary; however, these people constantly push the limits of common knowledge. Visionaries take us to places we would never go and help us see the world in a manner we would never imagine on our own.

Characteristics of visionaries include:

- They see what others don't see and have a knack for making critical connections.
- They possess enormous foresight and understanding of human behavior and the use of technology/science as well as the ability to anticipating future usage.

- They possess a keen sense of timing and know when to move.
- They are bold and take risks in order to realize their vision.

Visionaries constantly push the limits, often challenging common assumptions and introducing a new view of the world. They are bold and willing to share their vision with others. They have tremendous will and an overwhelming drive that enables them to turn their dreams into reality. They are the consummate risk takers and have the courage to share their vision, regardless of the opinion of others.

When we think about our lives and the wonderful tools and luxuries we have at our disposal, many of them came from the mind of a visionary. Think through something as simple as a Starbucks coffee shop and how in 10 years this business blossomed into a national icon. Someone took the simple idea of repackaging coffee and creating a unique retail experience and created a national craze. Think about the concept of bottled water. We all drank water prior to packaging it in a bottle, but someone came along and took something that we consume on a daily basis and presented it a little differently. As a result, bottled water is now a billion-dollar industry.

The same idea applies to the concept of 24-hour news. Although we had local/national and sports news before, networks such as ESPN and CNN revolutionized the entire news industry. Now U.S. households are able to track and monitor events 24 hours per day. Visionaries shape and mold our world. They span all aspects of our everyday life. They include our musical artists, writers and poets, visual artists, scientists, and businessmen of all types. Visionaries influence our daily lives and are the driving force behind all of the wonderful creations in our world today.

Ted Turner, Visionary

Ted Turner not only has exceptional confidence in his abilities, he is persistent in his drive. As with most visionaries, Turner has the ability to foresee what people want, and, as he demonstrated with the creation of CNN, he has an uncanny ability to connect the dots. Turner transformed himself into a modern-day icon whose work has made a major impact globally. He single-handedly launched the beginning of 24-hour news and information.

As he foresaw how cable and satellite technology would transform television, he ushered in the era of unprecedented change in the lives of individuals across the planet. He firmly believed that he was on to something. He once proclaimed, "I am the right man in the right place at the right time. Not me alone, but all the people who think the world can be brought together by telecommunications." He had a vision of life and a global reach not only in telecommunications, but in his championing of global disarmament.

In 1970, Turner bought a small television station, WJRJ (Channel 17 in Atlanta), that was known for broadcasting wrestling, reruns, and old movies. At that time, it was one of the worst stations in the Atlanta market. Turner made a deal that took the assets of Turner Advertising public by joining them with the assets of Channel 17 and formed a new company called Turner Communications. Realizing that watching sports on television would be big business, in 1973 the Atlanta Braves were being broadcast on the station. Within three years, Turner had Braves games broadcast via satellite across the country. By 1976, the station that Turner had built was being broadcast worldwide. Turner then brought on Atlanta's professional basketball team, the Atlanta Hawks.

In 1980, Ted Turner founded the Cable News Network (CNN). Critics said it would never work, but Turner never wavered in his vision. CNN was not an immediate success; however, it became well respected fairly quickly. CNN laid the groundwork for other stations that Turner would eventually own. In 2001, Turner Broadcasting merged with Time Warner, one of the biggest mergers in history.

As a private citizen and businessman, Turner attacked the philosophy and propaganda of the Cold War and fought for peace between the Soviet Union and the United States. To further these efforts, in 1986 he created and founded the Goodwill Games. With former Senator Sam Nunn, Turner now co-chairs the Nuclear Threat Initiative, which he also founded. Turner also has made a difference worldwide with his philanthropic efforts. Since 1991, the Turner Foundation has donated millions of dollars to environmental and preservation initiatives. In 1998, Ted Turner made an astonishing gift to the United Nations of $1 billion. With this gift, the UN Foundation was created and now serves as a platform for connecting people, resources, and ideas across the globe. This visionary giant not only rethought the way we use television, but has also focused his energy on making our world a better place.

What made Turner a visionary was not that he invented cable television, nor was he the first businessperson to launch television news reporting. Turner saw an opportunity to make some critical connections. He saw the powerful convergence of how cable TV would engulf our lives and how we would have an insatiable appetite for continuous information. He anticipated how cable television would consume the lives of millions of people across the planet.

Deal Makers: Making the Market

Michael and Steven Roberts are classic deal makers. They live for the transaction and over 30 years have built more than 70 business enterprises worth more than $1 billion. With beginnings in real estate, the Roberts brothers parlayed their holdings into a robust portfolio that includes holdings in real estate development, business consulting, wireless communication, television, aviation, and construction.

Deal makers make the market, serving as the conduit through which flows all that is created. They bring products, services, and new technologies to market. Deal makers are a critical part in the chain of commerce. They are our small business owners, our real estate brokers, investment advisers, and salespeople of all types. They are always intensely focused on making the transaction happen, regardless of what it may take.

Characteristics of deal makers include:

- They are transaction oriented, focused on closing the deal.
- They are rule breakers (and rule benders).
- They are highly motivated by compensation.

Conversely, I know many individuals who serve in a deal-making function or activity, but they are not truly deal makers. Life sometimes pushes many of us to obtain a job that does not fit with who we truly are. Don't you know someone in your family or circle of friends who is in a deal-making position but does not truly embrace and enjoy what they do?

Deal makers can't hide; they love the chase and close of the deal. In the world of commerce, they are akin to hunters. While visionaries get excited about innovating and bringing new approaches to light, deal makers are consumed and fully focused on the transaction at hand. They live for it! They prefer to be in an environment that enables, rather than restricts, their deal-making activities. They view rules, policies, and processes as a hindrance and barrier to business.

When leading deal makers, you must strike the intricate balance of giving them freedom while still holding them accountable for following the rules. For example, think of the role of stockbrokers or investment advisers. They play a critical role in ensuring that you invest in the most effective products that will help you achieve your financial goals. Although they are there first and foremost to serve the client, investment brokers are driven and compensated to transact, to make deals. Many things motivate investment brokers that inherently conflict with a client's objectives, which is why it is particularly important to place structure and boundaries around them.

Investment brokers are primarily concerned about closing the transaction, so they generally have a number of resources around them to ensure that they deal in the right way. They have administrative assistants, client support, and investment specialists on their teams to ensure that all of the administrative requirements necessary for completing the transaction are in place. These functions play a critical role in ensuring that the client is protected and his or her interests are furthered. The investment firm that an investment broker works for also has other critical functions—like compliance and operations—that support the broker's activities.

When interacting with deal makers, it is important to understand where their interests lie. This will not only aid you in understanding how they process information, but how to more effectively communicate with them. This will create a win-win for all parties.

Sustainers: Supporting the Market

Karen Sanchez-Griege is a nationally recognized high school principal from Albuquerque, New Mexico. As sustainers go, her work is critical to supporting growth in her community. Students at her high school take nontraditional courses that teach them practical life skills and help them learn aspects of personal finance and other skills such as film production. Ultimately, students at her high school will be better equipped to compete for jobs in an increasingly demanding marketplace.

Sustainers are the glue that keeps all the components together. In their support function, they serve as the foundation of any organization or system. They are accountants, laborers, technicians, lawyers, administrators, and a host of other functions. Sustainers, in contrast to Conceivers and deal makers, play a role that keeps all the components together. They serve as the foundation of any organization or system. They provide structure and consistency, ensuring that all organizational "mechanics" are operating as they should.

Characteristics of sustainers include:

- They are process oriented and highly organized and regimental.
- They prefer to operate in a structured environment.
- They are detail oriented.

Sustainers provide support for some of the most critical parts of systems, both large and small. They process, build, operate, and analyze. They may function as educators, lawyers, physicians, analysts, accountants, store clerks, technicians of all types, and individuals who operate in a customer service capacity (that is, those who do not sell through the telephone).

Or consider your accountant, CPA, or tax preparer. They live in a world of detail, and in order to work with them, you must correspondingly provide them with detail. A person in this profession enjoys interpreting tax codes and the process of determining how they apply to a specific client's circumstance. This discipline is very black and white, and is not left to too much speculation or interpretation. The rules are generally hard and fast and require them to extract from you all of the necessary details in order to get your tax situation right.

When interacting with sustainers, it is important to appreciate that anything absent of detail and specifics to them becomes an exercise in frustration. Therefore, in order to effectively work with these types of individuals, give them the nitty-gritty. Then you will find it easy to enjoy a productive and harmonious working relationship with them.

Sustainers can also straddle different industries or market functions. Let's take a lawyer, for example. There are many types of lawyers that serve in various capacities across industry types. You may have a lawyer who is just focused on terms and conditions and deals mainly in your run-of-the-mill contract work, or may be engaged in family law, personal injury, or even bankruptcy-type work. Or you may have a lawyer that operates in a deal-maker type of environment. This lawyer is always close to the transaction and loves to wheel and deal. He may be involved in mergers and acquisitions or real estate transactions, or may support investment brokerage/banking or even private banking activity.

Finally, you have those attorneys who support those in the conceivers space. These attorneys support the activities in arts, entertainment, and athletics, or may even be patent attorneys, supporting new innovations and ideas. The point here is to acknowledge that even if you may fit, from a skill perspective, in a particular job classification or area, you can leverage that skill across multiple types of activities.

THE INTERNET EXAMPLE

I am highlighting the emergence of the Internet and e-commerce because it provides a strong example of how the new HR model works from a functional perspective. Yes, the new HR model helps us understand how one's skills and abilities tie into the marketplace; however, those skills also align to key functions that drive commercial activities.

During the mid- to late 1990s, we were swept away with the dot-com bubble, or Internet boom. This period saw billions of dollars pouring into the market to invest in a myriad of ideas and exciting new innovations. Internet commerce, or e-commerce was hot. Venture capitalists and private equity firms salivated as they lined up to capitalize on the enormous financial potential of this new space. And they were not disappointed! Even those of us in banking took part in this green field of new opportunity as many of the top-tier banks quickly redeployed capital to participate in this new investment opportunity.

The emergence of the Internet spawned a host of new commerce. There were many visionary and groundbreaking ideas and companies that came out of this new technology from eBay to Amazon, from Google to Yahoo, and the creation of PayPal and YouTube. Many new companies and commerce were created from this new tool of technology.

As ideas emerged, private equity and venture capital were there step by step to provide the financial wherewithal to bring them to life. Providing the seed money necessary to get these ideas off of the ground was a key facilitator in bringing innovations to market. Private equity and venture capital has always been a critical facilitator of commerce, from the funding of the oh-so-familiar voyage of the *Mayflower,* through the funding of the leveraged buyouts of the 1980s. The use of capital to fund ideas is a critical aspect of the marketplace.

Finally, as new ideas and companies were created, a great deal of infrastructure was needed to support this new stream of commerce. I witnessed this firsthand at Wachovia as we built a new division called eCommerce. This new and exciting division of the bank was a critical channel in the delivery of products and services to customers.

To support these new activities, companies needed to build web sites and acquire the necessary technology, which included hardware and new applications. In addition to this infrastructure, organizations needed marketing and product functions, as well as other critical support functions such as accounting and finance, risk management, customer service, and a host of others.

We all know how important e-commerce is to us today, as it has become an integral part of our daily lives. In 15 short years, the Internet and e-commerce have become a social and economic marvel. In 2010, U.S. Internet advertising revenue alone was $26 billion, with total U.S. Internet sales topping $165 billion. According to eMarketer.com, U.S. e-commerce sales are predicted to grow from $225 billion in 2012 to $430 billion in 2017. And if that isn't startling enough, analysts are predicting an annual growth rate of 19.4 percent.

A NEW MODEL FOR EVALUATING TEAMS

Companies can optimize performance by purposely having a blend of personality traits in teams of all types (see Exhibit 8.3). This new model is a natural extension of the new HR model we saw in Exhibit 8.1. In today's organizations, when managers assemble teams at all levels, they consider many factors, like functional expertise, industry type, leadership competencies, educational background, and diversity.

CONCEIVER	DEAL MAKER	SUSTAINER
Highly experimental	Adept at making things happen	Structured
Out of the box and big picture	Transaction oriented	Requires clarity
Pushes boundaries	Bends and breaks the rules	Follows the rules
Requires little structure	Focus on speed	Process oriented
Idealistic	Pragmatic and opportunistic	Realistic

EXHIBIT 8.3   Functional Personality Types

However, I believe this process often omits a filter that, in my opinion, is a decisive factor in the quality of decisions rendered by teams or committees. This filter is the one of personality type. While often the focus of personality types centers on whether individuals will challenge a direction or be assertive in stating their opinion, more focus should go into understanding and assessing personality types.

Organizations leverage teams or management committees as a critical tool to make their most important decisions. These groups are charged with arbitrating a number of issues, like determining an organization's strategic direction or the way resources are utilized, or even setting the overall priorities for a business unit, division, or the enterprise. From the board of directors to a C-suite executive operating committee, from a divisional management team to a special task force established to address a specific business unit challenge. Committees are an important part of an organization's governance model and ultimate success.

I'm not certain how we've come to depend on committees and teams, but they play critical roles in governing organizational activities. Conventional wisdom is that having a team of people reflecting various points of view—whether they be functional or organizational—ensures that some of the most critical decisions on all levels go through effective filters. Having a team of highly skilled and capable individuals vet critical issues will often result in a higher-quality decision when compared to a decision by a single person. This not only insulates any one individual from the negative fallout that may result in making a poor decision, but, more important, ensures that multiple perspectives are at the table and provide input into a final decision.

The Criticality of Evaluating Personality Types on Teams

Having a diverse set of functional personality types is critical in any organization because quite often leaders surround themselves with people who think and see the world as they do. This common human tendency can be a critical roadblock to sustained organizational success because it undermines a team's ability to make important decisions leveraging the appropriate filters and lens. Whether it is at the board level, executive operating committees, steering committees, employee task forces, or routine management teams, ensuring a broad set of personality types is critical to the decision-making process. It improves the quality of decisions on any team.

By understanding the attributes of the leaders, managers, and employees who serve on critical management committees, an organization can remove those blind spots that hinder teams' effectiveness. Through carefully and deliberately designing a team's composition, organizations can ensure the right "tension" on the team, which often yields better decisions.

Quite often, on management committees and teams, the focus is on assembling a group of people who represent different business units; however, does this single filter ensure that various viewpoints are represented? For example, the fact that an individual represents the legal department does not mean she will be process oriented, follow the rules, and offer the lens of pragmatism and practicality. She could bring other personality traits to the table that quite often run contrary to what we have come to pigeonhole people in.

The Cost of Personality Types in Driving Value   John Maxwell is the CEO and president of APEX Corporation, a technology reseller and systems integrator firm headquartered in Memphis, Tennessee. APEX offers a broad spectrum of information technology (IT) products and services from leading IT manufacturers and sells to the government, corporate, and educational industries. Some of its products and services include new equipment sales and leases, network storage solutions, software licenses, maintenance and service contracts, and electronics.

The firm has annual revenue of $50 million, but for seven years has struggled to grow. This is due to the highly competitive nature of the reseller industry, where the primary driver is to be a low-cost provider. With shrinking margins, APEX is attempting to identify new ways to generate new revenue while maintaining its existing business.

John and his three partners have desired to grow revenue and determined they would do it by expanding their current portfolio of limited clients and to pursue an aggressive merger and acquisitions strategy. Over the past two years, an infusion of capital has enabled the firm to expand its footprint through acquiring two other firms, one on the East Coast and one on the West Coast. Even with its additional presence and diverse footprint, the firm's revenue is flat and even in retreat. Conversely, many of its competitors have generated increased sales by expanding products and services and are experiencing robust growth.

So why does John's firm struggle when several of its competitors are experiencing significant growth and APEX is merely surviving? A significant factor in its failure to perform is its management team composition. If we take a closer look at the makeup of John and his partners, we will find a window into what plagues this firm with so much potential.

John is a very capable and intelligent businessman. He is best described as a sustainer, as he is trained in technology in a supportive-type role. John is a stickler for details—he loves them. In addition to being the firm's chief, he also manages the financials. When the company experiences a problem with its technology, John is the first to be back in its computer room troubleshooting whatever problem has arisen. He seldom goes out on sales calls and is detached from customers and the marketplace. Instead, John prefers to administer the details of managing the home office.

John's first partner is also a sustainer, having come out of a similar background. Similarly, he is a technologist and is responsible for the firm's recruiting efforts. He also is very process oriented and a stickler for detail. The second partner is also a sustainer and very process oriented. His role is to drive business development by increasing the client portfolio. However, two years into the establishment of this new direction, the firm continues to struggle and build new revenue.

John's company highlights the importance of having a robust and well-rounded management team. There are no conceivers or deal makers on the firm's management team. The firm's strategy is being set and executed by only sustainers. While I believe sustainers can effectively run organizations, it's important for them to recognize who they are and what their limitations are. For this firm, having a blend of personality types would be beneficial, for it would provide the organization with the type of filters and perspectives to enhance its value.

A deal maker personality type would provide tremendous benefit in driving much-needed sales. A deal maker would understand how to make these happen and is very transaction oriented—a skill set that is critical to make things happen. Also having someone with the conceiver/creativity personality traits could also be a shot in the arm for John's firm. A conceiver would challenge the management team's conventional thinking and provide new perspectives for the company's strategy.

Leveraging talent to drive bottom-line results can make the difference in today's marketplace. This means ensuring that there is a robust and continuous process in place to put together diverse teams at all levels of the organization.

The process of understanding team makeup based on membership traits is different than assessing leadership competencies. They are two very distinct filters and points of reference. Leadership competencies are associated with behaviors and characteristics affecting a person's ability to effectively lead resources. Aspects of leadership competency include decisiveness, accountability, resilience, integrity, influencing, and partnering. Effective leaders can have personality traits that fit in any of the three categories: they can be creative, facilitative, or supportive. However, all leaders must possess a very clearly defined set of competencies.

THE DIVERSITY TRAP

Today, many companies are focused on ensuring that teams on all levels are composed of individuals with diverse backgrounds. These companies realize the power of a diverse culture. They also realize the positive impact diverse teams have in making critical decisions, as divergent and rich perspectives often lead to quality decisions. However, while diversity is critical, organizations should ensure that they evaluate diverse teams through an additional lens: personality types.

Yes, the richness and uniqueness of an individual's culture and experience add value; however, there are times when a person's personality traits dominate their perspective, approach, and how they view the world. Diversity alone does not guarantee that organizations will harvest the richness of an individual's experience and approach; they must also understand the personality types on these teams.

The issue of functional personality types in business decision making is similar to the dynamic that exists in individuals regarding race, gender, age, status, or sexual orientation. Just as individuals process certain information based on important social influences, the manner in which we process and analyze data is also influenced by our innate wiring or personality type.

During my corporate days, large groups of us went through diversity training. This important training provided us not only with a deeper understanding of the sensitivities and complexities of diversity in organizations, but also armed us with valuable skills. An important reality that we learned was the impact of our social identities in the discussion of race, gender, status, and sexual orientation.

This is critical in the discussion of diversity because it links social identity groups to systems of power and resources in society, which in turn has an important impact on the way we see the world. In social identity theory, our behaviors are divided into two groups—dominant or subordinate. Those belonging to dominant groups would benefit from being male or white due to advantages those groups have in society. People in subordinate groups are disadvantaged in society because they are female or may be people of color.

My social identities influence my thinking and the lens through which I process certain issues. Because I am a male, I at times process and see things through my male dominant lens. Because I am a person of color, I process and see certain things from a subordinate group perspective.

This same dynamic applies to the issue of who we are from a personality perspective when it comes to thinking through problems in a business context—or any context, for that matter. Regardless of our leadership competencies or the lens of our race, gender, status, or background that we see things through, a strong influence on the way we process and see the world is strongly linked to how our personalities are wired. Again, this orientation can be based on a number of factors, such as ancestry, experiences, innate talent, environment, and a host of other influences.

Because we leverage teams to assess critical data and find solutions to some of our most formidable challenges, this new approach offers much promise. It is exciting because it provides us with a new tool to evaluate the composition of teams at all levels and of all types. Assembling teams whose membership evaluates problems from varying perspectives and approaches only assists in enhancing the quality of those decisions. It fosters a healthy filtering process.

THE THREE FORCES AND THE NEW HR MODEL

The Three Forces—movement (change), balance, and repetition—also apply to the new HR model. Their relevance to individuals in the context of systems has a similar impact as they do in systems in nature. Whether you are a conceiver, deal maker, or sustainer, leveraging this new model to align to skills and interests is only half the battle. The model is brought to life when individuals apply them in a manner that propels their new direction. And only through a systematic process can this be assured.

Change and Movement

The impact of change and movement in our world is important to consider in the discussion of career planning or managing the career of any employee. As we observed with the most recent global recession, change was imposed on millions of individuals the world over with very little warning. The resulting impact of this change was seismic shifts in the marketplace, as the recession wiped away millions of jobs, many of which will never come back.

Today's marketplace requires new skills, thus demanding that displaced individuals retool themselves. These monumental changes, though fraught with unique challenges, have provided an opportunity for individuals to proactively consider where they are or even chart a new direction. Too often, complacency rules the day as we become comfortable, and only when forced to change do we reluctantly chart a new course. Our attempts are often too little, too late, placing us in a reactionary mode.

This behavior and our ultimate failure to proactively manage change professionally run contrary to dynamics of how we experience change in our daily lives. As discussed in Chapter 3, movement, and change that results from it, is a critical influence that substantially affects life on our planet. We live in a world that is continually shifting, moving, growing, and evolving. Everything in our world is in a state of constant change, from the Earth itself to everything living and existing within its plane. We must always be growing and moving, as nonphysical change in our world requires us to respond in a like manner. This process of growing and changing is cyclical and continuous throughout our lives.

We are bombarded by a continuous stream of information and images that both stimulate and influence us in many ways. Without consciously stepping back to process it all, this stimulation can play a significant role in influencing our behavior and attitudes. Think about how certain types of information and images can affect your political, social, or even spiritual views. Eventually, if we are not mindful of the subtle power and influence that this stimulus has on us, we can find ourselves moving in an unintended direction.

Experiencing change evokes in us new fears as well as aspirations. Change in its most fundamental state is therefore stimulating. Even the exposure to new realities and information creates change within us and to our world. By experiencing new realities, we begin to alter our position and quite often the lens in which we view ourselves and the world around us. Ultimately, this shift in our reality ignites new desires and stimulates us to think differently about the world and what we want in life. Let me provide you with an example.

Think about our efforts to raise our children. We spend countless amounts of time and resources to provide them with opportunities for learning. As they grow, we want to expose them to different experiences and activities. Why do we do this? It is my belief that we do this in an effort to provide them with a variety of opportunities to explore themselves and the world around them. I further believe that what actually happens is that this stimulation stokes our children's imagination, creating dreams and aspirations.

Exposing our children to stimulating experiences will ultimately result in a shift in their reality. This reality shift creates a new world for them, a world of expanded opportunities and new realities. They see and experience life through a different lens. There is no difference in the impact of change on our children and on us as adults. This is why after spending several years in a particular role, we experience the yearning for something different. As we gain new experiences, even as adults, this process, over time, may stoke new interests or even reconnect us to old passions.

It is important that leaders and managers create an organizational culture that encourages and embraces change. By creating an environment that encourages employees to incorporate change into their professional lives, it eventually serves to provide as a catalyst for strong individual performance, as well as organizational performance. Think of the A players in your organization and how they intuitively or sometimes with intent incorporate change into their work lives. This is often achieved through their efforts of continuing to update their technical skills, learning new skills, and/or staying abreast of the most recent trends in their industry.

Balance

Balance is an essential part of everything that exists in our world. It is a critical part of every system in nature and our man-made world. Balance is also an integral element that keeps everything in our world performing optimally. It is quite simply a very real and important part of our natural world, as everything in nature performs harmoniously and with precision to ensure balance. Think about the examples I used previously. All components are ordered in a manner to ensure that they provide equilibrium to the underlying system they support.

Achieving balance in our professional lives is essential to ensuring that we find enjoyment and meaning in our work. Let's face it—life today is complicated, as we have many competing priorities to manage through daily. However, through it all, we must maintain some semblance of sanity as these challenges can be overwhelming. As leaders, it's important to ensure that the concept of balance is woven into the fabric of an organization's culture because it can serve as a formidable force in driving employee satisfaction and engagement. Whether reflected in HR policies or business practices, this notion of balance ultimately results in impact to the bottom line.

The need for balance in our lives is very real and vital as it applies to our emotional energy. It is as critical in this aspect of our life as it is in others. Balance in our lives ensures that we keep it all together.

The Importance of Repetition

If you are considering making a career change and redirecting your efforts to building new skills, repetition can be a powerful ally. There is a transformative nature to repetition—it is one of the most powerful realities we have in this world. Repetition enables us to develop expertise and become keen practitioners of a particular discipline or set of skills. It facilitates the notion of mastering something.

When you consider your current skill set or area of expertise, think of what you endured to gain the particular knowledge. The expertise you possess may have been amassed through years of study, however, what makes you proficient is the continuous application of knowledge to a set of activities.

Therefore, the concept of repetition when applied to a career change or a new beginning can facilitate your transition. This can be helpful as it sets the stage for eventual success. Also think about the power of repetition as it relates to the messages that are embedded in our psyche regarding who we are and the perception we have of ourselves. Or think about its power in continuing bad and good habits: because we continue to return to the same cycle of a particular behavior, the habit eventually takes root and becomes a part of our reality. Practice does make perfect, and in the context of learning new skills, the power of repetition becomes a transformative tool.

SUMMARY

Leveraging the new HR model to align or think through an individual's skill set can be beneficial. It also provides an additional lens with which to consider how best to leverage talent in one's organization. Whether you are an employee or leader, evaluating and aligning skills in a manner that best fits with individual interests and key organizational activities ensures optimal performance.

As organizations construct teams as a means to tackle various challenges, it can be beneficial and highly effective to leverage the elements contained in the functional personality–type model. By designing teams of all types that leverage the personality type tool, organizations, managers, and leaders can build higher-performing teams. This will ensure another layer of diversity in thought and create a powerful tension, which can yield more quality decisions.

If you are contemplating a career change or looking to enter into the job market, you can leverage the new HR tool to approach career choices from a different perspective. The tool can assist you by providing you with an opportunity to align how you are wired with different types of jobs and opportunities. It may lead you to understanding how misaligned you are with your current job and who you are inside. Or, if you're a new graduate or are entering the workforce, you can gain a sound understanding of the direction or career you'd like to pursue.

QUESTIONS

1. Based on the new HR model in this chapter, what category best aligns with your talents, passions, and skills? Evaluate this in the context of your appetite for risk.
2. If you are a leader and have a management team, does most of your team reflect your personality and align with how you process and view the world?
3. Is your leadership team a mirror image of how you think and process? And if so, is there an opportunity to add leaders who reflect a different approach and thinking?
4. What steps can you take to better align your skills, talents, and passions with your career, and how can you constructively move toward this new vision of yourself?
5. What steps are you taking to ensure that the right type of leaders flourish in your organization? Are you managing out those who do not reflect what you desire in your leadership profile?

CHAPTER 9

Waking Sleeping Giants: The Importance of Empowering Employees

"**T**he whole is only as good as the sum of its parts." And as applied to the dynamics of organizational performance, employees play the most critical part. In today's competitive marketplace, an organization's ability to leverage and unleash the unlimited potential of its employees provides it with a distinct advantage. It's an advantage that has been brought to bear by the convergence of compelling forces such as the emergence of our knowledge economy, technological advances, globalization, and our most recent global recession. Mobilizing and, more important, empowering employees has become a strategic imperative, as the quest for meaning and purpose in the workplace has taken on a heightened significance.

THE EMPOWERED EMPLOYEE: THE KEY TO DRIVING PEAK PERFORMANCE

There is a giant waiting to be awakened in each of us; we possess tremendous gifts, talents, and abilities that lie latent within us, waiting to emerge. However, circumstances, experiences, and the vicissitudes of life get in the way, as many of us abdicate our personal authority to the powerful influences of family, society, and corporate culture and organizational dictums. This imposing force lies deeply submerged within us, like an unassuming iceberg floating aimlessly atop the ocean's peaceful waves, but whose magnificence and sheer mass is hidden far below the frozen sea.

Corporate culture, organizational systems, and the world around us have a way of conditioning us to rely on external circumstance and the actions of others to give us direction on how our careers and lives should be shaped. These powerful influences dull us, as we somehow lose our edge and our sense of who we really are inside. I cannot stress how dangerous this is and how pervasive this problem is in individuals, organizations, and society at large.

When I speak of personal authority, I am referring to the unlimited power that all human beings possess that enables us to not only know what we believe, but to act in every instance in perfect alignment with those beliefs. It is also an innate knowledge that serves as the foundation of true confidence, one that enables us to understand that our value as human beings is derived from within rather than circumstances and factors without.

Tapping into or rediscovering our personal authority leads us all to realize who we truly are and enables us to connect with our true talents and gifts. Exploring this issue in individuals can be a powerful exercise. Organizations that foster a culture that allows individuals to explore these issues can cultivate legions of empowered employees. Ultimately, this will translate into organizations' gaining a competitive advantage due to their ability to harness powerful human resources.

Unlocking the unlimited potential of employees and human resources is a strategic advantage in a highly competitive and dynamic marketplace. In many organizations, achieving this goal is driven through many corporate directives such as talent identification and development, as well as training and skills development. However, in my mind, these activities should be a part of a laser-focused effort that is centered on employee and individual empowerment.

Empowerment is at the core of unleashing the true potential of employees and individuals. It is also a key differentiator and can be a strategic advantage to organizations that understand this, for what is a corporation? Is it not an assemblage of hundreds, if not thousands, of individuals who are charged with executing certain tasks on behalf of the entire organization? Cultivating and harnessing the talents, energies, and rich resources of individuals can only benefit the whole. We must always remember that organizations, as complex and sophisticated as they may be, are in their basic form a network and conglomerate of people just like you and me.

Employee empowerment is a strategic imperative today because of several critical factors:

- *The power of technology* and how easy it has become for employees from everywhere and on every level to participate in critical organizational activities and challenges.
- *Market uncertainty.* As millions of people across the world have lost their jobs and have transitioned into new careers, many look toward the future

with enormous trepidation. We've lost our way, as individual confidence is waning. Even people who still have jobs are rattled when they read the gloomy headlines. Employees across all industries have lost confidence in the marketplace and their own organization's ability to compete in a highly unpredictable economy. This reality has also created a vacuum of confidence. This lack of confidence extends to our economy, as leading consumer confidence indicators reflect an emotionally exhausted society.

- *The powerful role of employees* and their connection to customers and the critical value-driven processes that they manage.
- *The prosperity we experienced at the beginning of the twenty-first century* cultivated a sense of entitlement in individuals and dependency on the organization.
- *The knowledge economy.*

It is important to recognize the low confidence many have in the system—or, for that matter, their employer—because it can lead to a tremendous level of organizational inertia. Employees and managers uncertainty of the future and their individual lot in the organization can have a significant impact on performance. It is a natural tendency to retreat in times of uncertainty. Focus is often on surviving rather than thriving, leaving many defensive and protective of their turf.

It's the default survival instinct. Meanwhile, empowered employees will press forward with confidence and thrive in uncertain times. This "attitude," if you will, is a key catalyst in driving peak performance in individuals despite organizational and marketplace uncertainty. It also translates into powerful results in times of prosperity.

Empowered employees not only take more accountability for their work and careers, but they view themselves as the primary architect of their life. They also take action rather than waiting for things to happen. They provide sometimes bold and courageous leadership in solving insurmountable challenges. We have reached a stage where we must individually and collectively take more ownership of not only our personal challenges but also the challenges that face us as a global community.

What does an empowered individual or employee look like? Empowered individuals derive authority from within. They possess personal authority. They typically are comfortable in their own skin and have a strong sense of purpose and understanding of who they are and what they are good at. They do not look to others, position, and status for authority and take accountability for their own destinies. An empowered individual can be a critical change agent in moving the corporate agenda forward.

Too often, the focus and role of human resources (HR) has been on the cost side. This is especially true as we slowly emerge out of our most recent

EXHIBIT 9.1

recession as companies continue to focus on cost and expense reduction. However, today leaders should focus on creating and leveraging human resources to deliver increasing value to the marketplace. This objective can be achieved by arming them with the tools, technology, and training to provide them with additional skills. Driving enhanced employee performance by equipping them with critical tools and empowering them will only boost overall corporate performance.

As we move further into a knowledge economy, harnessing the significant upside and untapped resources employees possess becomes more critical. There is no doubt that the role of the employee has evolved over time when we consider his/her role in the Agrarian/Pre-Industrial Age to our present Knowledge Age (see Exhibit 9.1).

During the Agrarian/Pre-Industrial Age, very little formal education occurred. Learning focused on reading, writing, and mathematics, while the Industrial age ushered in an era of mass education. This time highlighted a period that required more abstract knowledge and a logical approach. The Industrial Age was also marked by the need for individuals to learn trade- or industry-related job skills and focused on more routine and manual tasks.

Today, which is considered the Post-Industrial/Knowledge Age, is heavily influenced by the speed of information and requires workers to know, access, and retrieve information quickly. These new requirements demand that workers be highly innovative and creative, while also placing heavy emphasis on cognitive skills, which are used for complex problem solving. Value is not solely driven by production, as a greater emphasis is placed on creating value through knowledge and information. While physical inputs and natural resources do matter, knowledge is king!

CITRIX SYSTEMS INC.: CULTIVATING A CULTURE OF EMPOWERMENT

Headquartered in Ft. Lauderdale, Florida, Citrix Systems has cultivated a world-class culture that focuses on empowering employees. With regional and local offices that span the planet, Citrix can be found in global hot spots from Silicon Valley to Hong Kong. Since 1999, Citrix's CEO, Mark Templeton, has made fostering a culture of empowerment a top priority.

The focus of its corporate culture is to rally around a common set of values, which translates into all of its processes being built off of a common set of operating values. With this intense focus, there is also clarity around what's important, and it's Citrix's people. The three core values its corporate culture revolves around are humility, integrity, and respect.

Templeton has also created an environment that is contrary to your traditional command-and-control management model and has instead emphasized a culture that fosters an entrepreneurial spirit. Why? Because its focus is on people and supporting their values, which in turn empowers them. These efforts cultivate a sense of purpose that everyone can rally around, as it is Templeton's belief that people deeply desire to become a part of something much larger than themselves. He believes they are searching for a greater purpose, to be a part of something that gives them a deep sense of belonging.

Citrix's approach is supported by clear and consistent communication and a deeply entrenched system of accountability. Everyone holds each other accountable, as employees understand what is expected of them. The company even goes as far as placing a bright light on violators of the company's core values. This accountability mechanism sends a strong message, reinforcing the company's values.

Wherein most companies focus on technical skills and abilities, Citrix takes it a step further regarding the need to recruit and retain individuals that can best reflect the company's DNA. Regardless of technical abilities, the top priority is to determine if a candidate's characteristics will fit within the corporate culture. This approach ensures that the culture is supportive of creating an environment that ensures that things get done.

CEO Templeton also has identified specific criteria by which he evaluates talent. They include the normal skills criteria that focus on intellectual agility and technical expertise, but go much farther to include factors such as curiosity, scars, and leadership.

- *Curiosity.* In individuals and prospective employees, this exemplifies self-motivation and a person's willingness to explore and further develop himself both professionally and personally.
- *Scars.* As evidence of wisdom and experience, an individual's scars provide a window into how in their life they may have gone wrong and what they have done to correct their path or mistake. An individual's scars demonstrates how experiences both positive and negative shape our values and beliefs. Templeton realizes that many prospective candidates have many facts and information; however, he places more emphasis on the individual journey and how one handles adversity and challenges in their life.

- *Leadership and motivation.* This is where an individual is independent and freely expresses her own opinions, rather than parroting leaders or telling them what they want to hear. This goes to the fact that an individual has opinions of her own. Further, does she have a vision, and can she motivate and align people to that vision?

There are other factors that are a part of the formula for creating a culture that empowers individuals at Citrix. At the company, employees are encouraged to work, learn, and help one another. Citrix also actively promotes a flexible work environment, where employees can work anywhere, anytime, and in any manner that fits within the employee's lifestyle. Another example that sets the company apart from others is that at events in which it celebrates company successes and achievements, an employee's significant other is encouraged to attend.

The approach taken by Citrix is the focus of many companies across the globe. It is a strategy that recognizes the convergence of two powerful forces: (1) how through our knowledge economy, tapping into the unlimited potential of individuals or employees has become a strategic imperative; and (2) the transformative impact of technology on virtually every aspect of our lives. As the new era has ushered in new requirement, this also translates into the need for organizations to think differently about their cultures and how to create work environments that support these efforts.

ADAPTING TO A MOBILE WORKFORCE

Meeting the requirements for employees in the twenty-first century also requires that companies adapt to a mobile workforce. While other new alternative workplace mechanisms, such as alternative work space and social responsibility policies are vital, ensuring employee mobility is at the top of that list. The times require employers to be flexible on the issue of mobility. A number of forces have changed workforce dynamics, including globalization, cloud computing and the consumerization of information technology (IT). Agility and flexibility have become a strategic imperative and an absolute necessity to compete. They are essential for the future workforce.

Mobility becomes a strategic and operational advantage. It has become a tremendous recruiting advantage. Why? First, because of the flexibility in allowing the use of personal devices; second, a flexible and economic workplace reduces expenses. Third, it increases productivity by allowing people to work anytime and from anywhere. However, the primary driver of mobility is a younger and mobile workforce, whose adoption and integration of technology into their daily lives has created this dynamic.

Work arrangements of the future will see more employees working from home and other locations such as hotels, airports, and other locations. Therefore, policies and practices must change in order to meet these new needs as it entails careful coordination and the integration of efforts. Personal devices include tools such as tablets, notebooks, laptops, smartphones, and other equipment.

EMPLOYEE ENGAGEMENT AND ITS LINKAGE TO EMPOWERMENT

An empowered employee is an engaged one. And by engaging employees I am speaking to the important aim of capturing their hearts and minds. In today's competitive marketplace, the focus organizations place on engaging employees requires the same effort and focus as its efforts to capture customers.

According to Gallup, only 30 percent of the U.S. workforce is engaged in their work, which means that approximately 70 percent of workers are not engaged. The rate of disengaged Americans in the workforce as compared to engaged Americans translates to a significant impact to U.S. industry, as two thirds of all workers are not reaching their full potential. This fact, having far-reaching effects, impacts U.S. companies as well as the economy.

The economic downturn of 2008 has caused the U.S. worker to become more reflective of work and other activities, as our collective confidence has been shaken due to the tremendous uncertainty that exists. The Gallup study also shows that there is a strong connection between employees' feelings of engagement and their health habits. That is, those having healthier habits are typically employees who are engaged.

The Empowered Shepherd Boy

Of all the great stories of individual empowerment that have been told, none stands as tall as the biblical story of David. It is a masterful story of unwavering belief in oneself. As the narrative goes, David was a teenage shepherd boy who tended to his father's sheep. From all accounts, he was not a physically intimidating presence. In modern vernacular, he was your average Joe! David was also an Israelite. As the legend goes, the Israelites were warring with the Philistines, who had an imposing figure on their side, a notorious giant and behemoth of a man they called Goliath.

The call went out to the Israelite army and to all of Israel for someone to fight Goliath. However, no one would respond to the call. The teenage, scrawny David, the shepherd boy, responded. All were surprised and amused, as David was hardly a soldier and in their minds ill-equipped for such a formidable task.

However, deep down David knew something that they didn't. David had a tremendous amount of personal authority! He was empowered!

As the Israelites finally succumbed to David's wishes to fight Goliath, they tried to equip him with the finest armor and weaponry of the day; however, all David wanted to use was his slingshot, a tool he came to depend on during his time caring for sheep on the rolling hills. David did not ask for a spear, sword, bow and arrow, or other weapon. All he needed was a slingshot and stones. As the story is told, David defeated the mighty giant with his slingshot and stones.

David was an empowered individual for many reasons. He had personal authority. In his mind, he didn't need any training to defeat the giant, for he knew that within he possessed the wherewithal and courage to defeat this imposing foe. David knew he had the necessary experience and skill to defeat Goliath. There wasn't a doubt in his mind! David believed and had the courage to stand up to the great Goliath.

Also think of the fact that those in the army—who had position, authority, the requisite military experience, and rank—didn't respond to the call. How could a mere shepherd boy not only respond to the call but defeat such a great and imposing foe? David was empowered! It's that simple! He knew deep within that he had the personal authority to defeat Goliath or, for that matter, any foe the Philistines or any other enemy placed on the battlefield.

Employees who view themselves as having tremendous personal authority will be of significant value to their team, department, division, and organization. Empowered employees take accountability for their careers and do not depend on the organization to make them happy. They look within for fulfillment and naturally are proactive in aligning their professional aspirations with what makes them happy. They can be strong leaders in times of uncertainty, providing a sense of calm and steadiness to all they come in contact with. Creating a corporate culture that encourages individual empowerment is a critical lever in driving peak performance in organizations.

Throughout history, empowered individuals have always ruled the day, from Joan of Arc to Mother Theresa, from the legendary actions of Susan B. Anthony to Harriet Tubman. The headlines are ripe with modern examples of individuals from every type of industry who, every day exhibit this fine quality. It is this spirit of empowerment that is the true difference maker.

A Wonderful Opportunity in Time

Where we are in the context of time provides organizations with a wonderful opportunity. This opportunity is for organizations to encourage employees to embrace the journey self-discovery. Why now? Well, while we must still contend and work tirelessly in organizations, the fallout from the economic crisis has forced people to think more carefully about who they are and what they truly want out of life. In times of prosperity, we tend not to carefully consider these things. It's just the way we are as human beings. But our current circumstances have caused us all to be more reflective. It is a perfect time for this!

Timing is critical in the process of self-discovery, for quite often we are so caught up in our day-to-day dramas that we have blinders on and are not ready to take a hard look at ourselves. Through the journey of self-discovery, we begin to connect with what we truly enjoy and the things that bring us fulfillment. This will lead to what I call professional and personal alignment, wherein what we truly enjoy and are good at aligns with what we do, enabling us to move toward a new direction professionally.

The times we live in have provided the opportunity for us to redefine ourselves. This means—after carefully reflecting on what we now want out of life—beginning to move toward a new career or job, either within our current organization or externally. Reinventing oneself can also be a powerful catalyst to individual empowerment.

The power in self-discovery is that it puts individuals on the path of true empowerment. How many of us know of family members, friends, and neighbors who have great disdain for what they do? Day after day, month after month, and year after year, they complain and whine about how unhappy they are at work and wish they could be somewhere else or do something different. But there are many forces and realities that keep them chained to their job.

It may be the house or car loan, school fees, status, credit cards, family commitments, or even misguided and unfulfilled dreams. While so many of us feel like slaves, tied ball-and-chain to a job or organization, we have lost ourselves. We forget who we are and what we truly love. We move away from the things that truly bring us joy and fulfillment and drift into a space where we become entrenched in the morass of false expectations and a state of contrived happiness.

The only way to combat this is for employees and individuals to embrace the process of self-discovery. There are many ways organizations can do this, as HR departments have rich resources to facilitate this process. I can speak firsthand of this process because there was a point in my career where I went through a very enlightening process of personal and professional discovery.

A PROFESSIONAL DEVELOPMENT JOURNEY

Before my last assignment at Wachovia (now Wells Fargo) I was at a major crossroads. I was unhappy with my career and unfulfilled professionally. As I contemplated several possible opportunities within the organization, my head began to spin as I quickly realized that many of these new assignments were not appealing over the long haul. At that time, I had a conversation with my manager and the head of HR about my career. This was very pivotal in that the three of us agreed on a plan, one that would enable me to explore myself and get a clearer understanding of my professional path moving forward.

This plan entailed a variety of tools, including working with a career-planning professional and completing career and professional development assessments. This process was so pivotal that it provided me with an opportunity to really self-reflect and parse through the personal and professional issues that I needed to at the time. But what made this exercise even more compelling was timing. It was at a point in my career when the blinders were off, at least partially, when I was truly in a place where I could reflect, assess where I was, and get to the bottom of what I really wanted out of life.

Although I do realize that I was fortunate to have the support of an organization that funded my process of discovery, the process does not have to be costly. There are many inexpensive HR tools that can be of great assistance to employees desiring to further explore themselves.

This experience taught me many things, as it gave me an opportunity to reassess my professional and personal aspirations. For years I had been moving steadily up the corporate ranks, taking on new assignments and building a strong track record. However, during this time I spent little time revisiting what I truly wanted personally out of life and if the success I was experiencing aligned with what I truly wanted. I also realized that I deeply desired to transition back into a role that provided me the opportunity to directly impact the customer and his or her experience. I had forgotten how much I enjoyed interacting with customers and being in the flow of daily business operations.

Through this process I also concluded that position, status, and rank did not matter as much as having the daily opportunity to impact the lives of people. After revisiting some of my core skills, gifts, and talents, I also realized that I desired to spread my wings and revisit some of the activities I enjoyed the most and had set aside for so many years. These skills, talents, and activities entailed problem solving, being of service to others, leveraging my suite of creative skills sets and engaging in daily activities that directly impacted the company's bottom line.

This opportunity also provided me with the additional incentive to forge my own new path and to seek out some of the more nonconventional opportunities in the organization. It was a time of great uncertainty, yet throughout it all I realized that I had gotten back to the basics, back to those things that truly brought me meaning and fulfillment in my professional journey.

Eventually, I landed a wonderful assignment that provided me an the chance to have a significant impact on customers and employees and enabled me to dust off more of my skills, talents, and gifts. And although the opportunity did not provide me with a larger office or increased position, it did provide me with the favorable chance to make an incredible impact to the organization. It was soon after I went through this process of professional and personal discovery that I serendipitously stumbled on to a capability that would profoundly impact my life. It was an incredible convergence of timing and organizational readiness, and, more important, tested my ability to truly seize such an opportunity. However, the greatest by-product of this experience was that it led me back to the things that I valued and cherished most. And set me on a path of true professional fulfillment.

REINVENTION AND THE INDIVIDUAL

Like organizations and our overall economy, as individuals, it is also important that we reinvent ourselves. It is an essential part of life on our planet. We live in a world that is in a constant state of change, and as individuals, in order to stay relevant, it is critical that we respond to these changes. Whether it is changes in our natural environment or changes in our physical world, our ultimate survival depends on our ability to keep pace and to stay in tune with new developments. Also at the center of the change that occurs in the world is our behavior as humans. Human behavior is almost always at the center of changes in both nature and our social and commercial lives.

Without a response to this constant change and reinventing ourselves, we may often miss out on critical tools or information that can assist us in our journey. For example, examine the advances over the past 30 years. Think about the various tools that we have at our disposal such as the cellular phone, e-mail/Internet, microwave oven, and voicemail. To keep pace and stay relevant with our current and emerging products, services, devices, and technology, we must learn new skills and reinvent ourselves.

Think about the transformation that has occurred in the music industry. Can you find an album on any shelf of a music or department store? We have moved from albums to CDs and now to downloadable music. Look at the workplace of today and how the workplace environment has changed over the course of the past 30 years. Very rarely does anyone send hard copy memos or letters anymore. Most people working in an organization today conduct communications via e-mail. Can you imagine functioning successfully in any company without knowing how to write and transmit an e-mail?

Consider the turn of the century and the invention of the Model T and how it transformed life in America and the globe. Prior to the creation of cars, people moved around by horse. The horse was a fundamental part of life across America for almost 100 years. The invention of the automobile ushered in the Industrial Revolution and drastically changed life for people in America. Think about the difference in life experiences for a family who owned a car versus one who didn't. Or the difference in productivity for a farmer or businessman who was able to drive versus those who still relied on horse power. Over time, having a vehicle became essential to stay relevant.

The need to innovate or reinvent is a fundamental function of any individual, organization, or system and has been a part of our world since the beginning of civilization. It is also fundamental to creating market and therefore must be kept in the forefront of how we move forward in all aspects of life.

THE LEARNING ORGANIZATION'S CONNECTION TO MOVEMENT AND CHANGE

Movement and change affect individuals as much as they influence performance in organizations. Employees as human beings are strongly affected by change and movement. There are many forces that shape and stimulate us. These critical forces are pivotal in determining our wants, desires, and aspirations. Employees as individuals are always growing, shifting, and changing. These changes evoke new desires and needs.

It is important to understand this dynamic, for it is the crux of understanding why it's vital for peak performance to build and sustain a strong learning culture. As employees desire new experiences and want to grow, these new desires not only serve the employee but can be very powerful to the organization. Creating an environment of continuous learning benefits both the organization and the individual. It is a highly symbiotic relationship! As employees acquire new knowledge, this new information can enhance organizational capabilities. These new learnings also energize the employee, bringing a wealth of resources and a winning attitude to the task at hand and to the organization as a whole.

The Cost of Complacency and Entitlement

In times of prosperity, organizations can become lethargic, as complacency and a sense of entitlement can take root. This occurs quite naturally as individuals become settled into certain behaviors and attitudes toward their work. However, complacency, entitlement, and organizational lethargy run contrary to the natural forces that dictate performance. These forces apply as much to the individual as they do to organizations and their cultures.

A Relatable Example

An example that comes to mind is a supervisor conducting the annual review. This was a process I dreaded because it entailed completing a litany of paperwork and formal HR requirements. However, this process provides a rich opportunity for learning and growth. But our natural instinct as human beings is to shy away from difficult dialogue that often can serve as a critical wakeup call and an important learning event.

I remember that on many occasions, as I conducted annual reviews with members of my management team, how they reacted not only to their performance ratings but also to the raise and bonus they would receive. For some of my managers, especially those who had spent many years in the organization, when it came to performance rating, it was *expected* that they receive only one of the highest ratings on the performance scale. Why would they expect anything else?

This is the rating they received throughout their entire corporate career! However, there were certain instances when I had to carefully and painstakingly explain that because the particular manager was now in an elevated role, it would require a different level of performance to meet the high rating they expected because of the role. Over time, this employee also had come to expect a certain level and amount of bonus, as well stock options and other perks. She came to expect this, even though at times the organization did not perform as well or our division had its challenges. It had become in her mind a right rather than a privilege.

I do admit that there were times when I had conversations with a strong performer about this very same subject and I eventually caved in because I wanted to keep the manager engaged and happy. This was incredibly wrong, and on occasion I missed a wonderful opportunity to provide that employee with a critical learning experience. Employees and key talent often become complacent and take on an attitude of entitlement.

This attitude is then enabled by managers who, in an effort to avoid confrontation and keep the employee happy, sidestep the difficult conversation. However, this is a great disservice not only to the employee but to the overall organization. Ultimately, the employee is stifled and does not learn and grow, and the organization is affected as some of its critical resources are being underutilized and not stretched to experience meaningful growth.

I remember also being on the other end of feeling entitled and complacent. After my first full year of being promoted to the executive ranks, there I was sitting in my manager's office for my annual review. The manager I was working for was a very capable and incredibly talented individual. However, as he proceeded to provide me with feedback, my eyes immediately shifted to a score I was not accustomed to receiving. There on one of his comments and feedback was a rating of 3—"fully meets expectations." Needless to say, I was livid!

I wasn't accustomed to receiving a 3 for my performance, and I would not accept that rating—not then, not ever! I had grown accustomed to exceeding my manager's expectations. Needless to say, I pushed back! It was a gentle push. However, looking back at that moment, I missed a wonderful opportunity.

Can you imagine how deeply entrenched into an attitude of entitlement I had become? There I was, only one year as an executive, and receiving a "fully meets expectation" as my performance rating. And I had the audacity to complain! Thinking about that experience only demonstrates how complacent and truly privileged I had become. I should have been grateful for that rating and provided the type of environment that would have encouraged my manager to speak more freely about my performance.

Not only did I miss an opportunity, but my manager also mishandled the situation by not providing me the critical feedback I needed at that time. As a new executive who was a member of the management team of one of the key divisions of the bank, I had much to learn. Nevertheless, instead of providing me the hard and constructive feedback he knew I needed, he instead conceded and changed his rating of my performance to a 4.

Yes, I developed an attitude of entitlement. I had come to expect certain performance ratings as well as a certain level in my annual bonus and other perks. And I wasn't the only one, as many of my colleagues expected the same. We all knew this, as we would discuss in general terms how our current year's perks compared to the previous year.

This sense of entitlement and complacency is not only at the management level but pervades most organizations as employees of all levels are conditioned to expect certain benefits. This encompasses issues and activities such as the level of pay, the percentage of annual salary increases, the size of cubicles, office space, and performance ratings. How many of us know individuals who year after year approach their job with the same lethargy as they did years before? They perform the same tasks and work rituals with the same effort, and expect to receive the same old paycheck and perks.

This type of attitude affects growth because the most valuable organizational resources are not fully optimized. The inactions of leaders and managers to address key development and learning opportunities for employees breeds a culture of entitlement. It sets the wrong expectations and is a tremendous disservice to individuals because it stifles their opportunities to thrive and learn.

And let us remember that organizations participate in a dynamic marketplace. They are not sole participants in the high-stakes game of commerce. The marketplace is fiercely competitive and it only become more competitive as we move forward in time. It is a marketplace governed by movement and change, as you can bet that the competition does not rest. They do not sleep! Organizations are always internally shifting, transforming, and changing in order gain a competitive edge. The natural ebb and flow of commerce dictates that opposing forces dynamically not only compete for consumers but also cultivate strong talent.

THE IMPORTANCE OF INFUSING NEW BLOOD INTO YOUR ORGANIZATION

Over time, internal organizational culture and systems foster an environment of apathy and staleness, as the challenges of day-to-day operations often crowd out opportunities for critical experiences that stimulate much-needed development. In this context, the necessary stimulation needed for development and growth is directly linked to realities that exist externally. They may entail key learnings and observations regarding customers (trends and behaviors), the industry, or particular employee discipline, technology, and overall marketplace conditions. The world around us is in a continuous state of flux, and it is essential to an organization's ability to survive that it keeps pace.

I've learned from my own experience how easy it is to become consumed by internal organizational priorities and demands. It's just how things work. There are the demands of internal stakeholders and partners, vital customer-related challenges, opportunities, and requests, as well as organizational, team, and departmental meetings. The pace is dizzying as many struggle just to keep their head above water.

However, becoming too insular, both from an employee and an organizational perspective, breeds a form of rigidity and nurtures a "groupthink" culture, thereby institutionalizing behavior and a mind-set that is not progressive and innovative. Unless an employee or internal group is actively engaged with external customers or activities that require interaction with the world around them, they are typically inwardly focused.

Creating an organizational culture that promotes the introduction of new ideas and fresh thinking gives an organization the chance not only to survive but to thrive in an ever-changing world. These realities dictate that we become exposed to new ideas, concepts, and thinking through experience and exposure.

This may entail encouraging and promoting the following:

- Participation in industry groups and/or committees.
- Active involvement in community and civic groups and organizations.
- Opportunities to network and share with competitors and industry peers.
- Promoting and encouraging continuing education, professional training, and other developmental opportunities.

EMPLOYEES DRIVING SHAREHOLDER VALUE

Cultivating an environment in which employees view themselves as a critical part of the organization is paramount to driving shareholder value. This entails putting in place several critical components such as:

- Providing tools and resources that enable employees to effectively carry out their responsibilities
- Implementing a continuous and robust employee feedback loop
- Ensuring that business decisions include front-line employee input

Ritz Carlton: Driving Value through Critical Employee Resources

The legendary hotel chain Ritz Carlton is renowned for its innovative and effective concepts centered on employee empowerment. Ritz Carlton views front-line employees as the key factor in its ability to maintain a competitive advantage over its competitors.

Over the years, the hotel has developed a sophisticated program that begins at the recruitment of employees and goes through to the day-to-day delivery of services to its customers. At the Ritz Carlton, prospective employees are taken through a rigorous selection process that focuses on identifying particular skills and attributes. Once hired, individuals are viewed as team members. They are even referred to within the Ritz family as "members" rather than employees.

At the Ritz Carlton, employees are given the freedom and authority to resolve problems independently. For example, should a problem arise during a guest's stay at the hotel, employees are given wide latitude to resolve the problem. Employees can commit up to thousands of dollars of hotel funds to fix the issue. The Ritz Carlton also has institutionalized an effective employee feedback process. It is not only robust and continuous, but the hotel actively encourages and rewards feedback.

How many organizations do you know that financially reward feedback? Because team members are closest to customers and know exactly what occurs in daily activities, their feedback is critical to the Ritz's internal operations. The Ritz even takes employee input a step further. Where there are organizational planning activities that will affect employees, the Ritz heavily involves these employees.

I'm sure the Ritz Carlton still has challenges in engaging and harnessing its human resources. However, there are critical elements that I believe they have right in how they engage and include employees in the process of managing the business. This approach can only benefit the overall organization at large. The Ritz Carlton, Zappos, and Amazon leverage other tools to empower front-line employees, including:

- *Robust data.* By creating a data-driven culture, these companies tap into the powerful insights and observations gleaned by employees and provided to them by customers.
- *Make their jobs easy.* Too often, employees are restrained and handcuffed by unnecessary internal barriers and obstacles. Front-line employees should have relatively easy access to the resources they need to make decisions and address customer issues.
- *Budget and spending.* Just as companies spend a significant part of their training dollars in training leaders, more resources could be allocated to training front-line employees.
- *Risk taking and experimentation.* Allow employees the latitude to make mistakes and errors.
- *Customer centric.* Encourage front-line employees to develop strong bonds with their customers. This will provide a greater opportunity for them to shape the customer experience and remain connected.

TAPPING EMPLOYEE RESOURCES TO ENHANCE VALUE

I'm often amazed when I hear of organizational efforts to put together a task force or group of individuals to address a particular set of challenges or new opportunities. These activities could range from finding additional efficiency or revenue opportunities to addressing specific pain points in an organization. What amazes me about this exercise is how very often it includes only top management or leaders and management-level employees.

Although leaders and top management in organizations possess a tremendous amount of talent, including individual employees from all levels of the organization provides a more powerful formula to address the particular challenge. Top leadership may attempt to collect the insights and perspectives of these employees; however, having them physically present in the room and in real time provides a rich exchange of ideas and problem solving.

Frequently, in organizations, when we are faced with our greatest challenges, we fail to realize that the individuals who are closest to our customers and key processes are best suited to provide the most effective solutions to these challenges. They possess a rich knowledge and understanding of customer needs, behaviors, and expectations as well as the issues related to key processes and activities.

In addition to providing the organization with tremendous benefit, including employees at all levels in such critical organizational exercises sends a powerful message. It demonstrates to employees that they are a critical part of the organizational community. It demonstrates through action rather than lip service that leadership is serious about creating a truly inclusive environment.

DO THEY HAVE A DOG IN THE FIGHT?: ENGAGEMENT THROUGH CREATING A COMPELLING VISION

Every contributor throughout the enterprise must have a dog in the fight. From the boardroom to the mail room, all participants throughout the corporate ecosystem must connect to the overall mission of the organization. The linkage must transcend organizational structure to resonate with every employee's individual tasks, penetrating through the corporate milieus and reaching them where they are. This is a primary force in driving employee engagement, as the ultimate goal is to capture the hearts and minds of the people we lead.

Whether it is a front-line employee, operations associate, middle manager, or senior leader, they all on some level ask the lingering question: What's in it for me? Yes, this going concern is deeply imprinted into the human psyche, and if as a leader you can answer this question for the "majority" of individuals in your organization, you will have won a major battle. However, creating a compelling vision entails not only articulating an end state, but also crafting carefully constructed linkages to issues and values that resonate with your employee base regardless of level or department.

Finding common ground or a set of issues that resonate across your enterprise provides a powerful unifying force. This also must be interwoven into every business unit and corporate initiative. An example that comes to mind ties in to my run-in in Chapter 7 with my Land Grabber manager.

There's an aspect of the story that underscores the importance of driving engagement by aligning employees around a common set of objectives.

The initiative I led was the implementation of a large enterprise program from 2006–2008, which we entitled Investment Rationalization. It was an initiative that delivered more than $120 million in profit-and-loss impact to the company's bottom line. At the end of its implementation, the initiative was heralded as one of the most successful change and transformation programs in the company's history. The Investment Rationalization initiative not only transformed one of the bank's most critical governance processes, but also addressed critical cultural challenges in the company.

However, what made this effort extraordinary was that it was not a top-down initiative, as most enterprise-level programs of this magnitude often are. It was not mandated by the CEO, our operating committee, or board of directors, but was an idea and initiative that took a bottom-up approach. It was an idea I introduced to my manager and our CFO. The initiative was eventually fully integrated into the company's operating environment.

The Situation

Toward the end of 2005, Wachovia, like any Fortune 100 corporation, was spending a significant amount of capital in implementing projects. These projects ranged from funding the construction of new bank branches to upgrading critical trading platforms in the brokerage and capital markets division. Projects also entailed upgrading important operating systems and other critical technology infrastructure issues across the enterprise. In 2005, our project portfolio was enormous, funding close to $3 billion in new projects annually.

Through the years, we created a review and approval process that ensured that these large projects were managed and governed in an orderly manner. At the center of this approval process was a steering committee made up of the CEO's operating committee. The committee was called the Enterprise Project Review Committee (EPRC) and oversaw the approval of all projects over a certain threshold. The EPRC met on a regular basis throughout the year as individuals and business units would present their projects to the committee for funding. This critical governance process was fraught with flaws:

- There was no formal process to ensure that capital allocation aligned with corporate priorities. This limited visibility into strategic directives, which did not cascade to the entire organization.
- A lack of standardized and rigorous evaluation criteria resulted in suboptimal investment decisions. This also produced a lack of rigor in

business case preparation as results in estimates significantly exceeded actual requirements or execution capabilities. Project benefits were overly optimistic.

- Project execution frequently took longer than expected due to resource constraints and portfolio prioritization. There often was too much demand for shared resources, which increased project costs and extended project timelines.
- Tracking of project performance and delivery of expected benefits was almost nonexistent. There was also limited tracking of spent dollars and their usage, resulting in poor visibility into project spend.
- There were duplicative processes, and the lack of adequate rigor resulted in overall process inefficiency and organizational burden.

What made matters worse was while annual spending for projects had doubled each year, the EPRC did little to weed out unworthy projects. Over a four-year period, the EPRC declined to fund only a few projects out of more than 600 that were presented to the committee. The weaknesses in the EPRC process were compounded by the sizable amount of capital that was expended on new projects.

However, at the heart of this issue was a commonly acknowledged passive-aggressive culture where being polite and noncommittal was the preferred way of interacting rather than being direct and candid. While the challenges regarding the EPRC persisted, many key corporate governance stakeholders grappled with how to address the many problems tied to the process. These governance stakeholder groups included various IT units, finance, risk management, corporate real estate, operations and program and project management.

The Solution   To address the issue we determined that we should leverage a capability termed Investment Rationalization (IR). It was an approach that was successfully leveraged at another Fortune 50 company with tremendous success. The approach and capability entailed initiating and executing on a series of initiatives that would reduce the current spend on projects. Further, the IR capability would provide us with the option to capture the savings and redirect the additional savings into higher-yielding investments or drive these savings toward the company's bottom line.

The initiative would also allow us to address a number of challenges surrounding the effectiveness of several processes that supported the project/investment portfolio process. We realized the initiative could not only drive bottom-line results but also assist in driving much needed change.

After conducting a thorough analysis of the prior year's spend, it was determined that we could reduce our investment in new initiatives at the very minimum of 20 percent. Critical to achieving this goal was broad support from a cross-section of key executive stakeholders. Through an intense and focused effort of sharing, syndicating, and receiving feedback from leaders across the company, a groundswell of support began to emerge from every facet of the organization.

However, to enable the new processes that supported this capability we had to find a common set of objectives/issues the key stakeholders could agree on. We also determined that these objectives, to ensure we could rally support, were ones that employees could identify with. To rally key stakeholders and employees around common themes we conducted meetings, surveying many individuals who were in some way tied to the entire process. And after a thorough "vetting" process we focused on four themes.

The four objectives included:

1. *Spend effectiveness*—to increase the financial returns of investments. This objective aimed at reducing the portfolio's capital commitment while substantially improving returns on capital deployed (i.e., "bang for the buck"). It would better align investments against strategic objectives.
2. *Portfolio management*—to achieve an appropriately balanced and diversified investment portfolio. This would provide more balanced execution, capacity, and risk by taking a portfolio view; reduce execution delays through improved prioritization; improve flexibility to react to market changes; and match human resources skills with project requirements.
3. *Process efficiency*—to ensure an appropriate amount of effort and rigor is applied to the investment process. Process efficiency would assist in freeing up human resources and management time by reducing complexity. It would also reduce decision cycle times by streamlining the approval process.
4. *Performance accountability*—to provide adequate transparency and accountability across all aspects of the investment process. This objective would improve the quality of investment decisions by increasing individual and business unit accountability. It would also reduce exposure from failing projects by gating funding decisions and leverage increased transparency to aid in development of talent and leadership skills.

We quickly realized that these four objectives were familiar to key stakeholders both in business units and the shared service organizations. The issues impacted and resonated with everyone, from line-of-business leaders to project managers in technology, from risk managers in operations to program leaders managing a key group of projects. Now that the key executive stakeholders were supportive, we received full funding to move forward.

To execute the IR initiative we also designed a process that pulled together various groups throughout the entire enterprise to participate in working groups. These working groups would own and be accountable for the design, processes, and execution of the entire initiative. The active participation of every key decision maker and stakeholder was required.

We realized that the integration of these working groups and the employees who supported key functions in the IR process would ensure engagement and buy-in. We also understood that to successfully institutionalize the new processes and capability, we had to engage stakeholders along the IR journey. This translated into ensuring that they were intimately involved from inception to full execution.

The Result   Toward the beginning of institutionalizing the capability, at an operating committee meeting, I was asked by the CEO to apply the methodology to our current portfolio in order to extract savings the company could apply for an immediate impact to its bottom line. Within two months we achieved success, due to the fact that we had several working groups actively engaged in the initiative and all ready working toward our common set of agreed objectives.

The company eventually reduced its annual spending on projects from approximately $2.8 billion to $1.1 billion. Within a year, the entire organization was abuzz with the IR initiative. Not only was there fanfare about the new project, but within 24 months a new governance process was institutionalized across the enterprise, and each business unit adopted the new process.

SEIZING THE OPPORTUNITY AT HAND: A MESSAGE TO EMPLOYEES

We operate in a highly volatile and intensely competitive marketplace. As we are mired in so much uncertainty and fear, embrace this opportune time to foster a culture that encourages self-discovery within your very own department, division, or organization. It will lead to cultivating employees who are empowered and have a tremendous amount of personal authority. Ultimately, empowered employees will provide you with a competitive advantage and help to drive bottom-line results.

As the times we are living in are changing and as the marketplace is going through tremendous shifts, many are rethinking their careers and, more important, what they want out of life. What a wonderful opportunity and convergence of events to launch such important work.

If, however, you are an employee who desires to create a more fulfilling career, now is the time to also embrace the opportunity to get on the path of self-discovery. It will lead you not only to professional fulfillment but will more importantly empower you and provide you with personal authority. Think about your current circumstances and where you are at this very moment. When you carefully consider your life's path and the many twists and turns along the way, where you are and the place you now find yourself was all orchestrated by you.

Many of us spend most of our days waiting for others to wave a magic wand to put in motion or bring to bear our dreams. As we idly stand by and wait for others, we fail to seize control of our own destiny, we prolong the status quo, and we miss out on the opportunity to find true fulfillment and meaning in our work.

This time of uncertainty has provided leaders and organizations with a unique opportunity. Organizations have the opportunity to nurture and fully develop and cultivate its precious resources. It is an opportunity to build your army of empowered individuals. Wake up your sleeping giants!

Here are ways in which employees can empower themselves:

- *Be a student of the game.* As a member of your organization, it is best that you pay attention to the forces that shape and influence the organization. Internally, that translates into understanding divisional and overall enterprise priorities, as well as keeping abreast of specific areas of focus, challenges, and opportunities. Externally, you can focus on being a keen student of the marketplace and industry your organization is a part of. Tracking marketplace trends enables you to keep pace with external change, providing you the opportunity to apply new developments to your career.
- *Read your organization's leadership tree.* Being a student of the corporate game also entails reading the organizational hierarchy and determining what it takes to become a leader in your organization. By examining the leadership branches, one can get a clear picture of how things work. This can be done whether your organization is a true meritocracy or not. If it is a meritocracy, determine what the backgrounds, track records, and path senior leaders took to become a senior leader in the organization. This is information that is very simple to come by. If it is not a meritocracy, still read the leadership tree and get an understanding of the types of behavior and track records that are recognized.
- *Follow the bread crumbs.* If your desire is to become a leader in the organization or even if you want to ensure a rock-solid career, follow the bread crumbs your organization's leadership leaves along the path. They always do this. I once worked for a senior executive who exemplified this best. He did things in a certain way; for example, he arrived early at a certain time, liked information presented a certain way, and was impressed

by leaders who would pay attention to the smallest of detail in his/her group or operations. Leaders in this organization also followed the same subtle dress code. His leadership team took cues from him and did the same. The behavior and expectations eventually cascaded throughout the entire division. Anyone who desired to get on this leader's and his operating team's radar had to follow these simple cues. If it does not go against your personal values and beliefs, then follow the bread crumbs!

- *Initiate action.* Be the initiator of action in your career. Don't sit idly by waiting for something to happen. I've found throughout my career that those who sit back and wait for things to happen often get left behind. Educate yourself, find a mentor or a sponsor, and make it happen. Create your own game plan and stick to it, ensuring that you hold yourself accountable for tracking progress against established milestones. Too often in the corporate game, people wait for things to happen rather than initiating action. If you choose to remain in an organization, spread your wings. Get to know others and network! Get on the radar!

- *It starts from the inside out.* Whether you want to become a leader or simply thrive as an individual contributor in your organization, remember that it starts from the inside out. Internally, you possess the wherewithal, resources, and fortitude to move mountains. Don't look to others to validate who you are and your value in any setting; your value and what you bring to the table is all determined internally. This dynamic is no different than the reality of corporate performance. An organization's performance in the external marketplace is only as good as how effective it is internally in its most fundamental processes. This pattern is replicated down through the organization, from enterprise, division, department, all the way to individuals.

However, the focus on the internal factors in employees has a lot more to do with individual forces that transcend technical knowledge and are centered on the intangibles, such as individual will, drive, persistence, hard work, and other determinants.

SUMMARY

Unlike natural systems, where anomalies and points of failures are counterbalanced by internal mechanisms that account for certain risks, organizational systems are dependent on human beings. People are the heart and soul of organizations, and only through a robust engagement approach can a company capture their hearts and minds.

Due to the power and emergence of technology, employees will play an even greater role in driving value to customers in the coming years. However, a critical part of this process is to equip and invest in your human resources, providing the tools and capabilities that enable them to thrive and grow as professionals.

QUESTIONS

1. Are the organization's strategic goals linked to individual performance?
2. Can employees link the overarching goals of the enterprise and trace how they impact performance from their place in the organization?
3. What mechanisms are in place to empower employees and their work? Do your HR and corporate practices enable a more flexible and highly mobile workforce?
4. Do informal and formal corporate practices encourage employee empowerment? For example, do you provide employees with the resources and tools necessary to make decisions faster and independently when appropriate?
5. Do your actions, through leadership and management appointments, match up with stated organizational values?

REFERENCES

Bradi, George. 2013. "IBM, Ritz Carlton and Yum Brands Empower Front Line Employees . . . Do You?" *Forbes*, April 17.

Bryant, Adam. 2012. "Paint by Numbers or Connect the Dots." *New York Times,* September 22.

Citrix. 2012. Mobile Workstyles Survey, "Workplace of the Future: A Global Market Research Report."

DeRose, Chris and Noel Tichy. 2013. "Here's How to Actually Empower Customer Service Employees," Harvard Business Review Blog. http://blogs.hbr.org/2013/07/heres-how-to-actually-empower-customer, July 1.

Gallup. 2013. "State of the American Workplace Report."

Hein, Rich. 2013. "How to Use Gamification to Engage Employees." CIO.com, June 6.

Reiss, Robert. 2009. "How Ritz-Carlton Stays at the Top." *Forbes*, October 30.

CHAPTER 10

The Shining Moment: Unlocking the Potential and Promise of the Twenty-First Century

We possess the wherewithal to create a world of unlimited possibilities, as the twenty-first century has ushered in a period of unique opportunity. When we also consider the pace, rate, and intensity of commercial activities, we live in an era where mastering risk will only intensify as we move forward into the future. Our evolved understanding of how the world works and our capabilities today supports this opportunity and allows us to create a promising future. To move forward with confidence and a strong sense of assuredness, we must consciously, and with intent, create the type of world we desire. At the forefront of this challenge is the role and importance of the twenty-first-century organization. Because so much is at stake, we can no longer squander precious resources and the wonderful opportunity at hand. We are running out of time!

HENRY FORD: RIDING THE WAVE OF CONVERGING FORCES

Known as the father of the automotive industry, Henry Ford was a transcending figure. He was a man whose vision not only significantly influenced his time but can still be felt today. Ford believed that cars should be affordable for the middle class and once proclaimed, "I will build a motor car for the great multitude." In 1908, he built the first Model T, which became known as the "everyman's car." Prior to the creation of the Model T, the automobile was a car only for the well-to-do. During the 19 years the Model T was in existence, Ford sold more than 15 million cars in the United States, 1 million more in Canada, and approximately 250,000 in Great Britain.

The son of prosperous farmers, Ford was the eldest of six children. He attended school only until age 15 and never learned to read or write well.

However, during his early years on the farm, he learned about the value of hard work and responsibility, a value he would continue to carry with him throughout his life. He was fascinated with watches and took on the hobby of watch repairing, a hobby he would continue to enjoy for the rest of his life.

In 1879, Ford left his parents' farm and became an apprentice for a machine company in Detroit, Michigan. Later, he moved to an apprenticeship for the Detroit Dry Dock Company. There, he was paid a salary of $2.50 per day, which was not enough for his room and board. Ford made up the difference by repairing watches at night.

By 1891, Ford began working for the Edison Illuminating Company, which was later renamed the Detroit Edison Company. He later became the chief engineer of the company, and while working there met and became friends with Thomas Edison. While at Detroit Edison, Ford spent his spare time working on an internal combustion engine for an automobile. His first car was finished in 1896. It was a small car that had two cylinders, a four-cycle motor, and had no reverse gear. The car was mounted on bicycle wheels. During these early years, Ford formed two automobile companies, both of which failed.

In 1903, with funding of $28,000, the Ford Motor Company was founded, and five years later the first Model T was produced. Originally, the car was economical, costing only $850, and was made in one color—black. Within four years, Ford was producing 40,000 cars annually. As he continued to optimize his production of the Model T, Ford started mass production in the industrial sector.

His significant development of mass production techniques enabled Ford to produce a Model T every 24 seconds. The improvements in mass production also enabled the steady reduction in the price of the Model T, which dropped to $600 in 1914 and then later to $360. In essence, his advances in mass production and the assembly line further fueled the Industrial Revolution.

In addition to his many accomplishments, Ford was a pioneer in advancing the cause of his employees. He believed that the leader of a company should have the ambition to pay better wages to his employees and that employees should work in a way that would make this possible. He proved that if the employee's time were used well, the higher wages would not matter.

As a result, wages for Ford's employees quadrupled in 20 years. Ford also believed that a factory should work as close to 100 percent capacity as possible. He made this possible by making variations in production and material transfer almost zero. Ford's system was common sense—if there was time to save, it was implemented.

OUR WORLD THEN AND OUR WORLD NOW

What makes Henry Ford's contributions interesting is when we consider his achievements in the context of time. During the turn of the twentieth century, transforming forces converged to create the perfect storm that served as a major catalyst of his success. These influences would go on to serve as the springboard of the economic progress and conditions of the twentieth century. Comparatively, some 100 years later, complementary forces are in motion, dramatically shaping our new millennium as they revolutionize our commercial and social lives.

Let's explore the period in which Henry Ford lived a little further. From the late nineteenth century and moving into the twentieth century, the U.S. economy dramatically shifted from an agrarian economy to an economic giant. With the emergence of electricity, during the 1870s the second industrial revolution occurred. Due to electric power, the ability to power machines served as the stimulus to produce goods more inexpensively and at a much faster pace. These advancements resulted in the opening of more factories and therefore the production of larger quantities of goods.

Consider how these and many other contributions impacted innovation. Prior to and leading to the year 1860, the U.S. government issued close to 36,000 patents. This aggregate number of patents was issued over a nearly 100-year time span from the date when the first U.S. Patent Office was opened. Conversely, from 1860 to 1890, in only a 30-year period, over 400,000 patents were issued by the same office.

Henry Ford's Model T was revolutionary because it brought together and leveraged electricity and the emergence of mass production through the assembly line to produce higher-functioning automobiles. Further, prior to Ford's assembly line, car companies organized employees to work in groups to build one car at a time. However, what Ford's assembly line accomplished was to organize workers so they would perform different activities as the automobile moved through the process. Individuals became responsible for specific and unique tasks along the way of the production process.

Consider how in the mid-1990s the Internet began to take off, eventually spearheading a period of enormous growth. Through this phenomenon, not only have we experienced significant commercial success in the 18 years since its significant adoption, but we have seen tremendous innovation. Take, for example, the small window of time from 1995 to 2012. In 1995, the U.S. Patent Office received 228,000 patent applications and granted 113,000 of those applications. Now consider some 17 years later, in 2012, the Patent Office received a staggering 570,000 patent applications and granted more than 276,000 plus of them.

There are also additional patterns that were at the forefront of the transformation that occurred approximately 100 years ago that are shaping our world today. From the nineteenth to twentieth centuries, the forces that served as the catalyst of progress included industrialization, the demand for unskilled labor, immigration, electric power, technological innovation, and mass production. Similarly, today, influences that are spawning advancement include technological innovation, globalization due to the advances in transportation, and the Internet and how these factors have created significant interconnectivity, and the knowledge economy.

Technology, through its many forms, is shaping and will continue to dominate our new era. Through the Internet and other forms of technology such as digital computing and satellites, these capabilities have unleashed prodigious capabilities. Consider this advancement in the context of how mobile technology has influenced and altered personal and commercial activities and how we can conduct a myriad of activities at anytime and anywhere.

Think of how the Internet has significantly altered a generation of human interaction through social media and how this powerful platform offers even greater possibilities than we currently realize. Finally, consider how technology has impacted the assemblage of data and how far the reach of innovation and technology has taken us into uncharted territory, enabling us to instantaneously analyze and assimilate data from divergent points of reference. These new and ever-emerging capabilities have significantly altered how we market and sell products in every facet of business.

Imagine what is ahead of us in this century if we think of the progress that took place in the twentieth century. We're moving toward a world of unlimited possibilities.

THE CALL FOR TRANSFORMATION

We are on the cusp of a new era in the history of mankind. Consider life just 50 years ago and all that has transpired since then. Think through our many advancements and the significant progress that has transpired since that time. Contemplate the impact of the Internet.

Just as people living at the beginning of the twentieth century would be astounded if they saw life today, it would be the same as us waking up in the twenty-second century. The capabilities of life on the planet will advance exponentially because of the transformation of human beings to a more deliberate and conscious way of living and interacting with one another and our environment. Combined with our use of technology and science, we will be propelled far beyond life today.

When we compare the coming changes to the technological and scientific advances of the past 50 years, the possibilities are staggering. Imagine what life will be like if we finally come together in a more deliberate and conscious effort and harness our promise?

The fate of mankind remains in the balance. We are on a perilous course that threatens to destroy the future of our planet. Though we face a future of enormous possibilities, our challenges are also formidable. As we witness our planet changing, we, too, must transform not only how we manage her resources but the way we live and interact with one another.

Over the past several decades we've witnessed a crescendo in the humanitarian, military, and economic tension around the globe. Yet no end is in sight in eradicating these issues that continue to plague us. While many continue to come together in an attempt to provide answers to these issues, I believe that without a significant shift in the way we approach life on this planet, we will fail.

According to the World Bank, approximately 1.5 billion people live in poverty, which is defined as living on less than $2 a day. While we have made great strides in fighting poverty across the globe, our most recent global recession has stymied the world's efforts. We cannot significantly change our direction by applying the same model of thinking that created our current crises. We must come to the realization that there needs to be a seismic shift to alter our current course.

MASTERING CHANGE MATTERS MORE NOW THAN EVER BEFORE

We've come to a time of unparalleled change. From the beginning of time and spanning through the ages, the more man has enhanced his understanding of himself and the world around him, the more civilization has advanced. The dynamic of exposure to new information and new experiences has quickened the pace of change. Because the pace of change has intensified commercial and social interactions, we must respond in kind to manage it. Let's consider how this has played out over time (see Exhibit 10.1).

The Prehistoric and Ancient World

During the first phase, a period I will refer to as the Prehistoric and Ancient period, change occurred at a slow pace. It spanned from the beginning to approximately 1000 B.C. Life was relatively simple, as it took considerable time to move over great distances. Significant milestones during this time included the domestication of the horse and the invention of the spoke wheel and chariot to name a few.

IMPACT OF EXPOSURE TO NEW IDEAS AND EXPERIENCES

PREHISTORIC AND ANCIENT WORLD	THE EARLY–LATE AGES	ADVANCED/MODERN ERA	POST ADVANCED/ MODERN ERA
The Beginning–1000 BC	900–1750	1750–2012	2012 and Beyond
Slow Change	Moderate Change	Rapid Change	Unparalleled Change
Man experienced change, occurred over a longer time period	Enhanced social and cultural cross-border sharing of ideas, customs, and innovations	Significant developments in science, technology, warfare and politics	Intense globalization with intense cross-border financing, institutions. Also unparalleled insight and access to information across the globe
4500–3300 The domestication of the horse	Emergence of world conquerors and world empires	The Age of Discovery The Industrial Revolution. Underwater cables circle the globe	The Internet Age The Information Age
2200–1550 Invention of the spoke wheel and chariot	The Renaissance and Age of Enlightenment	Steam power, the railroad, commercial flight	
		Inventions of the telegraph/telephone, automobile, computer/internet	
		The launching of the first satellite and space travel	

EXHIBIT 10.1   The History of Change

The Early–Late Ages

Moderate change occurred during the premodern world. As mankind began to move, crossing geographic, tribal, and national borders, an explosion of the sharing of ideas, customs, and innovations occurred. This period was also marked by the emergence and dominance of world conquerors and empires.

The Advanced/Modern Era

The Advanced/Modern Era was marked by significant developments in the sciences, humanities, technology, politics, and warfare. This period has also seen the Industrial Revolution and is the Age of Discovery. Our Modern Era has also seen the inventions of the telephone, automobile, computer, and the Internet.

The Post-Advanced/Modern Era

A period of intense globalization, the Post-Advanced/Modern Era has evidenced a heightened level of cross-border sharing, as through the Internet we have gained unparalled insight into knowledge from around the world. This is also the Information Age.

ENHANCED CAPABILITIES DRIVING CHANGE

This phenomenon, which is the impact of learning/exchanging new information and the introduction of new ideas on a civilization, expands the prevailing thought and knowledge base. However, unless integrated into current practice and capability, it has little impact. Further, an expanded and enhanced understanding when integrated also advances a civilization's inventions, tools, and so on, offering new insights on how to improve capability. This dynamic has two distinct by-products: It enables more to be accomplished and drives the speed of activities.

Over time, enhanced capabilities, whether over a spectrum or singular disciplines, compress more activities into specified units of times. Therefore, this proliferation of activities, when viewed in the context of fixed periods of time, creates a dynamic that influences the pace of life or activities. Second, the speeds at which activities are conducted have been greatly enhanced due to the impact of innovations such as electricity, automation, computing technology, and the Internet, to name a few. Because more can be done within the same period of fixed time and at increased levels, life moves at a more rapid pace.

From approximately 2000 B.C. to now, there has been no change in how we measure and quantify time. There remains 60 seconds in one minute, 60 minutes in one hour, and 24 hours in a day. The only thing that has changed is the volume and speed of activities that have intertwined with our personal and commercial lives.

For example, in a social context, consider the transition from horse and buggy to the modern-day automobile. And remember that prior to Henry Ford's Model T, information from various parts of the world contributed to the knowledge and ingenuity of the modern-day automobile. Think of how with the horse there was only a limited amount of activity that could be achieved in a fixed period of time and over a specified distance.

Now, consider today, with the advancement of the automobile, how much more we do in that same period of fixed time and specified distance. Because we can compress so many activities in that specified period of time, there is much more to manage and do. This escalates the pace and dynamic of change. And remember, throughout the ages, the measurement of time has remained the same, but what has changed is the volume of human activity.

This also holds true regarding commercial activities. Think of how today, because of advancements in technology and the Internet, we can trade at a significantly higher volume, versus 20 or even 50 years ago. Trading volume has intensified because of the ability to conduct a higher volume of activity through the same fixed period of time. When we also think about where we sit today and the confluence of social and commercial activity, we can see this dynamic has quickened the pace of change. Again, this all would be impossible without the dynamic of integration, which is the catalyst and primary driver of advancement and change in our world.

While the impact of integration has throughout time advanced civilization and impacted the pace and intensity of activity, let's consider its promise in the context of organizations. In Chapter 7, I spoke of cross-pollination as a critical organizational lever with which to create new growth and activity. At the heart of the concept of cross-pollinating ideas is integration. Whether ideas are generated and shared internally or they are leveraged from competitors, they carry force only when applied in a new context. Companies typically do well in integrating external ideas into their internal organizations, but often miss the opportunity to integrate ideas and knowledge across an enterprise.

Just as in the broader context of how the exchanging and ultimate integration of ideas has done much for the advancement of our world, it can have similar impact in the context of organizations as systems. However, often because we view internal capabilities and processes through a bifurcated and silo lens, we forgo much opportunity. Within organizations, the integration and cross-pollination of ideas and approaches provide much promise as it relates to meeting challenges. This view ensures that you are developing new capabilities, and creating new products and services.

An additional dynamic to consider if we track change over time is how time frames have condensed. If you take a closer look at Exhibit 10.2, as man has moved throughout the different periods of time, learning, sharing, and understanding more about himself and the world around him, each time frame has shortened. Just consider how many years it took from the beginning to 1000 B.C. and how from one period to the next there continues to be a dramatic reduction in time. Think how in only 2,000 years during the period of Moderate Change significant advances were made, and how then during the period of Rapid Change it only took 200 years to achieve even more as a civilization.

What supports such rapid change are advancements in all disciplines and new knowledge. As a result, capabilities begin to multiply at an exponential pace. Can you imagine what the next 100 years will bring?

HUMAN BEINGS: OUR GREATEST NATURAL RESOURCE

The twenty-first century will be a time when the talents of human beings will be universally accepted as our greatest natural resource. It will be the new frontier, for the amazing gift of technology will enable all of humanity to participate in the flow of commerce and life on our planet. While we have severely impacted many of the planet's natural resources, we've failed to recognize and truly harness the greatest resource available to us—the human being. As we move ahead, we will begin to recognize this truth and place a greater emphasis on cultivating and leveraging human resources.

To ensure that we tap into this wealth of resources, the uplifting of people everywhere must be a priority. While we have demonstrated great humanitarian efforts across the globe, we have not done enough. There is much to do in addressing how we respond globally to people in crisis. We must place more emphasis on raising the living conditions, physical health, and education of all people.

A more intense and focused effort to eradicate the suffering of individuals not only is necessary to move us forward but is essential for the survival of the planet. If we truly recognized the intrinsic value in a single human life, we would be more responsive and compassionate to our fellow man in crisis. We would place more effort at proactively addressing the issues that go to the core of these challenges.

Organizations like the World Health Organization (WHO) and the United Nations Children's Fund (UNICEF) are dedicated to uplifting the conditions of people across the globe. These organizations and others like them emphasize instituting sustainable programs that foster a continuous effort that helps those in need on a daily basis. Rather than providing only financial assistance or physical resources, their efforts are aimed at teaching individuals how to effectively incorporate practices into their daily lives that will eventually eradicate their challenging conditions. Only this approach will have the type of lasting impact that eventually transforms individuals, allowing them to move to a more effective emotional and personal state.

As the conditions of individuals are raised, they can begin to focus on issues other than their day-to-day survival. They can draw their attention to moving forward to consciously construct the lives they ultimately desire. Moving individuals to a better place will ultimately bring other tremendous resources to fruition.

India is a shining example of the power of harnessing human resources. Less than 20 years ago, India's gross domestic product (GDP) was only US$180 billion, but it soared to $1.25 trillion by 2009—a ten fold growth. India's explosion onto the global economy is attributed to one dominant factor: its people. Not only is India a major player in the outsourcing industry, but its people are making significant contributions to the advancement of mankind around the globe. They can be found in the critical centers of technology, lending their ingenuity to developing leading-edge products and services.

While millions of Indians still live in poverty, a vast majority of them have access to quality training and education. Many Indians who are making significant contributions today came from extreme poverty. Their unique perspective has benefited us all. The country's investment and commitment to quality education has fueled the country's emergence as a global leader and positions it favorably far into the future. Moreover, her people are making critical contributions not only for the nation but for the betterment of mankind.

Now compare India to the dire circumstances that face Africa. Although many Indians live in poverty, they don't face the catastrophic challenges that grip Africa. Not only do many African countries face abject poverty, but they are also besieged with a host of social, health, and military issues, all of which threaten the very existence of millions of Africans. Think of the millions of Africans who struggle to survive on a daily basis and those who die each day as victims of their abject conditions. Imagine eradicating these conditions and having this mass of individuals participate in our global economy, contributing their unique gifts, talents, and perspectives to the betterment of mankind. A stable and productive Africa will only make the world better. This is but one example of the impact this cause can have when we view all people as treasured resources.

MAN'S COMING OF AGE

What makes our new era more opportunistic than periods before is when we consider how much we've developed as a species in the context of our technological, commercial, and social advancements. The confluence of the metamorphic forces discussed earlier takes on increased efficacy when we consider of how far we've come.

Furthering this arable moment in time is our enhanced and informed understanding of ourselves, our world, and our ever-expanding universe. Mankind's social, intellectual, spiritual, and emotional evolution has provided a unique opportunity considering our current trajectory. This unique opportunity allows us, with intent, to shape and influence our world like we've never been able to before.

An analogy that best describes mankind's journey is to compare our development and evolution to the growth and development of a human being (see Exhibit 10.2). There are several ways to segment the development of a human being; however, I've organized them into five stages. There are many models to choose from and on which these categories are based; they include conception to birth, infant and toddler, child, adolescence, and adulthood.

Similarly, as a species, we've gone through a comparable path of development and growth. Whether you believe in the Big Bang, which is more closely aligned with Darwinian evolution theories, or creation, this initial

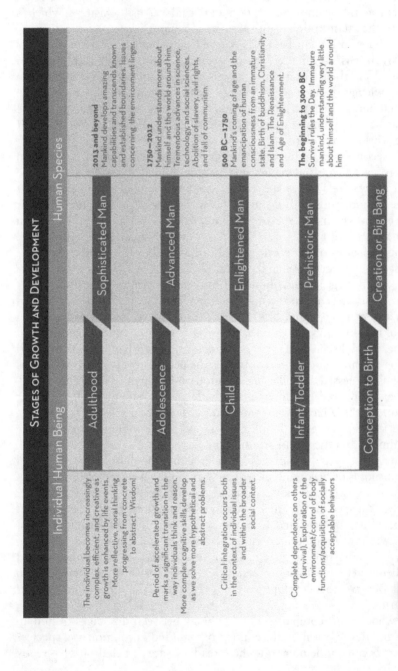

STAGES OF GROWTH AND DEVELOPMENT

Individual Human Being		Human Species

Adulthood — **Sophisticated Man**

2013 and beyond
Mankind develops amazing capabilities and transcends known and established boundaries. Issues concerning the environment linger.

The individual becomes increasingly complex, efficient, and creative as growth is enhanced by life events. More reflective, moral thinking progressing from concrete to abstract. Wisdom!

Adolescence — **Advanced Man**

1750–2012
Mankind understands more about himself and the world around him. Tremendous advances in science, technology, and social sciences. Abolition of slavery, civil rights, and fall of communism.

Period of accelerated growth and marks a significant transition in the way individuals think and reason. More complex cognitive skills develop as we solve more hypothetical and abstract problems.

Child — **Enlightened Man**

500 BC–1750
Mankind's coming of age and the emancipation of human consciousness from an immature state. Birth of buddhism, Christianity, and Islam. The Renaissance and Age of Enlightenment.

Critical integration occurs both in the context of individual issues and within the broader social context.

Infant/Toddler — **Prehistoric Man**

The beginning to 5000 BC
Survival rules the Day. Immature mankind, understanding very little about himself and the world around him

Complete dependence on others (survival). Exploration of the environment/control of body functions/acquisition of socially acceptable behaviors

Conception to Birth — **Creation or Big Bang**

EXHIBIT 10.2 Stages of Human Growth and Development
Data Source: Robert V. Kail and John C. Cavanaugh, Human Development, *A Life Span View,* 6th Edition, Cengage Learning, January 12, 2012.

period is akin to conception to birth in the development of an individual human. From the beginning to 3000 B.C. I've labeled as Prehistoric, which is similar to the infant/toddler time period in human beings.

This stage in human beings is marked by complete reliance on others for survival. It is also marked by a period of exploration and fascination with the physical environment as at this stage the infant and toddler have little knowledge of their surroundings. Corresponding to this time in the individual human being is a time period as a species during prehistoric time man was at a very immature state, understanding very little about himself and the world around him.

The second stage in human development is that of a child, a period in which critical integration occurs both on the individual level and as to the broader context relating to the child's social surroundings. Similarly, about the time period from 500 B.C. to 1750 was a period of enlightenment. It was an era in which as a species mankind came of age as we evolved from an immature state to a more advanced understanding. During this time, the major religions of the world were born as well as the emergence of the Renaissance and Age of Enlightenment.

The third stage in this model of human growth and development is the time of adolescence in the human being. This is a period of accelerated growth and marks a significant transition in the development of reasoning and thinking skills. As individuals, we develop more complex cognitive and sophisticated skills, enabling more abstract problem solving. From approximately 1750 through our present time is the period of Advanced Man. This period has witnessed a similar acceleration and growth in mankind as species when compared to individual growth and development. During our Modern Era, there have been tremendous advances in science, technology, and the social sciences as mankind has and will continue to learn more about himself and the world around him.

The final stage in human development is that of adulthood. This period in humans finds us becoming increasingly complex. We become more reflective and wise as our thinking shifts to a more abstract way of thinking. Similarly, as a species, we are at the dawning of a new period of time that I've labeled as Sophisticated Man. As we have witnessed during the past decade, we have become increasingly complex. Collectively, we have also moved to a more reflective state, as we've observed several critical global issues being vetted with more resolve. Moving forward, as a civilization we will observe the development of capabilities that transcend current boundaries.

So what of this comparison and analogy between the stages of human growth and development in the context of mankind's evolution as a species? It matters because it demonstrates how ready we are as a civilization—ready like no time in the history of our planet to fully harness and leverage our wonderful advancements.

Our civilization has reached a major point of inflection. When we consider the convergence of enormous forces that have shaped our world over time, it is clear that our time is like none other. Whether it is viewed through the lens of how mankind has matured and developed over time, the timeline of human activity, or the impact of change and movement and its impact on propelling us into our new paradigm, we sit at a unique juncture.

The times also signal the need to direct the velocity of life. While there is much to be gained in our world of unrelenting momentum, there is much to be lost devoid of a more intentional approach in this wonderful era. We must slow down!

WHAT WILL BE OUR LASTING LEGACY?

While human beings have created much of the calamity, destruction, and misfortune we've experienced as a species, man's creative spirit has also spawned many wonderful and miraculous things—from discoveries in medicine, such as penicillin and insulin, to our theories on germs and the discovery of anesthetics; in physics, from Newton's Laws of Gravity and Motion to Einstein's Theory of Relativity and groundbreaking insights into how light works. There are many other discoveries—too numerous to mention—in the fields of technology, science, business, and others.

In addition to these discoveries, think of how the imagination, will, and pure grit of individuals across the globe have altered the course of history. From Mahatma Gandhi's efforts that brought an entire empire to its knees, to Martin Luther King and how his devotion to recognizing the fundamental rights of every person and vision for a truly democratic nation ushered in a new era in America; from Mother Teresa and her tireless efforts to end the suffering of the poor, to Louis Pasteur, whose devotion to the study of germs created cures for a host of diseases including anthrax and rabies. Or even think of someone with the imagination and vision of Walt Disney, whose creative energy and legacy remains with us to this very day.

We all long for a world of peace and prosperity. This deep desire must be the basis of a new vision for the planet, a vision so powerful that each resident of Earth will embrace it. Only a transformative vision like this will usher in a new era of life on Earth.

The millions of Americans who preceded us left us with a rich legacy. Because of our limited natural resources, we must ensure that we use them judiciously, not only for today, but also for the many generations that will follow us. We also must do much more to ensure the health and welfare of everyone, as it is critical for us all to have access to some of the most fundamental services and needs that ensure that we can not only survive but thrive. What legacy will we leave generations of Americans yet to come? What will their America look like 50 or 100 years from now? And what are we doing as individuals to contribute to creating a brighter and more prosperous future?

From the inception of this country down through the mass influx of immigrants who came to our shores, people pursued the American dream with a very important goal in mind. This goal, although not unique to Americans, was focused on leaving a lasting legacy for the next generation, for in the coming generation lay their hope that they would carry their achievements even further. Even the newly freed slaves coming out of bondage deeply hoped that their efforts would one day benefit those who would follow them. We were a caring and nurturing nation, balancing our personal desire for success and prosperity with a strong determination to leave our children with a lasting legacy.

In the mid–twentieth century, Dr. Erik Erikson pioneered work in the field of psychosociology that led to his development of what is known as the eight stages of psychosocial development. In his model, there are eight stages in the life of all human beings, each stage leading to the next stage of development. What makes Erikson's work relevant to the discussion of our future were his findings concerning the seventh stage of the development model, a period called Generativity vs. Stagnation.

During this stage, which typically occurs between the ages of 35 and 55, Erikson observed that adults go through a period wherein there is a focus on the care of others and an innate desire to improve the surrounding community and society at large. Adults in this stage have a tremendous extension of love into the future, with a deep concern for the well-being and best interest of the next generation and all future generations. Conversely, in his model, stagnation occurs when there is very little concern for future generations. This state of mind is characterized by self-absorption, with only limited connection to others and little concern for the greater society. People in the stagnation stage also have no concern for social activism or volunteerism.

Erikson's observations on the period of generativity highlight a critical theme concerning the development of our great nation. America and all she is today is a direct result of the hopes, dreams, aspirations, and hard work of generations before. Erikson's work further calls attention to the rich legacy previous generations consciously created for our generation, and begs us to ask, "What legacy will we leave future generations?"

From 1612 to 1945, countless immigrants came to America. If we closely examine the ages of these individuals, many of them made the transition during their period of generativity. Yes, they carried with them their personal dreams and aspirations, but they also carried a strong determination to create a more prosperous life for their children and future descendants. Their attitude of providing for the greater good demonstrated a deep sense of care. Is it any wonder that we have been blessed with such a rich legacy and tremendous success? When we examine the foundation laid by previous generations, we must realize that it was all done in order to ensure that a lasting legacy would be carried throughout the ages.

The time has come for us to act! In Chapter 2, I highlighted the importance of the creative element in systems. The creative element is the catalyst that spawns all elements in the system. It is this same creative element that will be the genesis that will spawn and eventually propel a new direction for our nation and ultimately mankind. However, thought and desire is not enough—it is only the beginning. We need to act, and act now. Fear, selfishness, intimidation, divisiveness, and excess can no longer rule the day. And we must not wait on our leaders to forge a new direction; we must do it ourselves. Throughout the course of history, the more powerful movements were not initiated or led by formal leaders, but individuals who through choice determined that their voice should be heard. It is this same spirit of leadership and individual empowerment that will propel us forward.

THE WAY OF THE WORLD: REVISITING THE CORE ELEMENTS AND FORCES

This is the way of the world, that in nature and our man-made world all systems are composed of critical elements and forces that not only ensure they operate effectively but also govern their performance. These elements and forces, when combined, form a powerful strategic model to manage internal and external activities in organizations of all types.

In all systems, it is the creative element that serves as the catalyst, as it spawns the necessary elements that form its lifeblood. There are many examples of this in the world around us. We find it in nature, whether it is in the fundamental design of how ecosystems operate or how the process of pollination functions. It is also found in the life force that emanates from the reproductive systems in all mammals and our biological makeup. This reality is also evident in our commercial world.

In our commercial world, this ubiquitous and powerful element plays a pivotal role, as it is the primary driver of commerce and industry. Through the individual and our innate creativity, ideas and imagination serve as the force that brings to life innovation, new discoveries, and a vision for all of our creations. Whether they are new inventions, products, and services, or even a transformative vision of our world and how it moves forward with such force and might to eradicate so much of the suffering, injustice, and inequities we experience on this planet.

The facilitative element is the conduit that carries forth and enables all that is created. It promotes, facilitates, and ensures that the creative elements are dispersed to the places where they are needed. This applies to the air that flows through our bodies via our respiratory system as well as the blood in our circulatory system. In the stream of commerce, the facilitative element is driven by functions such as marketing, sales, and trading, to name a few. In our system of government, we see it at work through our monetary and economic policies, as they serve to enable the marketplace both domestically and globally.

The supportive element, serving as the foundation of it all, provides the infrastructure necessary for growth and sustainment, whether it is through the highway system that traverses this great nation of ours, or through our elaborate yet highly effective patent, trademark, and copyright system. In our commercial world, the supportive element serves as the backbone of any organization, whether private or public, as it spans functions such as technology, governance, and administration as well as accounting and legal, to name a few. And in nature, it is ever so critical as we understand the relationship of the land and Earth itself and its impact to our commercial ecosystem and to us as individuals—or, for that matter, when we think of our very own bodies, how our skeletal and muscular systems serve to support us so well.

Balance, movement, and repetition also serve as critical forces in the flow of all life on our planet. It is evident in how impactful the role of movement and change is to us as individuals and to the world around us; how movement and change must be accounted for in commercial activities and is responsible for how we grow and develop as individual human beings. Balance is essential to the life on our planet as the environment and our management of our limited natural resources will affect generations to come. In organizations, maintaining an appropriate level of change and set of activities is essential to ensure that it operates efficiently.

Think of the magic in repetition and how it mysteriously holds all systems in continuous motion, ensuring growth and sustainment as well. In organizations, it creates a strong culture of discipline through methodologies such as Six Sigma, and lean. Or even through management reporting or conducting periodic assessments. We also understand how the lack of repetition and organizational discipline has brought legendary corporate behemoths to their knees. Many corporations over the past 25 years could have averted a crisis by following simple processes. By leveraging the Three Elements and Three Forces, leaders, managers, and stewards of all types ensure that their organizations grow and are consistently sustained.

Yes, the world is transforming at a torrential pace. And modern man has leveraged the tools of technology, science, and mathematics to create a truly amazing world. However, as we move forward toward a world of mind-boggling possibilities and breathtaking progress, there are enduring truths that will remain the same. These truths are all around us and will remain throughout time. The strategic model introduced through the universal guide is one of them. This strategic model is timeless, one that can stand the test of time, for it was in place long before we showed up. Though we face formidable odds, we will eventually prevail and create a better world. Just as we are experiencing turbulent times, we will return to a time of much needed balance.

THE EMERGING STEWARD: WHY ORGANIZATIONS MUST LEAD FROM THE EDGE

Organizations sit at the hub of this critical crossroads. Whether it is in the form of their massive consumption of natural resources, or high dependence on human resources, companies of all types must lead the way. However, at the heart of it all is the requirement for a new type of leadership. It is a model and approach that consider organizational challenges from the perspective of a steward. And it is one that also demands that internal and external activities are coordinated in a more integrated and holistic manner.

While the Three Elements and Forces hold much promise for organizations in our new era, it is also important that we leverage them in the form of the universal guide to shape the companies we lead with intent. By approaching the challenges we face in organizations from a systems point of view, we capture more synergies and exploit untapped opportunities. Moving toward this holistic and integrated thinking enables us to better manage the intensity and complexity of our new world.

Supporting this approach is the need to up the ante on what is required of leaders and those in a position to manage precious resources. They ultimately are stewards! The most important piece of a high-performing organizational puzzle is putting in place leaders with the competencies and wherewithal to break through the old managerial paradigms. This equates to tearing down organizational barriers by effectively communicating and partnering with peer leaders, sharing resources, and unleashing human resources under their control through meaningful engagement strategies that resonate with and empower their employees.

However, this all comes together by a focused effort on creating a robust corporate culture. It should be a culture rooted in accountability, beginning at the boardroom and finding its way through every group and individual contributor on the organizational chart. Reinforcing and holding leaders accountable not only reinforces corporate values but, equally important, drives companies closer to delivering consistent performance. Quite often, significant resources are squandered and not fully optimized due to a lack of organizational and leadership resolve in making the tough call. Demanding accountability in organizational systems also sends a message throughout the enterprise and fosters a culture of trust.

THE MASTERS OF OUR FATE

I began this journey by sharing with you how the truths and realities in nature hold the key that will improve our man-made world, and so will I end it with this same theme. I did this on purpose, as I desired to highlight two very important themes regarding the natural and man-made world we live in:

Integration

The first is the importance of integration. The central theme of *Mastering Strategic Risk* is to extract critical lessons from natural systems and applying them to organizational systems. As discussed in Chapter 1, this thinking follows the approach we've taken in building our world as we have assimilated many lessons from nature into every facet of life. Integration has and will continue to drive progress in our world as there is much to learn from so many points of reference.

The more we explore and uncover fresh insights, we unearth profound knowledge that advances understanding. This perpetual cycle of discovery and the incorporation of new observation serve as the engine of advancement. This occurs in the form of sharing cross-cultural, discipline, and systems knowledge as well as others. As we continue to explore our universe and worlds beyond it, we will continue to leverage the knowledge acquired to inform us.

Great opportunities exist in organizational systems as often a siloed and divergent mentality serves as a barrier to integration and holistic thinking. Yes, shared services organizations and functions provide the opportunity to view activities from a cross-functional perspective; however, opportunities may exist when we consider assimilation pertaining to innovation, product development, sales, and services.

Polarity and Duality

The second is the theme of duality and polarity. The way of the world also ensures there is an ebb and flow to life, an innate polarity in all systems in nature. It is a rhythmic and continuous dance that permeates all life. As one force or reality leads, another is soon to follow. There are many examples that come to mind. Can there be male without female? Or, for that matter, darkness without light? Or could animals and plants have inhalation without expiration? Consider the realities and benefits of heat and of its exact opposite, the cold. They are distinct yet inextricably bound by their interdependent relationship.

Nature is filled with these polarities, for it is indeed the way our world is designed to operate. They are a part of an intricate system that enables the wheel of life to turn. Understanding this very important truth concerning the existence of polarity and duality in nature is also critical when considering the realities of our man-made world.

These dualities exist in our marketplace and world of business as in accounting there exist bedrock principles such as debits and credits, profit-and-loss statements, equity and liabilities, or capital and expenses. These concepts extend into broader economic market principles such as market contraction and expansion, or the nomenclature we use when reporting budgets and trade in the context of deficits and surpluses.

Supply is worthless without its opposite, demand, and there can be no production without consumption, no positive without negative, and so on. There are many examples. However, as we experienced a great era of prosperity during the early to mid-2000s, it was inevitable that we would one day experience a period of loss and economic challenge. And while we must always manage our resources prudently, it still follows both in nature and in our man-made world that as there are times of abundance, difficult times must follow.

However, as there are these periods of contraction, we must also remember a time will soon follow that returns us to a more positive position. Let me provide you with an example that strikes close to home.

The U.S. stock market crash of 1929 ushered in a worldwide depression. It was the greatest economic collapse of the twentieth century and one of the most severe ones in modern history. Unemployment in the United States rose to a staggering 25 percent, while in other countries it topped well over 30 percent. In various accounts of the Great Depression, many in our nation and across our world were filled with great despair.

In the United States, there were stories of starving children in Appalachia who chewed their fingers to the point of nearly drawing blood because of starvation; men took their lives as they saw their fortunes wiped out. Many children left school to work in order to support their families. It is estimated that in the 1930s alone, more than 2 million boys and girls between the ages of 10 and 18 worked in coal mines, factories, and farms nationwide. Millions of individuals across the planet were mired in devastating economic circumstances with little hope for the future.

However, as we know, this catastrophic worldwide event was followed by an incredible era of global prosperity, advancement, and progress. Can you imagine those who died during the time of the Depression coming back to life some 25 years later and witnessing a country that was experiencing such economic success? Many couldn't have imagined it at the time; however, as we now know, through events such as the start of World War II and key actions taken by leaders both in the United States and globally, we eventually made our way out of those dark days.

SUMMARY

This is also the way of our commercial world; it is governed by the same forces that dictate the realities in systems of nature. As the benefits of prosperity meander effortlessly through the stream of our lives, so, too, must the realities of adversity and barrenness. This ebb and flow in the state of commerce is an integral aspect of our reality and will continue throughout time. However, this reality never precludes us from improving systems and learning critical lessons from our shortcomings and the mistakes of the past.

As it was in the early twentieth century, so, too, is it with the fate of man today. The state of the planet is in flux, and hope has waned as the dark clouds of despair loom ever so near to our seemingly fragile existence. We yet contend with tepid economic growth and a lingering global recession as formidable social, environmental, and health issues assail us both domestically and across the planet. There are tensions everywhere as the saber rattling between nations continues at fever pitch, and as politicians bicker over positions of power, all in the spirit of self-aggrandizement and political posturing.

We need not despair or lose hope, for this is the way of *our* world. From today and well after we leave this existence, there will always be an ebb and flow to life, a mysterious cadence that permeates all living things. Yes, this is the truth that exists in all things, both in nature and in our man-made world, that must grow and be sustained. For the enduring truth is that we will contend and manage through these challenging times, though formidable they may be. We need not lose hope or faith in the future, for our fate lies in our hands.

No, modern man is not relegated to some predetermined fate, nor are we held captive to some ancient prophetic prediction that is propelling us toward perdition. Nor is it a given that the strong winds of strife and global tensions will obliterate us from this existence. We hold the key to the future—the future of our wonderful planet—in the palm of our collective hands. We can, through deliberate and conscious intent, and with the force of our will, create a world of peace, a world of amazing abundance. A world that in the end will shape the future for generations to come. The markets? Oh, how they rage! Yet despite their raucous fury, we will contend and emerge a more resilient and triumphant world!

REFERENCES

Hoare, C. H. 2002. *Erikson on Development in Adulthood: New Insights from the Unpublished Papers.* New York: Oxford University Press.

Iacocca, Lee. 1998. "Driving Force: Henry Ford—He Produced an Affordable Car, Paid High Wages, and Helped Create a Middle Class. Not Bad for an Autocrat." *Time,* December 7.

Levinson, William. 2009. "Henry Ford's Proven Lessons for American Industry. *Industry Week,* 258, no. 7 (July): 16–17.

Mitchell, Dan. 2013. "When Patent Trolls Were Simply Sharks." *Fortune,* June 7.

Sokol, Justin T. 2009. "Identity Development throughout the Lifetime: An Examination of Eriksonian Theory." *Graduate Journal of Counseling Psychology* 1, no. 2 (Spring).

U.S. Patent and Trademark Office, U.S. Patent Statistics Chart, Calendar Years 1963–2012.

About the Author

A business strategist and former executive, Joel McPhee is a keen student of understanding how organizations as systems work. Through a holistic and integrated approach, he provides consulting services to Fortune 500 companies. A former senior leader at Wells Fargo, Inc., Joel was the chief risk officer for the company's 18,000-member Operations and Technology division, as well as heading its Global Delivery Center. During his more than 20 years of experience, he has held critical roles at other top financial institutions, placing him at the forefront of addressing some of the most formidable challenges facing the banking industry. He has also worked at the Huntington National Bank and JPMorgan Chase. Joel brings his rich background and fresh insights to each client. Joel and his team provide consulting services in the areas of strategy, risk, and change management.

Joel, who is also an attorney, co-authored the article "Why Government Regulators Need Corporate Boot Camp" for the *Washington Post*. He is a sought-after industry expert and speaker and is quoted regularly in industry articles. His thoughts on off-shoring banking processes and services were published in *Bank Technology News* in the article "A Reversal of Fortune." Learn more at www.JoelMcPhee.com.

About the Companion Web Site

This book includes a companion web site, which can be found at www .wiley.com/go/MasteringStrategicRisk (password: objectives123). The companion web site contains tools and resources that will enable you to build your knowledge of new concepts introduced in *Mastering Strategic Risk*. Here, you can further explore models such as the Three Elements and Forces, the universal guide of governance, our commercial ecosystem, and the individual contributor framework, to name a few. Feel free to download and utilize these models, or try to create your own and compare.

The web site also contains chapter goals and exercises, chapter summaries, key term flashcards, and PowerPoint instructional materials.

To access the site, go to www.wiley.com/go/MasteringStrategicRisk (password: objectives123).